ART ESSENTIALS

LOOKING AT PHOTOGRAPHS

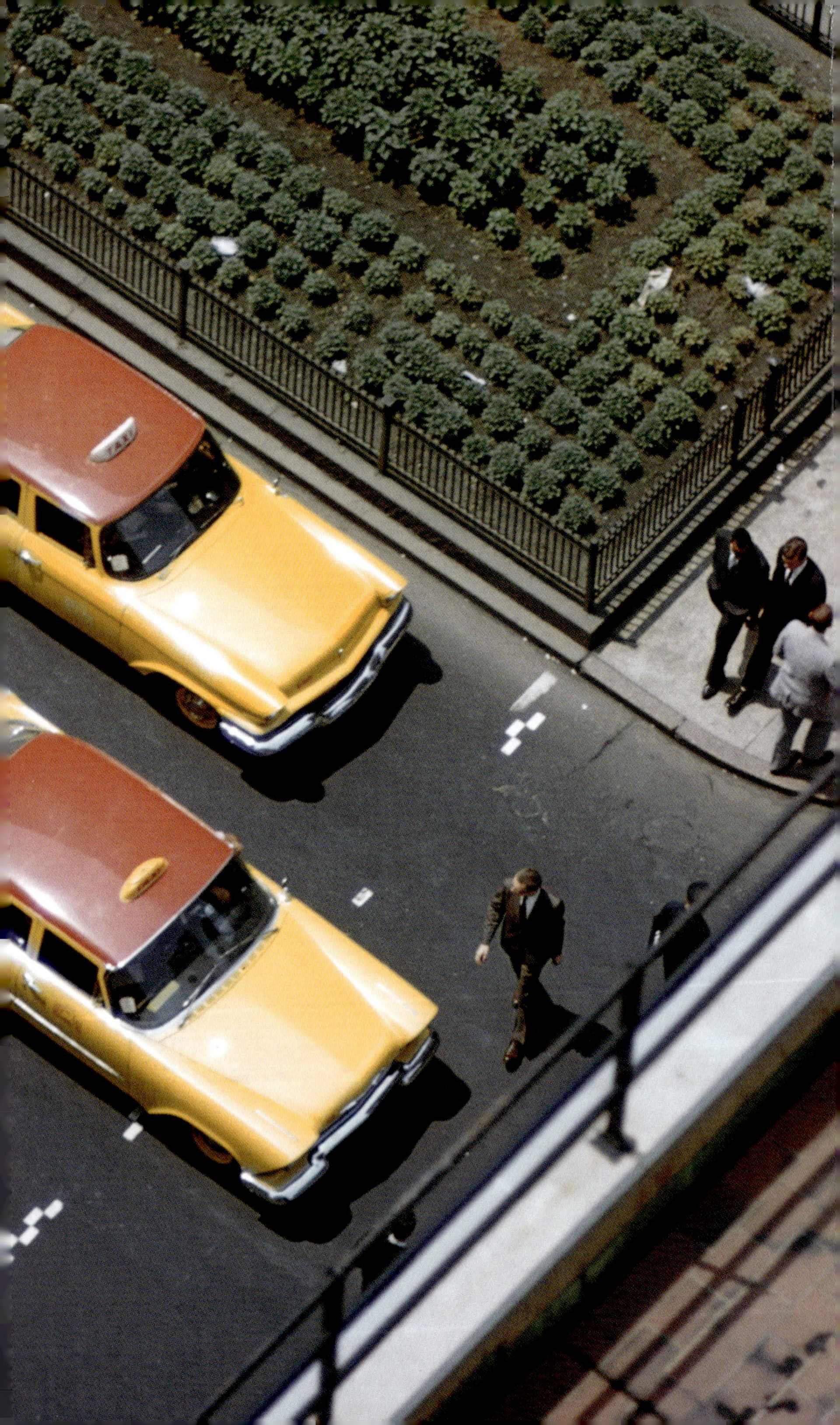
TAXI

ART ESSENTIALS

LOOKING AT PHOTOGRAPHS

—

LAURENT JULLIER

—

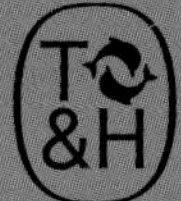

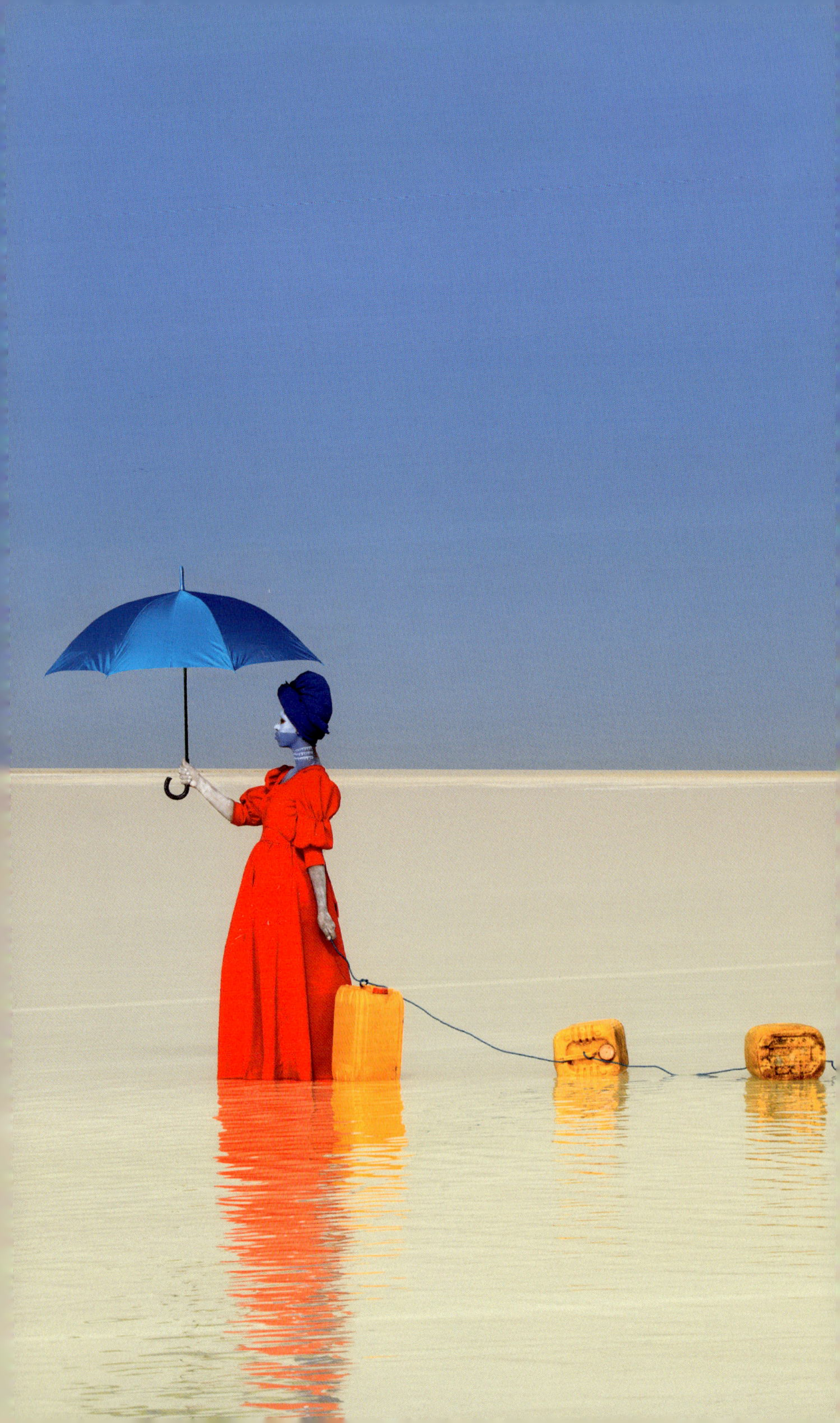

CONTENTS

INTRODUCTION

If photographs didn't offer such an accurate representation of the world, perhaps we would spend more time looking at them. But they are like little windows, behind which time stands still, so we are often content simply to recognize what they depict.

However, a photograph is not a window. Whether it is posed or unposed, figurative or abstract, it is first and foremost a *way of looking*. Of witnessing. Someone saw something, whether in front of them or in their imagination, and they are showing it to us. In this sense, a photographer is more than just a witness: they offer us a new pair of glasses through which we can see the world. The question, however, is how far we can trust them...

The first two chapters in this book explore this question in detail by comparing pictures that are considered to be straightforward representations of the world with those that are doctored in some way – although, as we will see, this is an overly simplistic opposition. The three following chapters show that every aspect of a photograph is important, not only the objects and people that are depicted, but also the way in which it represents its subject matter, including the use of shadow and blurriness, the position from which it was taken, and finally its relationship with time, the way in which time leaves its mark on a photograph. Analysing these elements in detail will allow us, in the final two chapters, to explore ideas that go beyond photography, but in which it plays an important role: the theme of identity, seen through the lens of portraiture; and how we form perceptions of events based on photographs when we have not witnessed them directly.

It is true that, today, photographs rarely surprise us: we see so many of them every day, whether printed or on our screens. It is time we looked at them in a new way, and this book is designed to help us do so. Whether you simply enjoy looking at photographs or take pictures as a hobby, this book is an invitation to examine your own relationship with images. Why does this photograph have this effect on me? What do I see when I look at it? These are some of the questions that this guide will help you to explore.

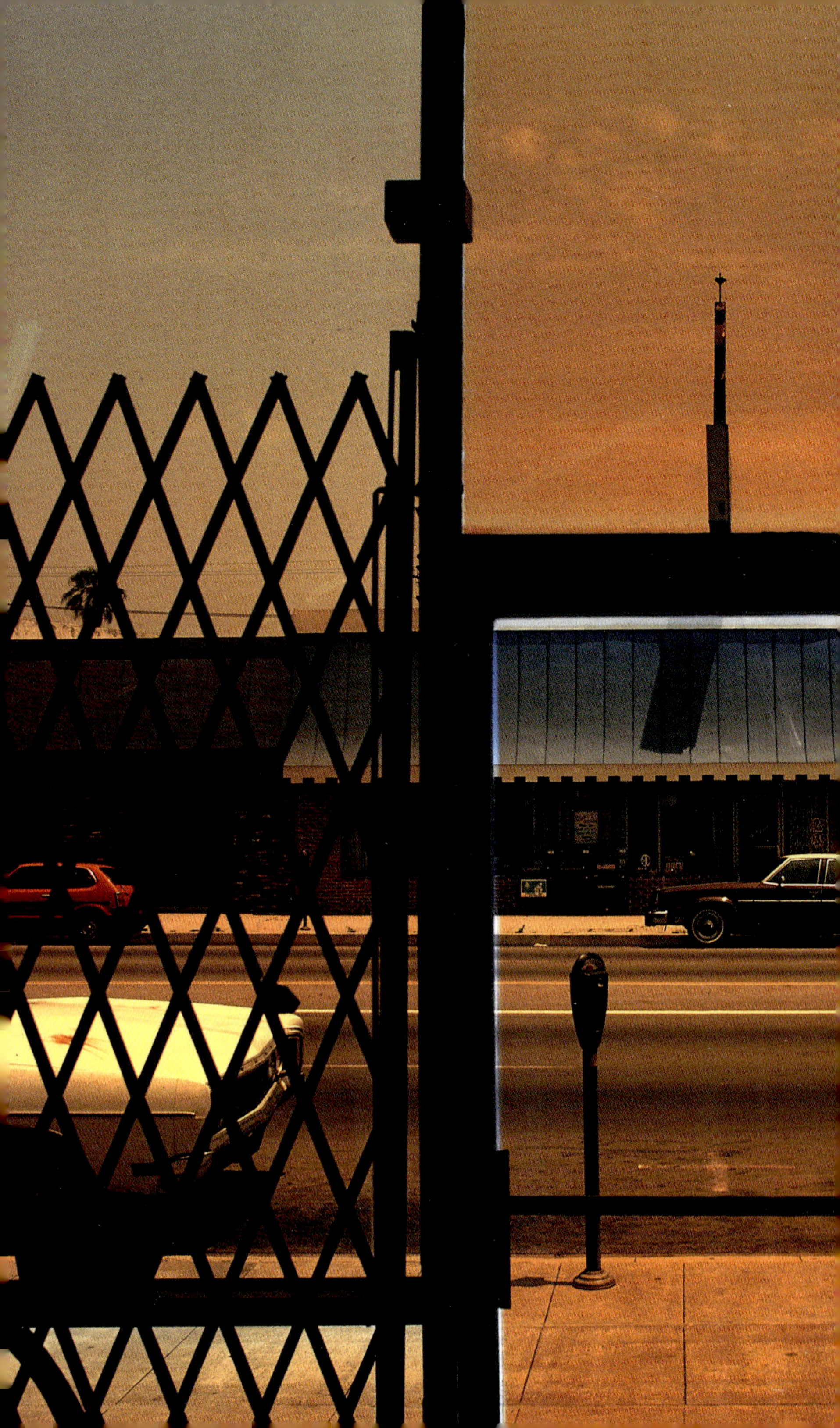

REPRESENTATIONS OF THE WORLD

-

It's purely intuition. There's no concept. Things attract me and it works both ways. I'm fascinated by the miracle where things come together in a way where things make sense to me, so there's very little thinking

-

Harry Gruyaert

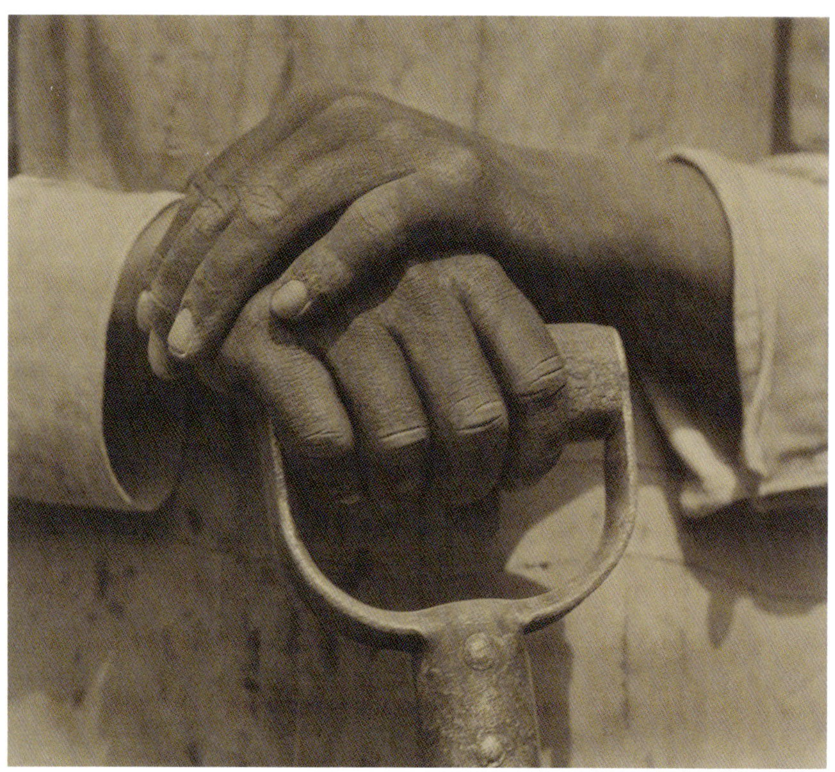

Tina Modotti
Manos de trabajador (Worker's Hands), 1927
Palladium print,
19.7 x 21.6 cm
(7¾ x 8½ in.)

Perhaps he is taking a break, or possibly the photographer asked him to pose for her? In either case, we wouldn't have looked so closely at his hands.

Caravaggio, one of the great sixteenth-century Italian painters, was criticized because, in some of his paintings, he depicted the dirty nails and feet of the men and women he used as models. He was behaving like a photographer: reproducing what was before his eyes, including the imperfections of the people who posed for him. Why on earth did he not improve on reality?

In the 1920s, when the term 'the seventh art' began to be used across Europe to refer to cinema, there were strangely only a few voices pointing out that photography had been forgotten. The commonly accepted classification of fine arts included architecture, sculpture, painting and drawing, music, literature and – grouped together – theatre and dance. The seventh spot should have been given to photography, invented around sixty years before cinema. Photography and cinema both have a mechanical, automatic aspect that is not found in the other art forms, but it was as if the magic of reproducing movement made up for this 'flaw' in cinema. However, in this chapter, we will see that photography definitely deserved to be recognized as an art form.

TRIVIAL THINGS

Photography is an art that depends heavily on technology – now including computers – but does that mean the human hand has no part to play? Of course, in everyday life, the work of the photographer is not always obvious. If someone hands you their phone and says excitedly, 'That's my cat!' or 'Look what I ate!', you will talk to them about the cat or the meal, not about the framing or sharpness of the photos. But in some cases, it can be useful to think about the *mediation* involved in the act of taking a photograph. Someone (the photographer) and something (the camera) are placed between us and the world. The first thing to do, when looking at a photograph, is to recognize that it is also a representation of this action – the act of mediation.

Take, for example, this motionless labourer (opposite), leaning on the handle of his shovel. If we had passed him on the street, would we have stopped to look at him? At the most, we would have cast a momentary glance in his direction, not noticing anything that might make us stop and think. But on that day in Mexico, the Italian-born photographer Tina Modotti (1896–1942) slipped between him and us.

Tina Modotti, who had been a silent-movie actress in Hollywood in the Roaring Twenties, had recently joined the Mexican Communist Party and her work was published internationally in the left-wing press. However, in this photograph she did not follow Karl

Marx's published guidance that 'the actual pressure must be made more oppressive...the shame must be made more shameful' (1843), meaning that artists should emphasize the suffering of exploited workers. Quite the opposite. These hands, marked by manual labour and caked in dust, are folded on the shovel's handle like a gentleman would fold his hands over his cane. The dirty jacket, with its uneven sleeves, isn't important. The composition creates a sense of balance and insists on the dignity of its subject. Rather than Marx, it evokes the words of the ancient Greek philosopher Epictetus: the master depends on the slave to live, but the slave does not need the master. This means that the slave has a kind of moral superiority.

Tina Modotti was later criticized for taking these kinds of photographs by proponents of Social Realism, who thought that an artist's only concern should be to spread communist ideals in the simplest way possible, the easiest way to understand.

Anna Atkins
Plocamium coccineum (in fruit), 1850, from *Photographs of British Algae: Cyanotype Impressions*, 1843–1853
Cyanotype

***Plocamium* is a red seaweed that often gets wrapped around the feet of swimmers. Here, however, the infinite ramifications of its tree-like structure transform it into an object of fascination.**

Perfections in form

As soon as photography was invented, it was criticized by many artists and intellectuals because it captured every detail, even those they didn't want to record. This is very useful for scientists or anyone who wants to create a highly precise record of a visual memory, so that they don't forget the smallest detail. However, the mechanical nature of photography, the way in which it seemed not to rely on human hands, meant it was not accepted as an art form. Instead photographs were seen as a kind of trace or imprint, like footprints left on the ground. The focus was on how they used light to capture the way something looked. One of the pioneers of photography, the British chemist William Henry Fox Talbot (1800–1877), called the first pictures that he took in 1835 'sun pictures' or 'words of light'. At the time, people did not recognize that there could be an element of artistry in this simple chemical reaction. After all, our skin is also a light-sensitive surface, which can reveal the outline of our swimming costume after a day at the beach.

Day after day, whether because we lack the time, the patience or the interest in trivial things, we pass by scenes that are crying out to be photographed, scenes that would take on a greater depth if only we stopped to look. For almost two centuries, some photographers have specialized in rescuing these very objects from banality.
The first photography book, printed in 1843 and then in subsequent volumes, was made up of pictures of algae (opposite). It was the

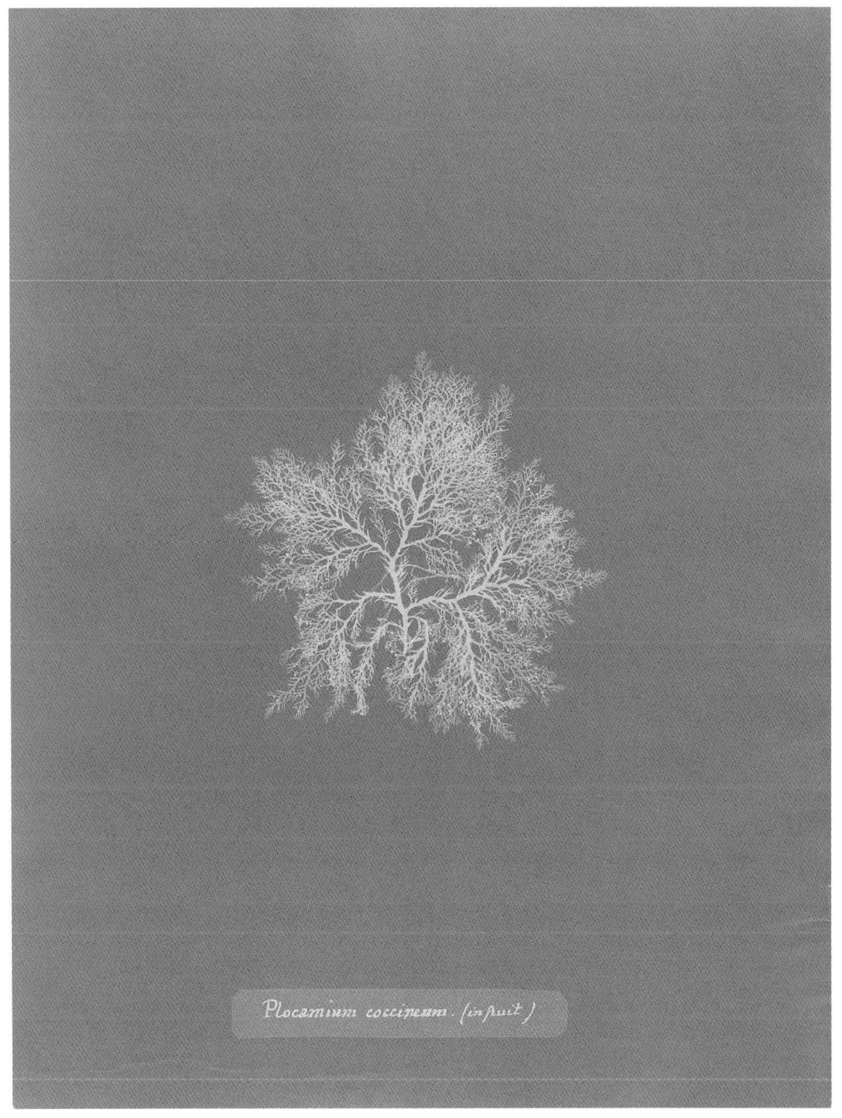
Plocamium coccineum. (in fruit)

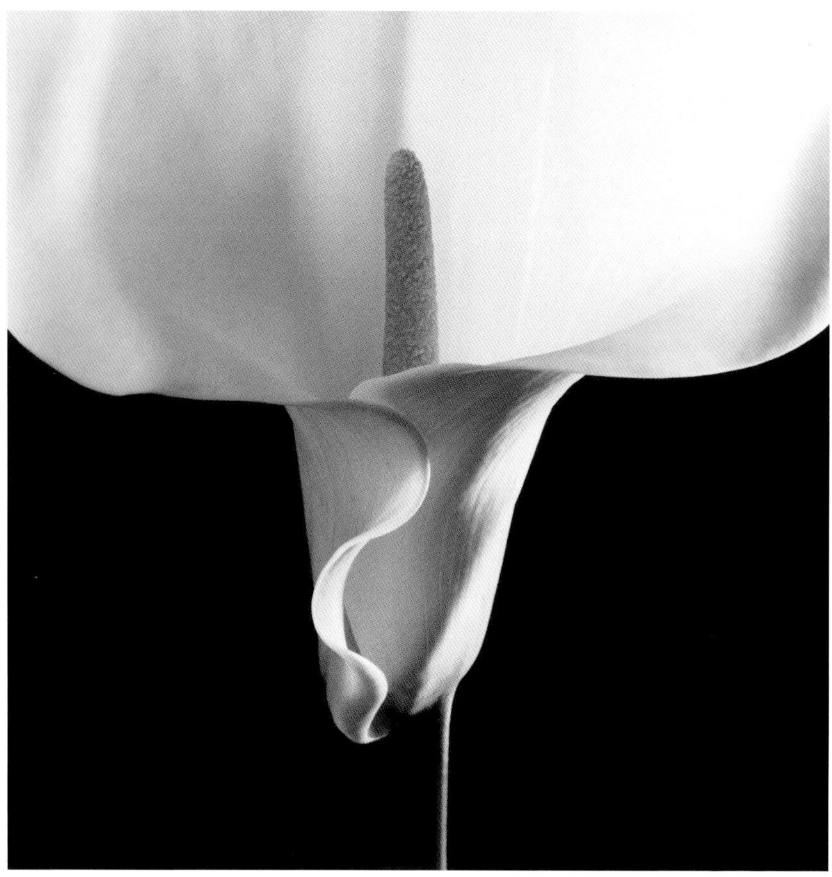

Robert Mapplethorpe
Calla Lily, 1988
Gelatin silver print

The Song of Songs in the Bible contains a reference to the calla lily, which is still used today in bridal bouquets to represent purity and given to mourners to symbolize everlasting light. Here, captured by Robert Mapplethorpe's camera, the flower has a much more sensual feel.

work of Anna Atkins (1799–1871), a British botanist who had the idea to adapt the technique of cyanotype photography – utilized at the time by engineers and architects to copy their plans – and use it to photograph her aquatic plants. She placed the plants on paper soaked in Prussian blue, and the sun did the rest. Stripped of its colours and its environment, the algae took on a new existence: it became pure structure, a pure explosion of infinitely dividing lines. Atkins had created a new way of looking at it.

A century and a half later, the American photographer Robert Mapplethorpe (1946–1989) began a similar project immortalizing flowers (opposite). No colour, no context, just a close-up shot highlighting ordinary details that are usually lost in the overall silhouette. Paring the flower down to its essence emphasizes its resemblance to human sexual organs, a similarity that becomes even more striking given that Mapplethorpe took numerous photos depicting scenes of gay BDSM sexuality. Though widely shown throughout his career with little or no issues, in the year after his death, some of these images were presented as part of an obscenity trial (which determined that they were not obscene), in the context of the culture wars of the 1990s.

These images of plants serve as a reminder that there is a limited number of shapes present in nature. The British scientist Alan Turing, known for his pioneering work in computer science, proposed equations, still used today, to explain how cells develop to form certain shapes and not others. Hence the calla lily recalls certain shapes in the human body, shapes that are visually interesting to artists. Mapplethorpe understood this: 'I'm looking for perfections in form. I do that with portraits. I do it with cocks. I do it with flowers. It's not different from one subject to the next.'

PICTURES AS EVIDENCE

Because we tend to see photographs as representations of the world, it is also tempting to search for evidence in them. Just as a burglar leaves behind his fingerprints as traces of a break-in, people and objects leave traces on the film as proof of their presence in front of the lens. That is the premise of Michelangelo Antonioni's film *Blow-Up* (1966). While on a shoot in a park, a fashion photographer accidentally captures what looks like a murder in the background of a photo. But although he blows up the photograph, he is not able to identify the people in it, or make the leap from the image to the real world. He may have captured a trace of something, but he is unable to go back in time to understand exactly what happened on that day.

If, like Anna Atkins, he had only been dealing with plants rather than people, perhaps the hero of *Blow-Up* would have been calmer. When a photograph is not burdened with the complexities of human behaviour, we feel freer to inhabit the small world that it offers up to us. We stop wondering what is he thinking about? Where is she going? What happened to them after the photo was taken? However, we are still very used to seeing individuals in photographs. The Belgian photographer Harry Gruyaert (b.1941) said that in his early days, those who were dissatisfied with his photographs asked him, 'But where are the people?' Gruyaert does not consider any of the elements that appear in his works to be more important than the others: 'For me, the light, the landscape, etc. are just as important as people. I believe that we are not all that important. No more so than trees, the sky, animals.'

In this photograph (below), Harry Gruyaert nods towards the Rule of Thirds that governs the composition of classical paintings, which are often divided into three equal sections, both vertically and horizontally, with the main subject placed along one of these dividing lines. This photograph is clearly divided into three vertical sections, but there is no subject placed on the two black lines. The barriers closing off the space feel oppressive: only the central rectangle offers a means of escape to the outside, and immediately beyond that, on the pavement, is a parking meter, a machine that also governs the

Harry Gruyaert
Los Angeles, 1982

We are in a place that is protected from thieves by railings, and protected from sunlight by a tinted window. As for the shop opposite, that is protected by an awning. This obsession with protection has the effect of saturating the colours and making them seem artificial. Reality is seen through filters, as if it cannot be faced directly.

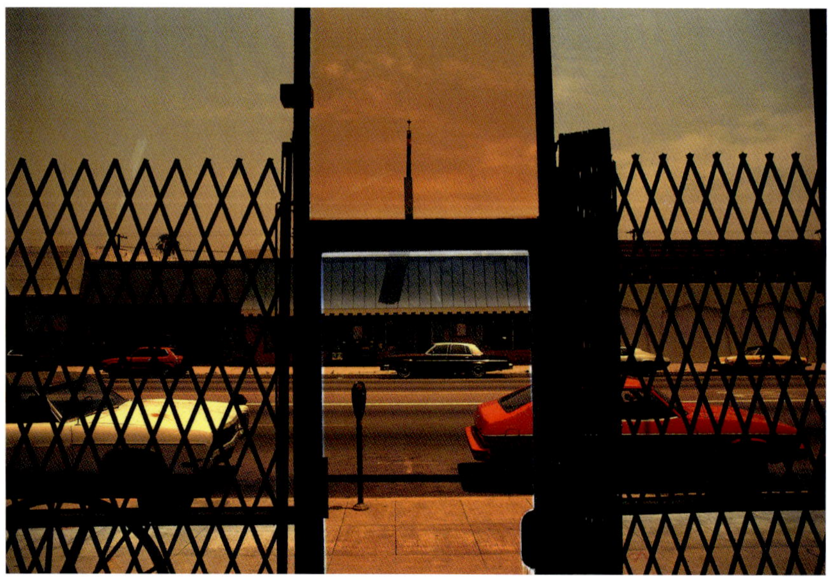

use of space. From a compositional perspective, next we notice two pairs of objects facing each other, creating perpendicular lines: the horizontal line created by two red cars and the vertical line created by the narrow cross-section of a sign that looks like a chimney, its shadow on the awning drawing the eye towards the parking meter. This is a world dominated by regular geometric shapes so oppressive that no person seems to want to venture into it. 'I was excited visually but on a human level pretty sad,' Gruyaert said of his photographs taken in the United States.

Photographs furnish evidence

Since it was invented, as we have discussed, photography has been of interest to scientists because of its ability to create visual records. Anna Atkins was a member of the Botanical Society of London, and in 1844 William Henry Fox Talbot wrote in his book, which had the revealing title *The Pencil of Nature*: 'The plates of this work have been obtained by the mere action of Light upon sensitive paper.' He capitalizes 'Light', as if to show that it is infallible, that it could never make a mistake when creating an image of an object on paper.

Many religions use images as part of their worship, and some of the faithful have also looked to photography, and its implications of scientific objectivity, as a way of conferring legitimacy on their beliefs. The story of the Holy Shroud, or the Shroud of Turin, the winding sheet believed to have been used to wrap Jesus's body in the tomb, is the most well-known example. What makes this relic unique is that it only really developed a global following thanks to photography.

A lawyer and mayor of the Italian town of Asti, Secondo Pia (1855–1941) was also interested in photography. He was commissioned by the Church authorities to take a photograph of the shroud (overleaf), which he did on 25 May 1898. At that time, the shroud itself was already believed to be a kind of photographic film. The energy unleashed by the Resurrection was believed to have been so great that the blood and sweat of the crucified Christ functioned as developing solution and fixer, printing the shape of his body onto the fabric. Over time, the shroud had faded, and only a few pale, vague traces remained. Imagine the photographer's surprise, therefore, when the negative showed a face similar to the one seen in traditional representations of Christ. At the time, no one thought to print positive images of the photograph; it was one of the rare cases in the history of photography when the negative is

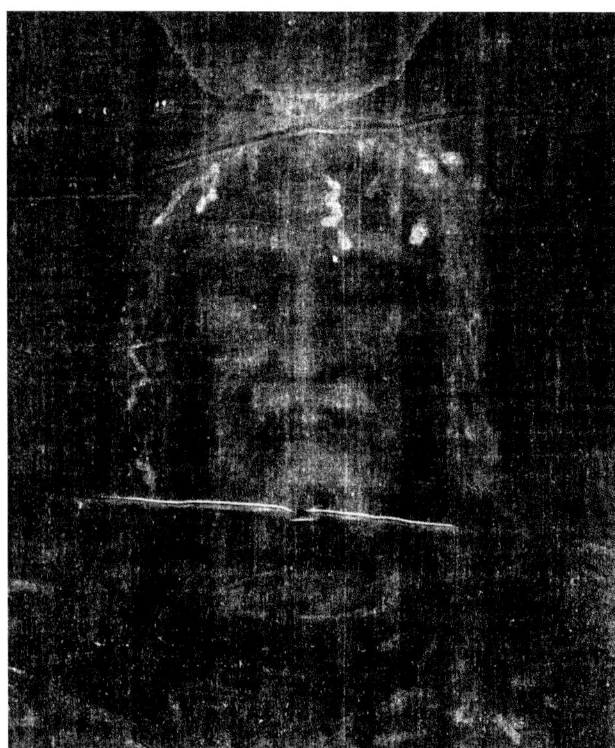

Secondo Pia
The Turin Shroud, 1898
Original negative

The photographer used a process that consisted of shining a light on the shroud and capturing its image on glass plates measuring 60 x 50 cm (23⅝ x 19¾ in.) coated with a photosensitive layer. The image that we see here, and which has been circulated online and published in countless books, is therefore the positive photograph of a negative that appeared on the glass plate.

more famous than the positive, to the extent that few people even realize they are looking at a negative.

In the late nineteenth century, the invention of photography also gave rise to various flights of fancy linked to the idea of 'proof', moving it further away from its scientific roots. People believed they could see images of the dead in a window pane or a mirror, captured by flashes of lightning; or that you could see the face of a murderer in their victim's eyes, if you quickly 'developed' their retina like a reel of film. 'Photographs furnish evidence,' wrote the American intellectual Susan Sontag (1933–2004). 'Something we hear about, but doubt, seems proven when we're shown a photograph of it.' Of course, sometimes a picture can be evidence, but can it still be seen as proof if it has been staged?

THIS MIGHT BE A PIPE

One of the first self-portraits in the history of photography was staged. The pioneering French photographer Hippolyte Bayard

(1801–1877) lies back languidly in a flattering pose (below), surrounded by props – a hat, a figurine. It is definitely him, it is the image of his body, but there is also a theatrical element to this photograph, a sense that it has been *posed for the camera*. Bayard named the picture *Self-Portrait as a Drowned Man*, implying that he had committed suicide because he had not been recognized as the true inventor of photography. He probably also realized that his chemical process was not perfect and that it damaged the paper – it feels like we are looking at a decomposing corpse. Bayard warns us, in a message written on the back of the print, that we shouldn't look at it too long, 'for fear that your sense of smell may be affected, because Monsieur's face and hands are starting to decay, as you can see.' A smell leaves an even stronger impression than a visual record.

In his last book, Roland Barthes, one of the leading French thinkers of the late twentieth century, turned to the subject of photography. However, although *Camera Lucida* (1980) runs to two hundred pages, its author never considers photographs as anything other than a record of 'something that was there', in front of the lens. He sets up an opposition between photography and painting, referring to *The Treachery of Images* (1929), also known as 'This is not a pipe'. This famous Surrealist painting by Belgian

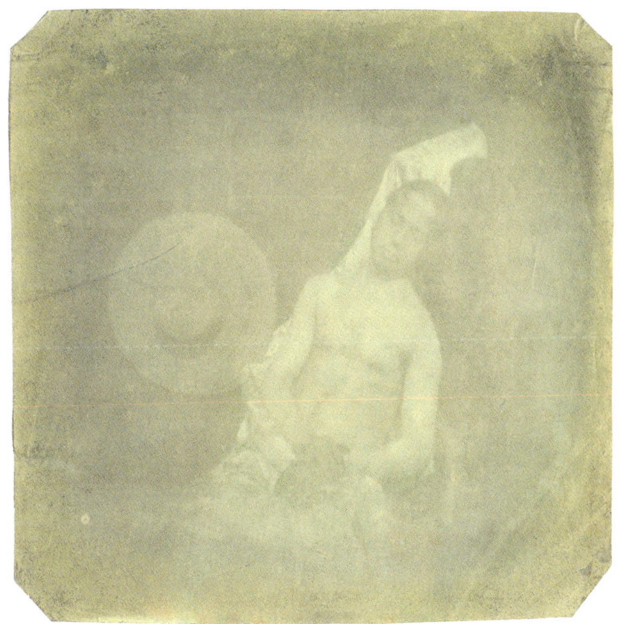

Hippolyte Bayard
Self-Portrait as a Drowned Man, 1840
Direct positive print, 18.8 x 19.2 cm (7½ x 7⅝ in.)

The different shades of grey on the subject's face and torso remind us that our skin behaves in the same way as photosensitive paper, and that a nineteenth-century gentleman would not lie out in the sun, so although his face and hands may be slightly tanned, the rest of his body is pale.

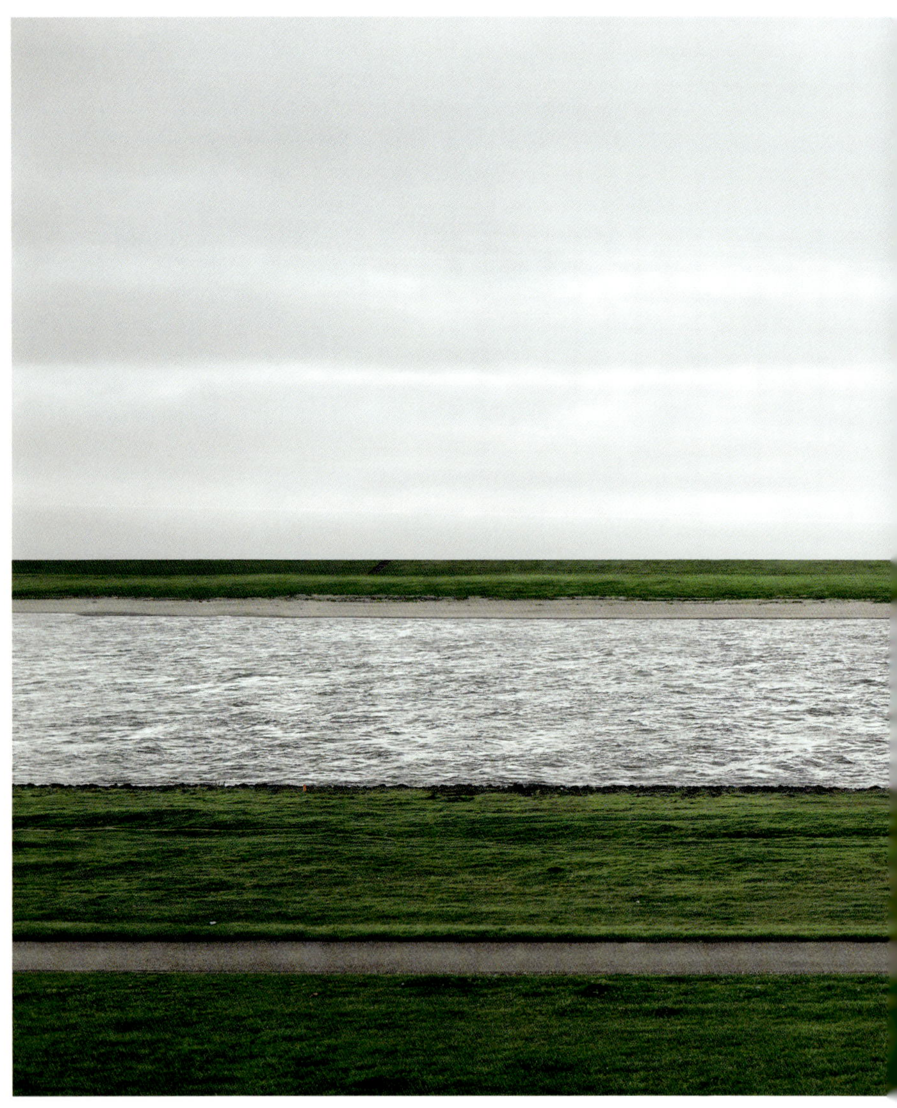

Andreas Gursky
Rhine II, 1999
C-print, 206 x 356 cm
(81⅛ x 140¼ in.)

(1801–1877) lies back languidly in a flattering pose (below), surrounded by props – a hat, a figurine. It is definitely him, it is the image of his body, but there is also a theatrical element to this photograph, a sense that it has been *posed for the camera*. Bayard named the picture *Self-Portrait as a Drowned Man*, implying that he had committed suicide because he had not been recognized as the true inventor of photography. He probably also realized that his chemical process was not perfect and that it damaged the paper – it feels like we are looking at a decomposing corpse. Bayard warns us, in a message written on the back of the print, that we shouldn't look at it too long, 'for fear that your sense of smell may be affected, because Monsieur's face and hands are starting to decay, as you can see.' A smell leaves an even stronger impression than a visual record.

In his last book, Roland Barthes, one of the leading French thinkers of the late twentieth century, turned to the subject of photography. However, although *Camera Lucida* (1980) runs to two hundred pages, its author never considers photographs as anything other than a record of 'something that was there', in front of the lens. He sets up an opposition between photography and painting, referring to *The Treachery of Images* (1929), also known as 'This is not a pipe'. This famous Surrealist painting by Belgian

Hippolyte Bayard
Self-Portrait as a Drowned Man, 1840
Direct positive print, 18.8 x 19.2 cm (7½ x 7⅝ in.)

The different shades of grey on the subject's face and torso remind us that our skin behaves in the same way as photosensitive paper, and that a nineteenth-century gentleman would not lie out in the sun, so although his face and hands may be slightly tanned, the rest of his body is pale.

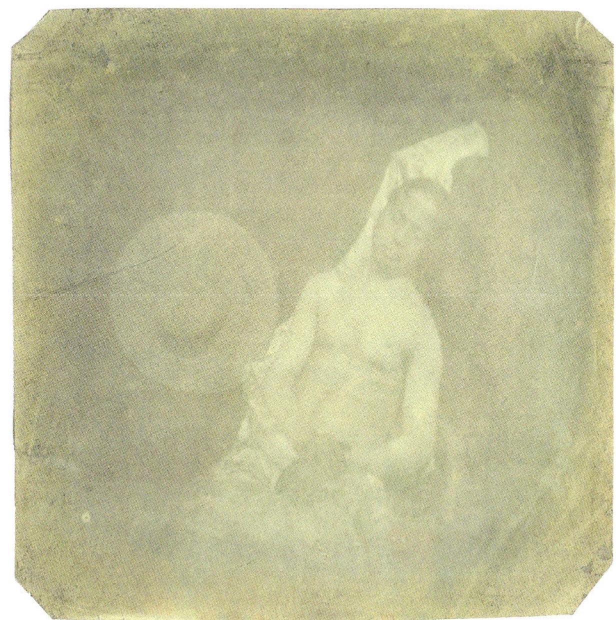

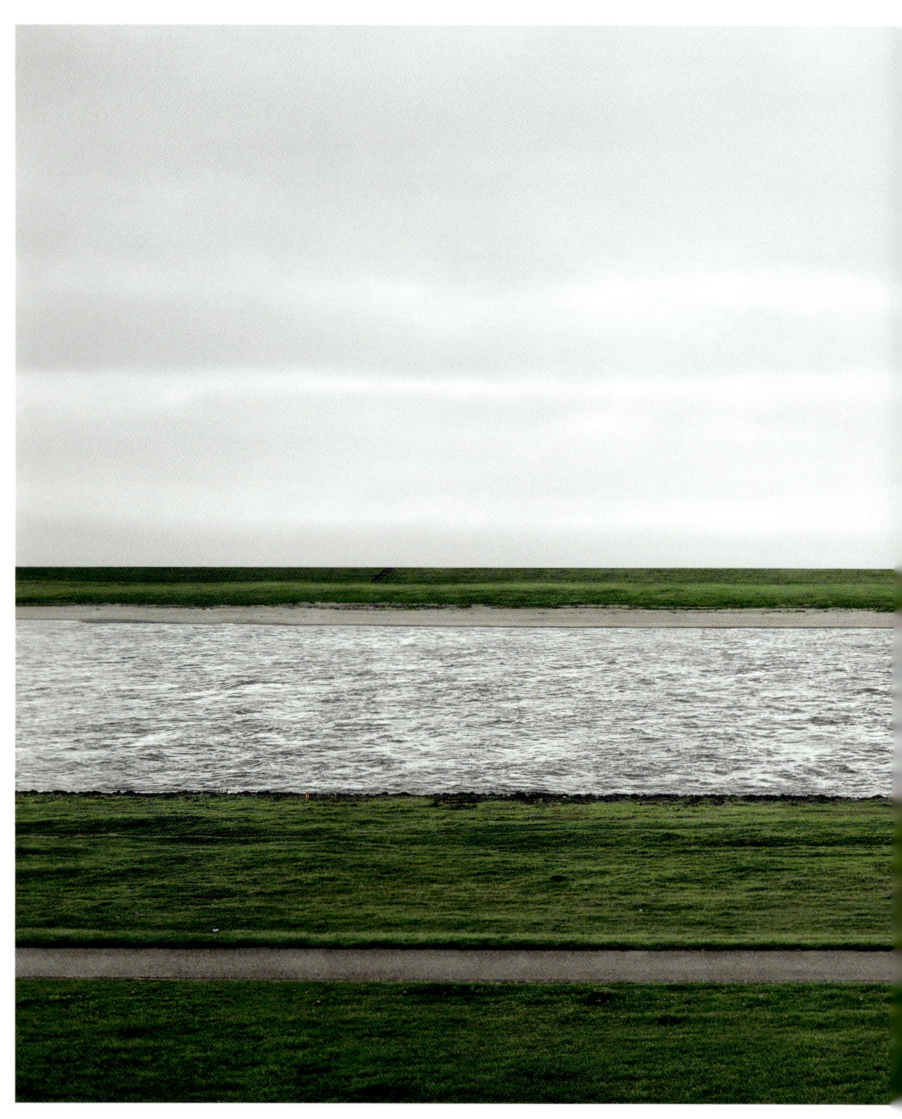

Andreas Gursky
Rhine II, 1999
C-print, 206 x 356 cm
(81⅛ x 140¼ in.)

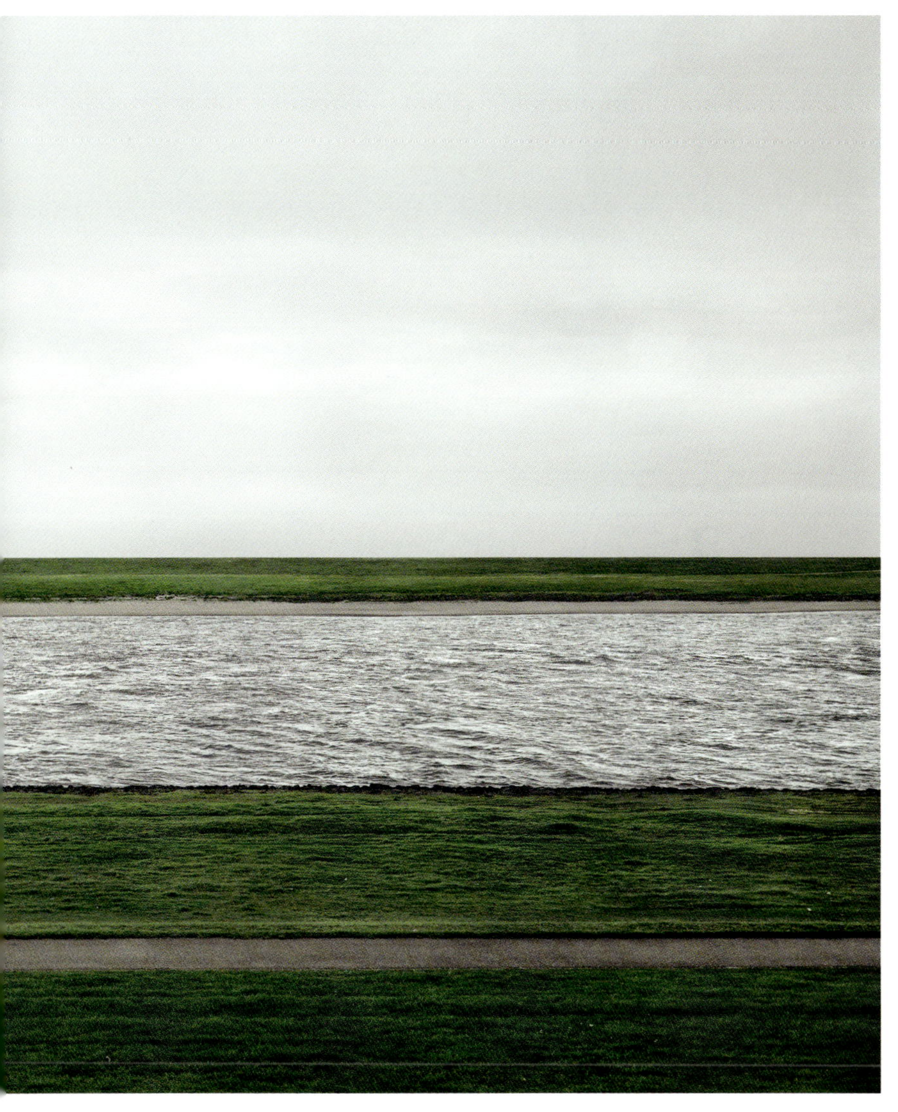

As in a French formal garden, the composition plays with symmetry: the horizon bisects the frame exactly across the centre, the strips of land create a sense of balance.

artist René Magritte reminds us that we are looking at a depiction of a pipe, and not a real pipe, even though it is painted in minute detail. Barthes writes that, in photography, it is a different matter: 'A pipe in a photograph is always a pipe.' But this is very strange. Despite the writer's reputation, I suggest that he is assuming too much, especially if we apply his analysis to the modern world. The number of doctored images that individuals post and send each other every day on their phones is huge, and people are becoming more sceptical about the 'truth' of these pictures, stopping to think and question them. Of course, our initial response is to view these images as records of the world, but that is by no means the same thing as believing everything they say.

Visual depictions of ineffable feelings and sensations

In order to be able to believe fully, without any reservations, that a photograph is an exact record of a part of the world, we need more information about its context than the image itself can offer. How can we know whether the very presence of the photographer has impacted things, even if they were very discreet? How can we be sure that what is depicted in the photograph matches reality? Let's take an example from the art world, one of the most expensive photographs of all time: *Rhine II* (pages 20–21), by German artist Andreas Gursky (b.1955). Gursky is often associated with the Düsseldorf School, whose members rejected close-ups in favour of large-format prints showing locations that were not usually considered worthy of contemplation – places that had been dismissed or abandoned, where people just passed through. Looking at *Rhine II*, it is tempting to think: 'You know what, I could have taken that photo! I would have walked along the Rhine from the centre of Düsseldorf, then, at some point, far from town, I would have set my camera on its stand and pressed the button.'

But this landscape never existed in the real world. It only exists in the artistic realm, in the form of this photograph, and in our minds. When we look at it, we picture ourselves standing at the edge of the path, sighing as we look out at the grey sky and the indifferent stretch of water. In fact, this photograph was made by combining images and deleting elements, digital manipulations that are so subtle they remain invisible, even though the image is both very sharp and enormous. There is something inhuman about the sharpness of the image: if we had been there, we would never have been able to see so distinctly, in a single glance, the blades of grass at our feet and the fields on the other side of the river.

Instead of seeing photographs as records of *what was there*, it is often more useful to see them as visual depictions of ineffable feelings and sensations that would be difficult to express without the impression of reality created by photography. From this perspective, strictly speaking, *Rhine II* does not depict the River Rhine on the outskirts of Düsseldorf, but rather, depending on who is looking at it, melancholy Sunday afternoons in autumn, the human obsession with pitting ourselves against the lush anarchy of nature and taming it into straight lines, the world when there is no one there to look at it.

RETOUCHING AND TOUCHING

Many people are happy for painters to take liberties with depicting precisely what was there, but they won't allow photographers the same freedom to deviate from reality. It is true that we are used to photographs that simply show what was in front of the lens when they were taken. These are the kinds of photographs that are accepted by the legal and justice systems, for example, when we supply an ID photo to the authorities to get a passport. But what about when a photograph's subject is not a person's face, but the emotion they are feeling?

Dorothea Lange's *Migrant Mother* (overleaf) is one of the most famous photographs of the twentieth century. It was taken by Lange (1895–1965) when she was working for the Resettlement Administration. This American federal agency, founded in 1935 by President Roosevelt as part of his New Deal, commissioned some of the greatest names in photography to document the living conditions of the working classes.

The context is well known: the subject's name is Florence Owens Thompson. At the age of thirty-two, she was already a mother of seven. In the wake of the Great Depression, her family, like many other seasonal workers, were forced to travel great distances in search of work. But the photograph doesn't tell us that. What it expresses are the questions playing on this mother's mind: 'Where will I find something for us to eat? Where are we going to sleep tonight? And tomorrow night?' or even: 'What kind of society would let this happen to us?' The baby's dirty cheeks, the mother's torn sleeve and the hole-riddled jumper worn by the child on the right, every detail in the picture whispers this message. The injustice is all the more shocking because Mrs Thompson is Native American: although her people had nothing to do with the causes of the Great

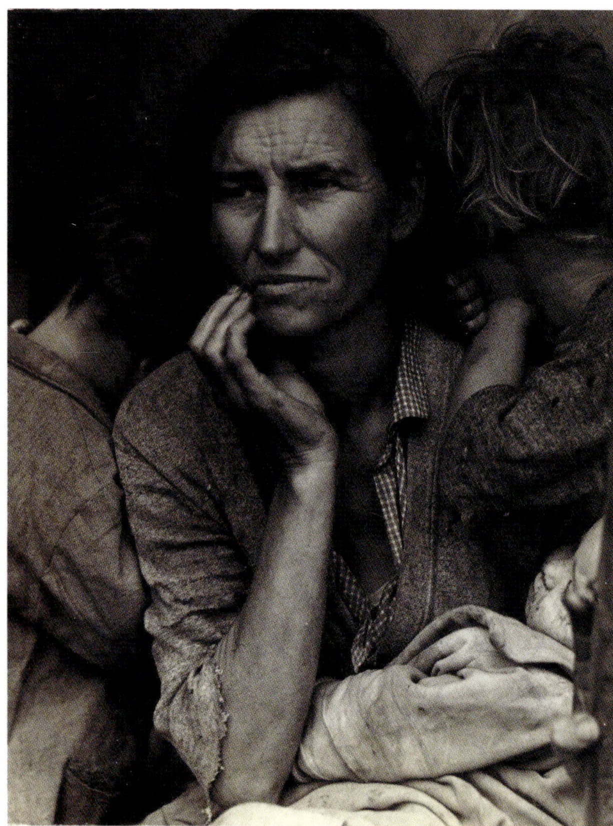

Dorothea Lange
Migrant Mother, Nipomo, California, March 1936
Digital file of original negative

This photograph is a trade-off between between creating an accurate record and staging an impactful shot: the subject's anxious gesture, raising her hand to her mouth, was natural, while the children turned their heads away because the photographer asked them to.

Depression, they were severely affected by it, and the media at the time was ignorant of their suffering.

As well as being deeply affecting, this famous photograph has all the characteristics of an unstaged documentary photo. It bears witness to the appalling suffering in a particular part of the world at a specific time. But that does not mean we can consider it a transparent window onto the world. Not only has Lange intervened in the normal course of events by asking the children to turn away, but, as was discovered in the 1960s, the most well-known print of this photo, created in 1939, was also retouched. In the bottom right corner, an unknown person's thumb could originally be seen grasping the tent pole, but this has been removed in the print. Lange probably thought that the thumb would ruin the composition, just as the tiniest of blemishes on a beautiful face irresistibly draws the eye. This should not be held against her, as photographs are a means of seeing through someone else's eyes, with everything that implies about subjectivity.

Dorothea Lange
Migrant Mother, Nipomo, California, March 1936
Digital file of original negative retouched in the 1930s

Here, in bottom right corner, the thumb that was grasping the tent pole has been removed by retouching.

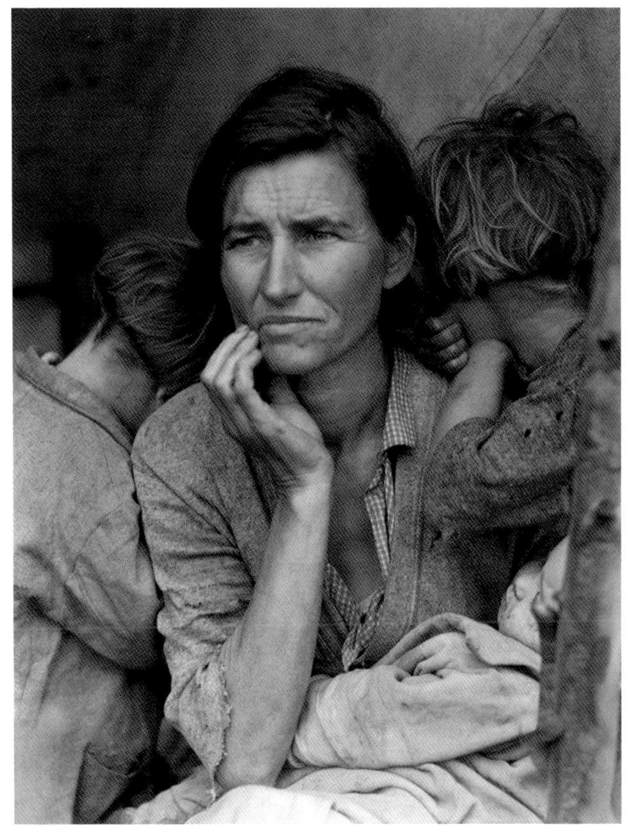

Every photograph is a fake from start to finish

The only photographs that we can truly say are not staged are those that are the result of sheer chance – when you press the button without looking through the viewfinder, without framing the shot. In every other situation, even if the photographer doesn't intervene in the real world by asking the subject to smile or adjusting a drooping flower, the mere choice of framing is in itself a subtle form of staging. As the American photographer Edward Steichen (1879–1973) wrote in a 1903 article for the journal *Camera Work* sarcastically entitled 'Ye Fakers': 'In fact, every photograph is a fake from start to finish, a purely impersonal, unmanipulated photograph being practically impossible.' Since then, of course, this has become even more true. The art of retouching is as old as photography itself, but in the past it required advanced technical skills, whereas

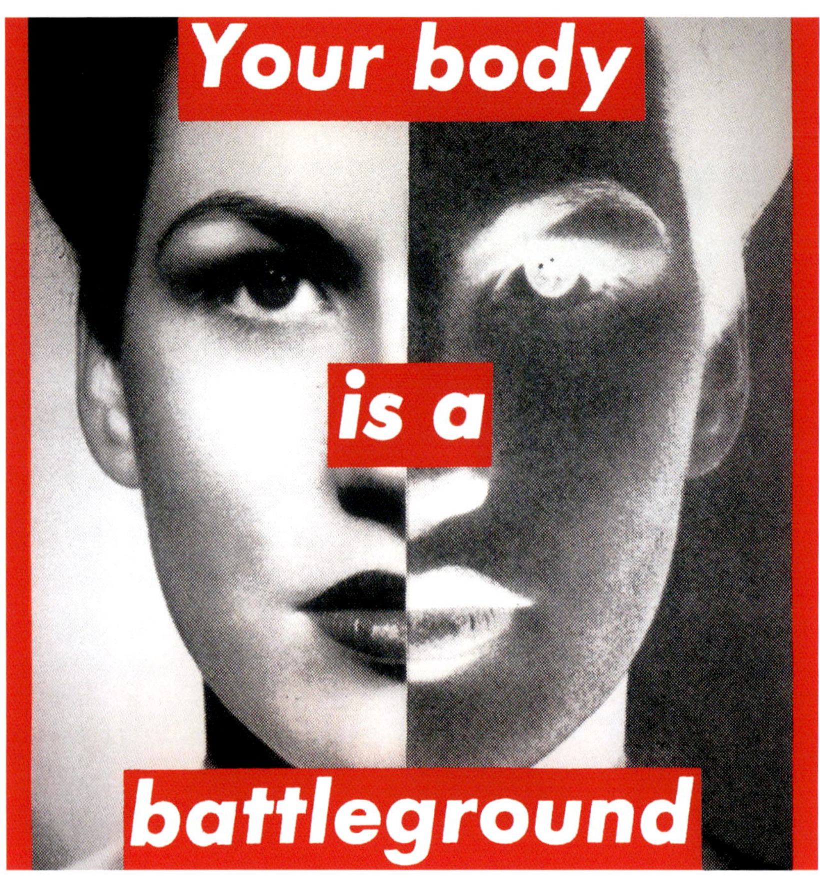

now easy-to-use software makes it simple to erase a thumb or any other unwanted detail. What's more, staging and retouching are not restricted to pictures: they are also found in the real world.

The most important thing is that we, as viewers, do not allow ourselves to be manipulated and unwittingly believe a lie. This is why photographs that invite us to question the line between reality and fiction are so intriguing. The two pictures illustrated here offer an opportunity to reflect on the question of staging by exploring one particular aspect of it: the staging of the self.

The above work by the American conceptual artist Barbara Kruger (b.1945) was first distributed in the form of flyers at a protest against reforms to abortion law in the United States, which took place in Washington in November 1989. Kruger altered an existing photograph by changing it to black and white, leaving the grain visible if you look closely. She then added a slogan written

Barbara Kruger
Untitled (Your Body is a Battleground), 1989
Photographic silkscreen on vinyl, 284.5 x 284.5 cm (112 x 112 in.)

This image is divided in two, with one half showing the positive, the other the negative. It is the same face, but what is white on one side is black on the other; it is the same woman, but she is seen as a criminal by those who would like to take away her right to an abortion.

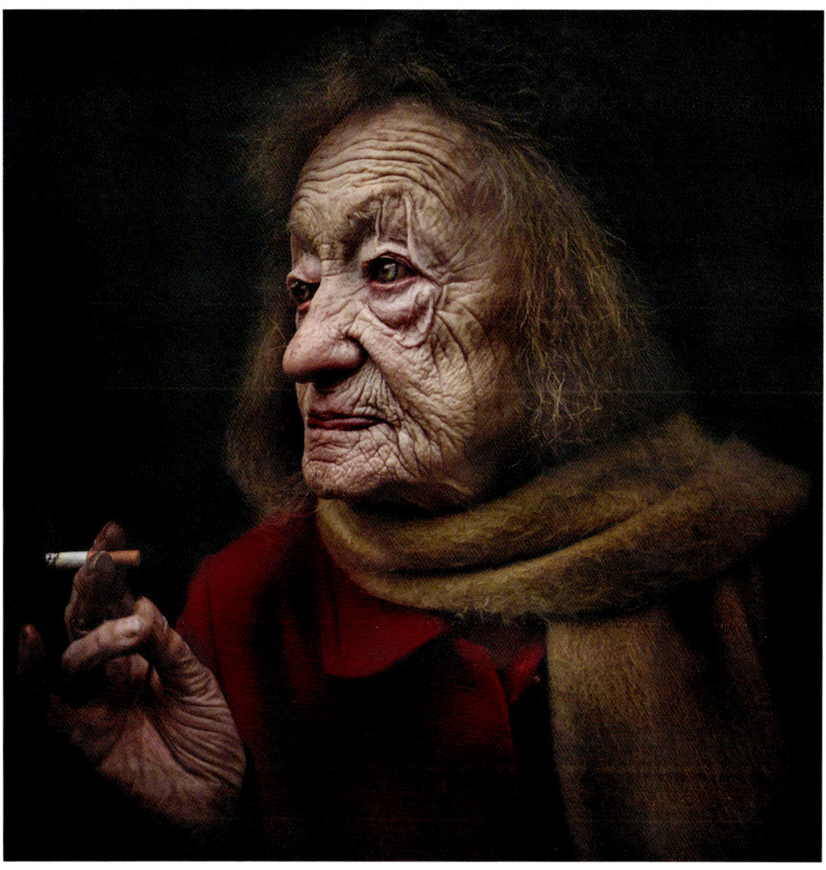

Lee Jeffries
Autumn, 2016

The camera meticulously captures the extraordinary network of wrinkles, like the twists and turns of a life that we imagine must have been eventful. A far cry from the perfect models used in fashion and advertising shoots, this picture of Autumn elegantly holding her cigarette shows that beauty is not necessarily to be found on the surface.

in white letters on a red background, in Futura, a font she often uses in her work. Women's bodies have become a battleground; it is tempting to expand the scope of this slogan beyond the question of abortion laws. The fact that the subject of the edited photo is wearing make-up points to the cosmetics industry and the commercialization of cosmetic surgery, both of which use glamorous photos to advertise their products or services, as though a smooth and wrinkle-free face was synonymous with happiness. Kruger refuses to allow her own image to be used in the media: 'Thank God I'm an artist and not an internet or TikTok or movie star,' she recently said.

In contrast to the perfect face used by Barbara Kruger, Autumn (above), a penniless woman posing for British photographer Lee Jeffries (b.1971), has shunned the beauty industry by allowing nature to leave its mark on her face.

IS THIS FOR REAL?

In the 1960s, Guy Debord was already using the phrase 'society of the spectacle' to describe a world in which everything we do is designed first and foremost to be seen. Today, this trend has only become more widespread: it is likely that many scenes would play out very differently if no one was there to photograph or film them.

That doesn't bother most amateur photographers, who take out their phones again and again to record what is in front of them, as if they no longer trust their memory. But many professionals are suspicious of this phenomenon and prefer to shed light on something that has not been set up as a conscious performance, or simply something that usually goes unnoticed. That is the case for the Spanish photographer Cristina de Middel (b.1975), who likes to go against the grain, for example by taking pictures of prostitutes' clients rather than of the prostitutes themselves.

In her series 'Poly-Spam' (opposite), De Middel seeks to give visual form to something that is usually only seen inside our minds: the pictures we imagine when we take the time to read one of the tantalizing spam emails that arrive in our inboxes almost every day. A fortune teller assures us that a stroke of luck is waiting just around the corner, if we will simply allow her to guide us. Perhaps we just need to give a small amount of money to a stranger so that they can access a huge inheritance; or, as here, a mysterious Nigerian lawyer assures us that a distant relative has left us shares in the oil company Texaco. Cristina de Middel creates real pictures of the scenes that only existed in her imagination when she read these words which, usually, are designed to get money out of us.

When we are looking at a photograph, rather than a spam email, our imagination is stimulated in the same way, although pictures tend to restrict it more than words. Even when looking at a photo feature in a magazine, we can't help but wonder more or less vaguely *what it is like there* or *how it would feel to be there*. It is the same, of course, when we hear about wars, disasters, terrorist attacks and other dangerous events that we would prefer to keep our distance from as long as we are not involved. Looking at photos taken of these occurrences is a way of safely travelling to the places where they are happening.

For example, we can visit Beijing on a day in June 1989 (pages 30–31), where Chinese students are calling for freedom of speech and freedom of the press. They have just erected a statue similar to the Statue of Liberty in Tiananmen Square, and the Western media have rushed to christen it the 'Goddess of Democracy'. But the authorities send in the army. On the second day of the crackdown,

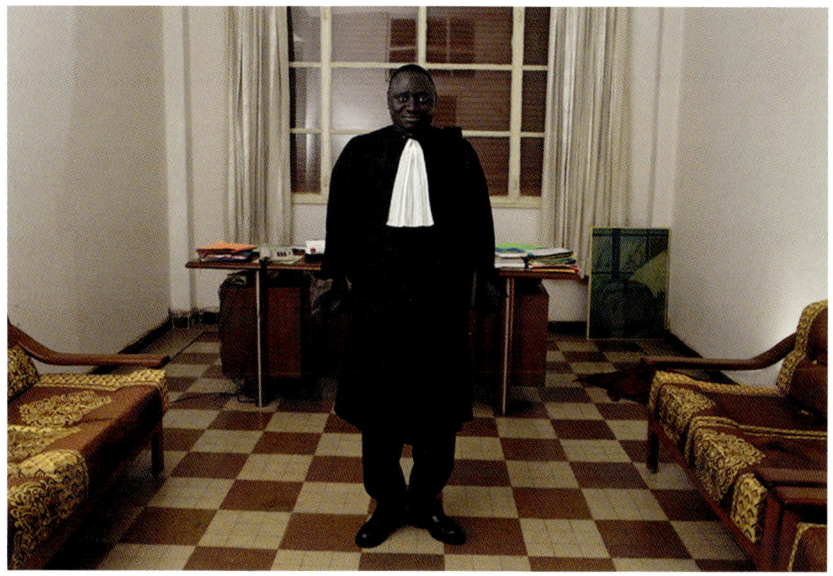

Cristina de Middel
Barrister Fagbemi Lateef, from the series 'Poly-Spam', 2009

'My name is Barrister Fagbemi Lateef I am a solicitor at law. [...] Thank you in advance for your anticipated co-operation.' We are being offered a chance to earn 3.5 million dollars. De Middel imagines the small, humble office where the author wrote this message.

one man stood bravely in front of a line of tanks, to stop them from moving forward. We don't know his name or what became of him, but this picture has been seen around the world.

The Czech artist Pavel Maria Smejkal's (b.1957) act of erasure (page 32) may be interpreted in a number of ways. It creates a world that exists in the past conditional, in which well-known events might not have taken place. It also highlights how famous photographs suffer from overexposure – we have seen them so often that they end up conveying nothing to us, and they function like advertising logos, which we can identify without even needing to see the whole image. Finally, the 'Fatescapes' series echoes the way in which dictators use edited photos to try and erase certain images from the collective memory. Over the years, this specific work has taken on a political meaning because the Chinese regime has sought to erase all traces of the Tiananmen Square protests.

Swiss-based artists Jojakim Cortis (b.1978) and Adrian Sonderegger (b.1980) play an even more dangerous game with historical truth. In their aptly named series 'Icons' (page 32), they imagine how the most iconic photos of the twentieth century could have been staged in a studio – including those that were later discovered to be faked. That is the case for the photo of Nessie, the Loch Ness Monster, published in the *Daily Mail* on 21 April 1934. It is an accurate record of what was in front of the camera,

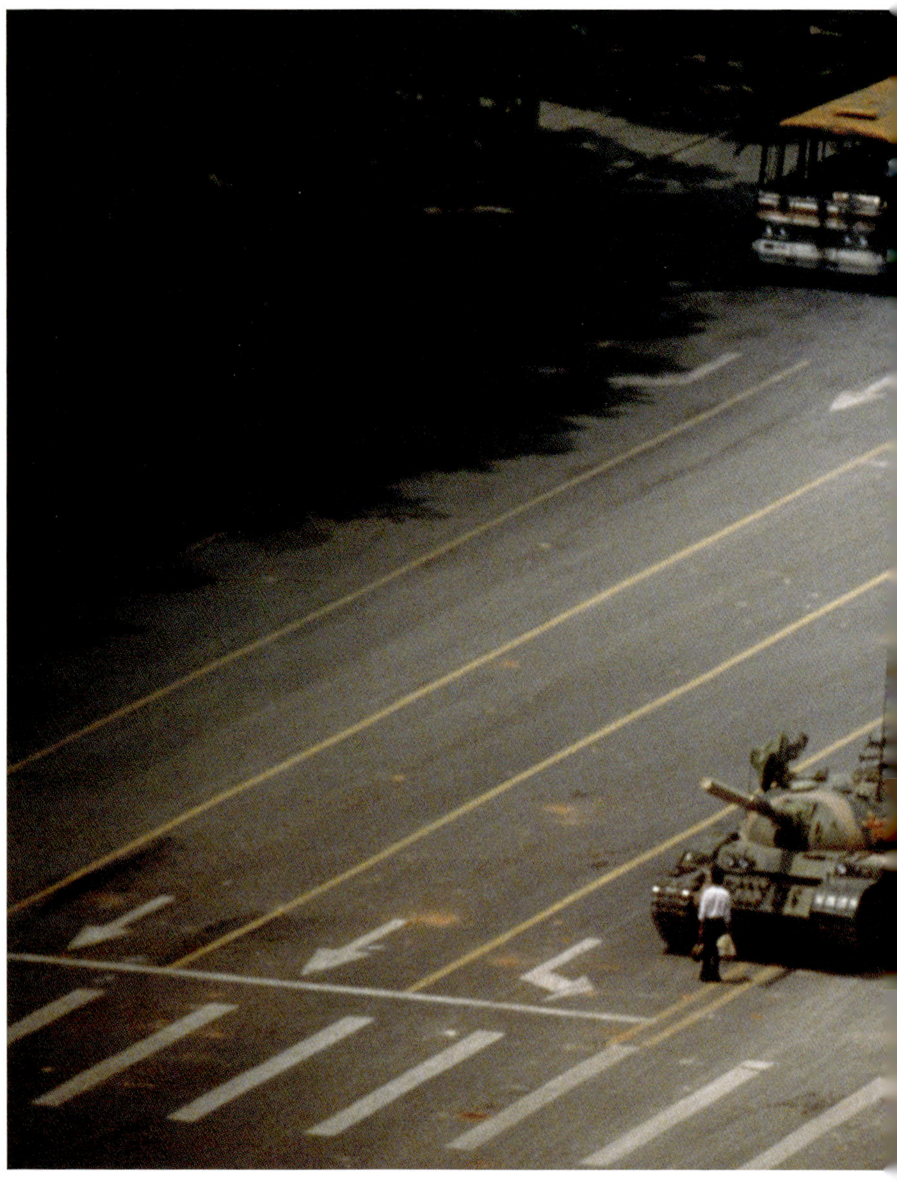

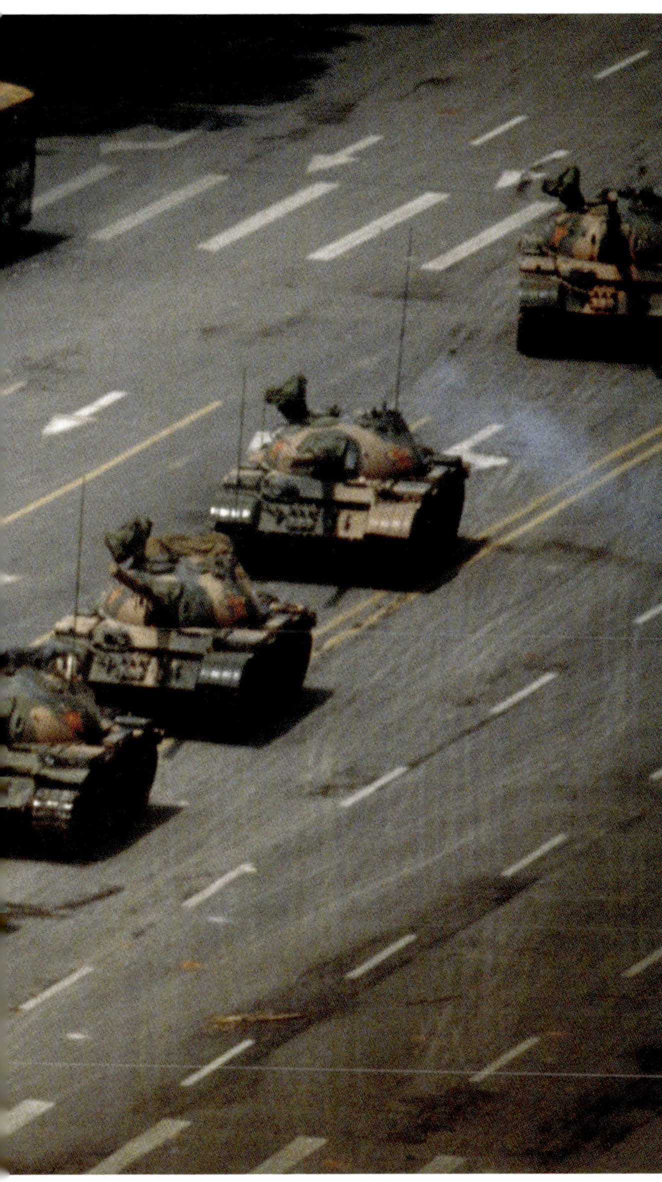

Stuart Franklin
'The Tank Man' stopping the column of T59 tanks in Tiananmen Square, Beijing,
4 June 1989

When he took this shot, British photographer Stuart Franklin (b.1956) did not think it would be very interesting because he was too far away from what was happening. In fact, it is the empty space all around the subject that makes the photograph so poignant. A close-up would have left us imagining a whole host of other objects outside of the frame, whereas here, the man seems tiny, isolated, vulnerable.

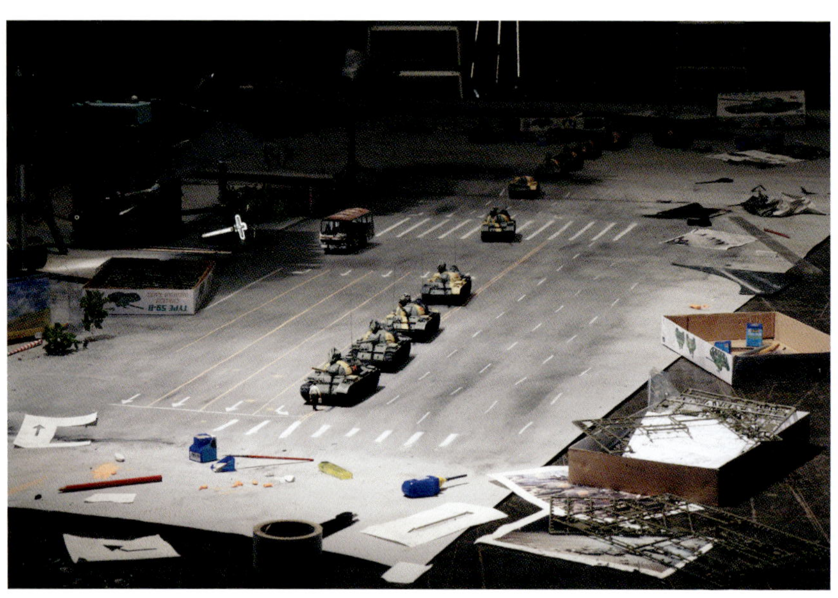
TYPE 59-B

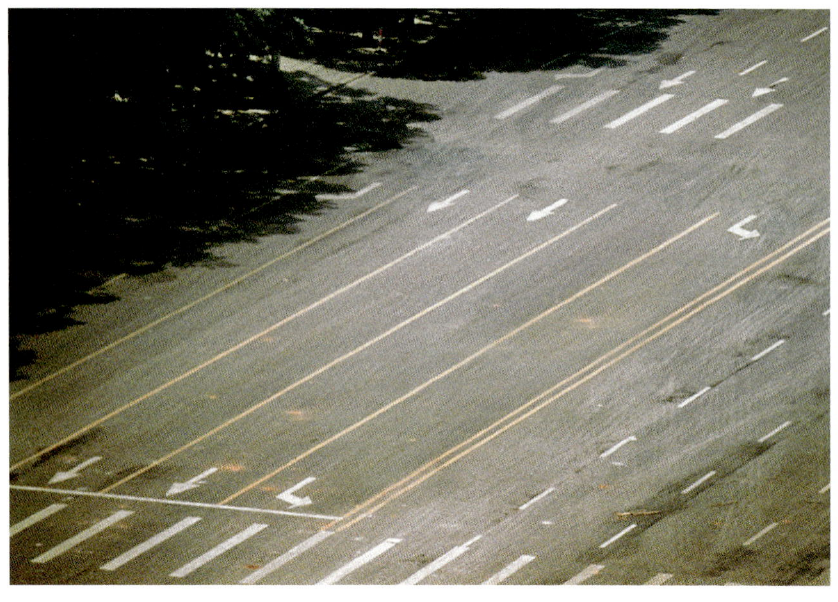

Jojakim Cortis & Adrian Sonderegger
Making of 'Tian'anmen' (by Stuart Franklin, 1989), from the series 'Icons', 2013
C-print

If the framing had been tighter, this photograph would not have included the pots of paint or the packaging for the model tanks. In a similar way to 'Fatescapes', the series 'Icons' reinterprets famous photos, some of which are shown in this book, such as *Death of a Loyalist Soldier* (p. 162) and *Rhine II* (p. 20).

Pavel Maria Smejkal
1989 Beijing, from the series 'Fatescapes', 2009–13
Archival pigment digital print

In his series 'Fatescapes', Pavel Maria Smejkal takes famous photographs – including the 'Tank Man' and two other pictures reproduced in this book, *Death of a Loyalist Soldier* (p. 162) and the execution of Nguyễn Văn Lém (p. 157) – and edits them, leaving just the background.

not an edited photo; however, it does not show a plesiosaur but a toy submarine with a neck made of putty. Cortis & Sonderegger invite us to question *all* pictures, even those that have been proven credible by trustworthy witnesses.

This warning is perhaps a little exaggerated, although, of course, it is not an artist's responsibility to encourage moderation. Instead of constantly doubting everything, it is more useful to ask ourselves what a photograph could express beyond accurately representing objects for us to lazily identify. In this sense, Franklin's original photograph of the 'Tank Man' offers a visual representation of the distance that separates us from this man who had the courage to put his convictions into action, and whose identity still remains unknown.

KEY IDEAS

Just because photographs offer an accurate representation of the world, that doesn't mean they are simply a duplicate of it.

A photographer sometimes works in the same way as a painter, a sculptor or a director.

Not knowing how a photo was created does not mean we can't appreciate it.

KEY QUESTIONS

Is it a photographer's responsibility to create records of the world?

Can we always see photographs as evidence of what has happened?

When a photographer repositions their subject to create a picture that is more faithful to their vision, does that necessarily distort reality?

In photography, are all means justified in the quest to create the desired image?

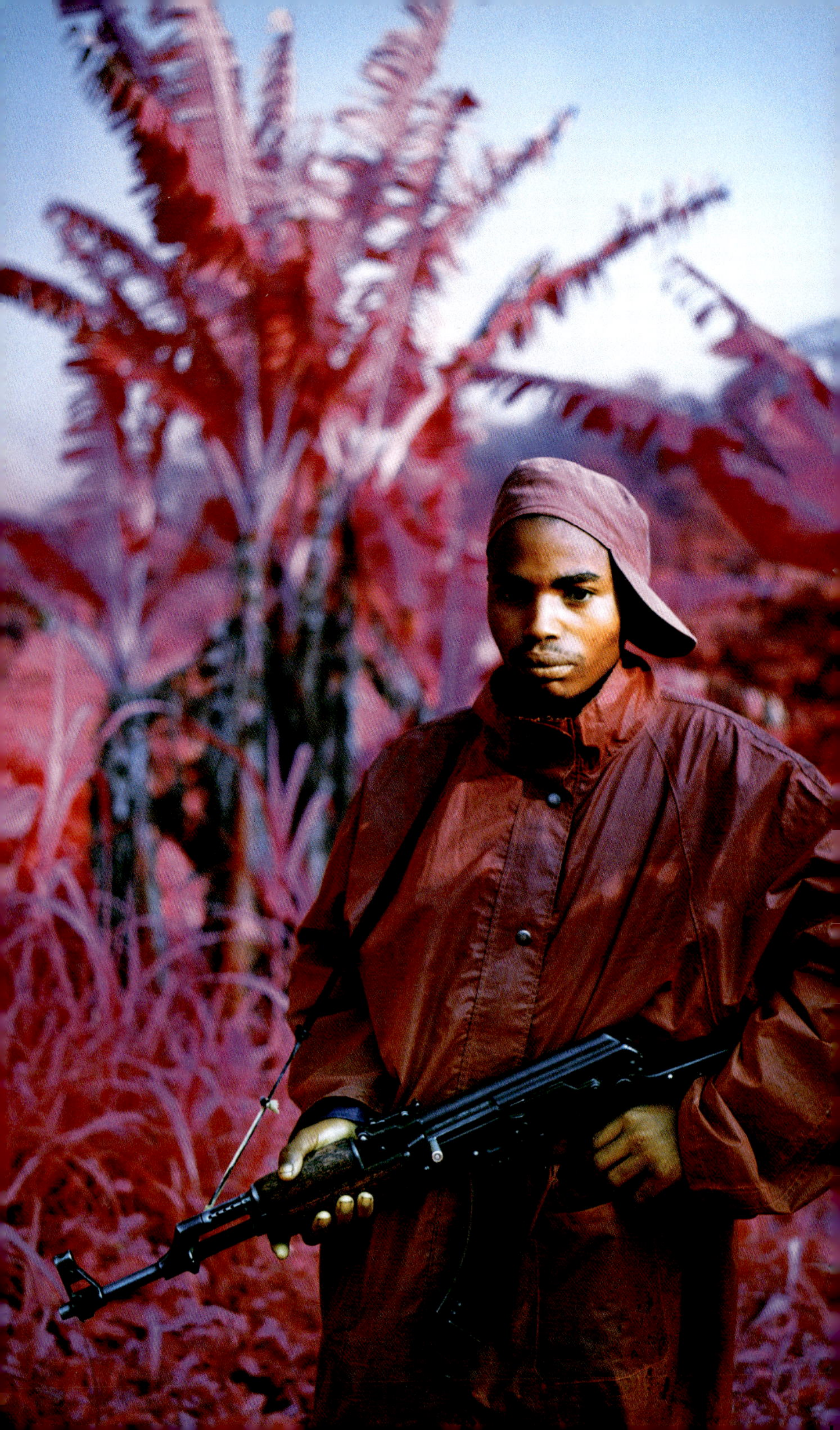

DOCTORING AND DEFAMILIARIZATION

-

When you see the same image again and again, you develop a certain response. I wanted to create work in which we have no automatic response

-

Richard Mosse

Many people believe that photographs should be like windows opening onto the world. These kinds of photographs do not add or remove anything from the scenes that they show. People looking at them do not feel tricked or manipulated; instead, they feel like they are being told the truth. The rules of the famous press photography contest World Press Photo, which has been held since 1955, stipulate that: 'Manipulation which adds, rearranges, reverses, distorts or removes people or objects from within the frame is not permitted.'

There are many press photographers who think this is the right approach. Stuart Franklin, who took the photograph of the Tank Man, is a member of the famous Magnum photo agency. For him, the most a photographer can do if they want to bear witness to the state of the world is to reframe the image and lightly correct the colours or the exposure. No more than that. But he wrote that in 1991. Since then, the digital revolution has made retouching and doctoring easy, commonplace and sometimes playful. As early as 2001, the German photographer Thomas Hoepker (b.1936), also a member of Magnum, complained that 'people tamper with images all over, muddying the public's perception of photography as documentary evidence'. This was still before the advent of artificial intelligence, which is now able to generate photos on demand, without a camera or a photographer, sowing doubt and discord among competitors at photography contests. At the Sony World Photography Awards in 2023, a prize was awarded to a photograph created in this way. But this is all simply a question of how an artist chooses to express themselves. A photographer who bears witness to the reality of the world armed only with their camera and a photographer who uses digital technology are not doing the same job. In photography, as in fine arts, controversies only arise when someone is found to be lying about how an image was created.

PAINTERS WITHOUT PAINTBRUSHES

In the history of photography, the first movement that openly challenged this view that photographs should be accurate records of reality was Pictorialism. The movement was born out of certain photographers' desire to compete with painting. They no longer wanted to be restricted to faithfully depicting what the world looked like, or seeking to achieve an impassive objectivity, but instead to use images to evoke feelings and impressions (opposite). Henry Peach Robinson (1830–1901), one of the movement's leaders, was vehemently against the window model of photography.

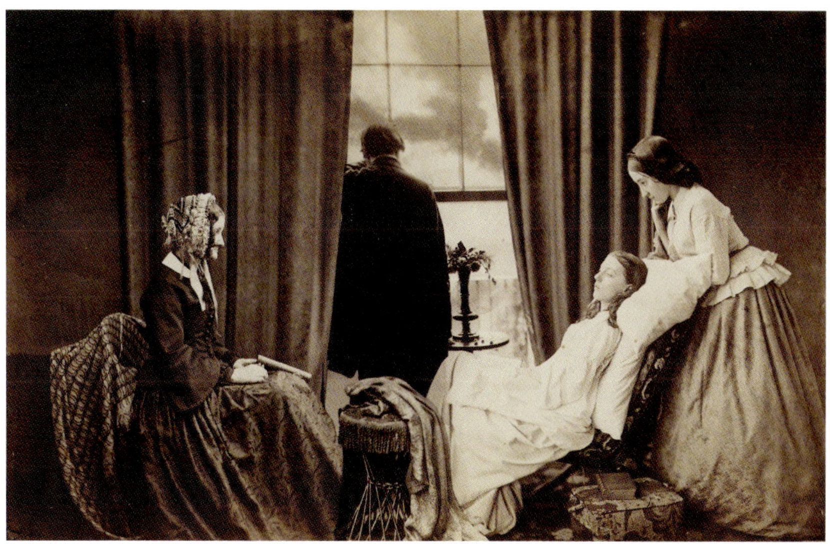

Henry Peach Robinson
Fading Away, 1858
Albumen print,
23.8 x 37.5 cm
(9⅜ x 14⅞ in.)

Note the bouquet of wilted flowers at the centre of the frame. This reflects in plant form the human drama being played out in the foreground. As the young woman's life drains away, the stems droop and the flowers fall onto the side table.

In his book published in London in 1869, *Pictorial Effect in Photography: Being Hints on Composition and Chiaro-Oscuro for Photographers*, he writes: 'But any "dodge, trick, or conjuration" of any kind is open to the photographer's use, so that it belongs to his art, and is not false to nature.' The question is exactly what he meant by 'nature'. Does the word refer here to the world as it is, or to the world as the photographer sees it, through the prism of their beliefs, their desires and their emotions?

Robinson looked to theatre for the performance skills (the young girl is pretending to die, like an actress) and to painting for the techniques of chiaroscuro. He also used the art of collage, as *Fading Away* is a photomontage created from five different negatives. Although this is not visible to the naked eye, there are two clues that give it away. Firstly, each of the three women is perfectly lit, but the source of this light is not the open window. Next, the perspective of the horizontal surfaces: the side table in front of the window, the stool on the left and the footrest on the right all seem to be the same distance from the lens, although they are spread around the room. Although the sky was photographed separately, it seems to be a representation of the 'dark thoughts' that are emanating from the standing man. Is he the girl's father? In any case, he seems to have half-opened the curtains to allow a little sunlight into the house and instead found only a sad and cloudy dusk – Robinson is truly talented at staging a scene.

Making reality speak

The French photographer Gustave Le Gray (1820–1884) was also concerned with staging scenes, although not in the theatrical sense of the word. At the time when he created his works, very few people suspected that they were the product of complex manipulations. To use modern terminology, Le Gray was an expert in the art of compositing, which Andreas Gursky would also embrace a century and a half later to create his photograph of the Rhine (pages 20–21).

In his seascapes (a term borrowed from the world of painting), Le Gray used a technique that he called *ciels rapportés*, which translates as 'skies added in' (below). The sea and sky here are from two different negatives, which were not taken in the same place or at the same time. The aperture must not have been opened to the same width in both shots, because the upper half is lighter than the

Gustave Le Gray
Marine, bateau quittant le port (Seascape with a Ship Leaving Port), Sète, France, 1857
Albumen silver print from glass negative, 31.3 x 40.3 cm (12⅜ x 15⅞ in.)

The setting sun is on the right, behind the clouds. But instead of creating a diagonal line from right to left, as we may have expected, its reflection is parallel to the vertical edges of the frame: the photograph is clearly doctored.

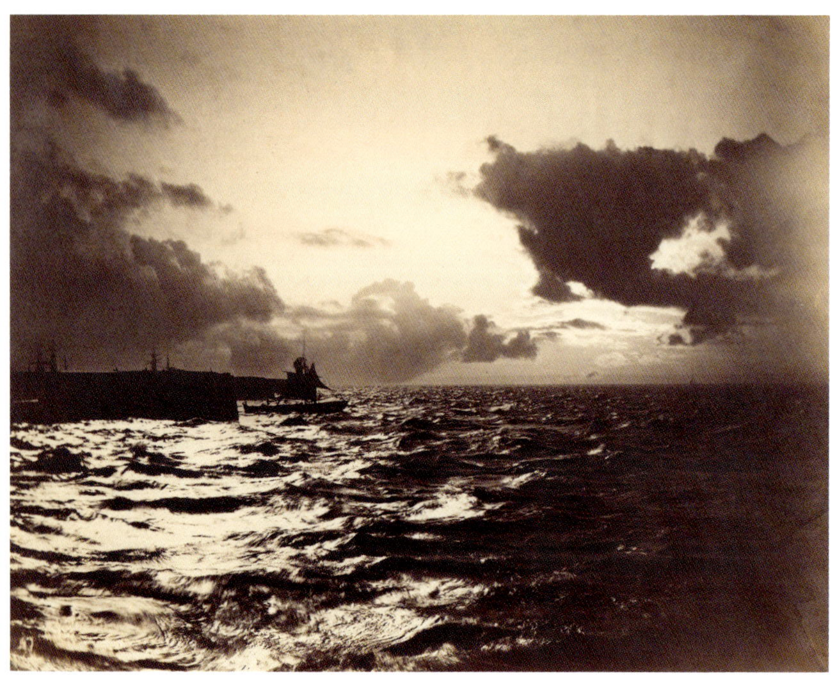

lower half. Looking closely at the picture, you also notice that on the right-hand side, the sea and sky overlap slightly. When Le Gray realized that the boat and the pier overlapped – because these two elements were taken from different negatives – he used a razor to cut into the 'sky' negative to allow the boat to show through!

In a way, the Pictorialists, with their desire to improve on reality or 'make it speak', using sophisticated techniques that were inaccessible to mere amateurs, anticipated the mocking response of professional photographers to the launch of Kodak's famous slogan: 'You press the button, we do the rest!' In 1898, one of their company magazines parodied this slogan: 'You jab the jigger, and we'll finish the mess!'

GHOSTS IN THE MACHINE

According to Henry Peach Robinson, as we have seen, a photographer is allowed to use any means at their disposal to depict 'nature'. But not everyone agrees on the definition of this word. Various reasons – religious faith, a penchant for the supernatural, belief in folklore or simply a desire to fight against the disappointments of the world – could lead someone to include all kinds of things in their definition. Things that cannot be seen, at least not by those who don't know how to look or who refuse to admit that science and rationalism cannot explain everything. For example, think of the wave of spiritualism that swept through Europe and the United States in the 1870s, which claimed that the dead are still with us, ready to speak to us, if only we can find a way to communicate with them.

At first this communication was facilitated by a medium, someone who carries messages between the worlds; then the role was fulfilled by a camera, which was, at least on the face of it, less susceptible to trickery. Spirit photography was born, and hundreds of fraudsters extorted money from parents whose children had succumbed to illness, or from grieving lovers, in exchange for photographs where the shadow of ever-present loved ones floated beside them. *The Ghost of Abraham Lincoln*, a photograph taken in 1872, is one of the most famous examples, showing the ghost of the American president standing beside his widow Mary.

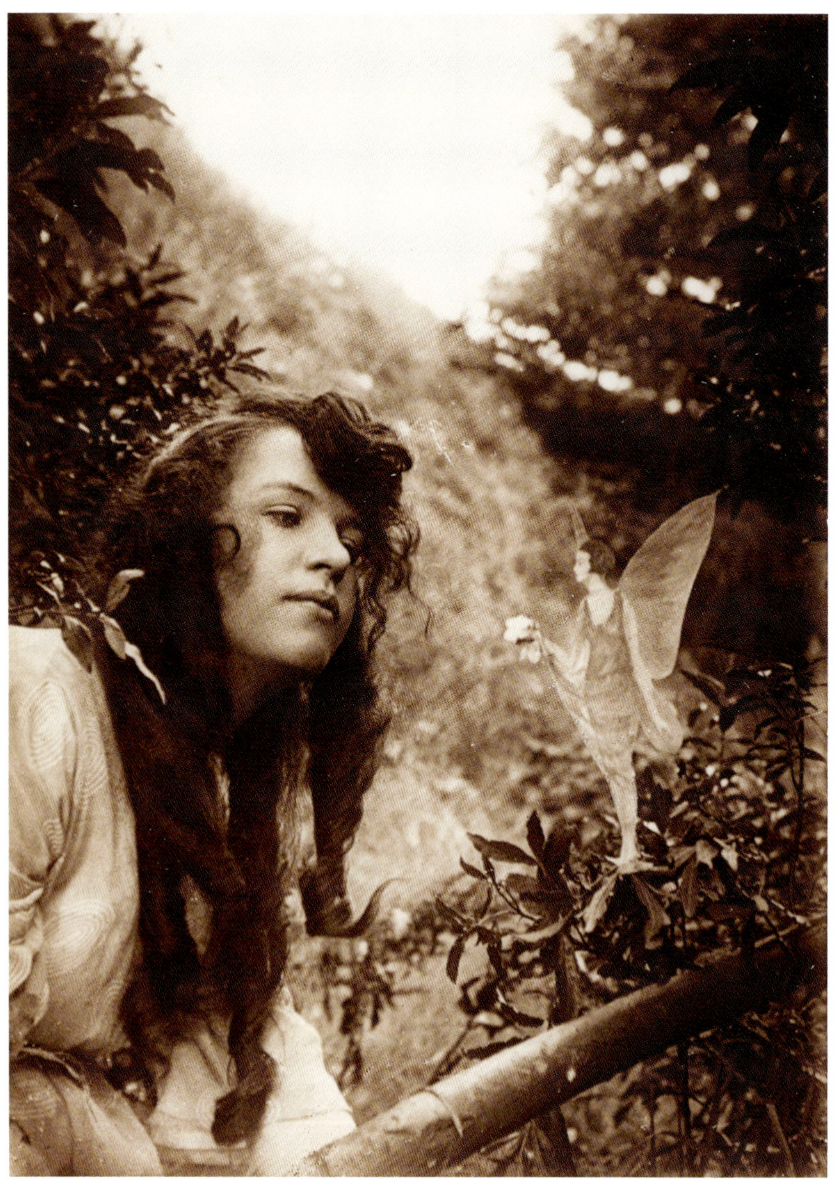

Elsie Wright and Frances Griffiths
Fairy Offering Flowers to Iris, August 1920
Gelatin silver chloride, 15.5 x 11.4 cm (6⅛ x 4½ in.)

The genius of these mischievous young girls was to photograph themselves with fairies made from paper stuck onto pieces of cardboard instead of trying their hand at layering two different exposures on top of each other – in any case, they did not know how to develop or print photographs.

People seeing that which is invisible to others

You don't need the technical skills of Henry Peach Robinson to create a credible faked photograph. The affair of the Cottingley Fairies is proof of that. In 1917, Frances Griffiths (1907–1986), aged nine, was staying with the family of her cousin Elsie Wright (1901–1988), aged sixteen, in Cottingley, a village in West Yorkshire. One day, when Elsie had borrowed her father's camera, the girls came back from a walk in the garden with photographs of fairies.

The fairy photographs (opposite) became more famous in Britain when the writer Sir Arthur Conan Doyle wrote an enthusiastic article about them in the Christmas edition of *Strand Magazine* in 1920. This was followed in 1922 by a book, *The Coming of the Fairies*, in which he wrote: 'There is nothing scientifically impossible, so far as I can see, in some people seeing that which is invisible to others.' The creator of the detective Sherlock Holmes was firmly convinced by spiritualism: he had posed for spirit photographs, and would publish a very serious *History of Spiritualism* in 1926. However, there is some ambiguity in his stance; he passes quite quickly over the difference between seeing that which is invisible and making it visible to those who lack the same supernatural gifts. In the case of the Cottingley Fairies, Frances and Elsie would have had to change the nature of the fairies in their garden, modify their 'luminous vibrations', as Doyle puts it, so that the camera could capture them.

Photographs of fairies and spirits played into a desire to regain some of the magic that had been stripped away from everyday life after the industrialization of society. In *Peter* [Pan] *and Wendy* (1911), J. M. Barrie, another British author, writes: 'Every time a child says, "I don't believe in fairies", there is a fairy somewhere that falls down dead.' Perhaps these young girls were only trying to slow down their extinction.

The questions raised by these photographs are not so much about technique as about belief. We might compare them to religious faith: a believer whose faith depends on material, scientific proof is not a true believer. If you're really convinced that your dead child is present in your home in the form of a ghost, you don't need a photo to prove yourself right.

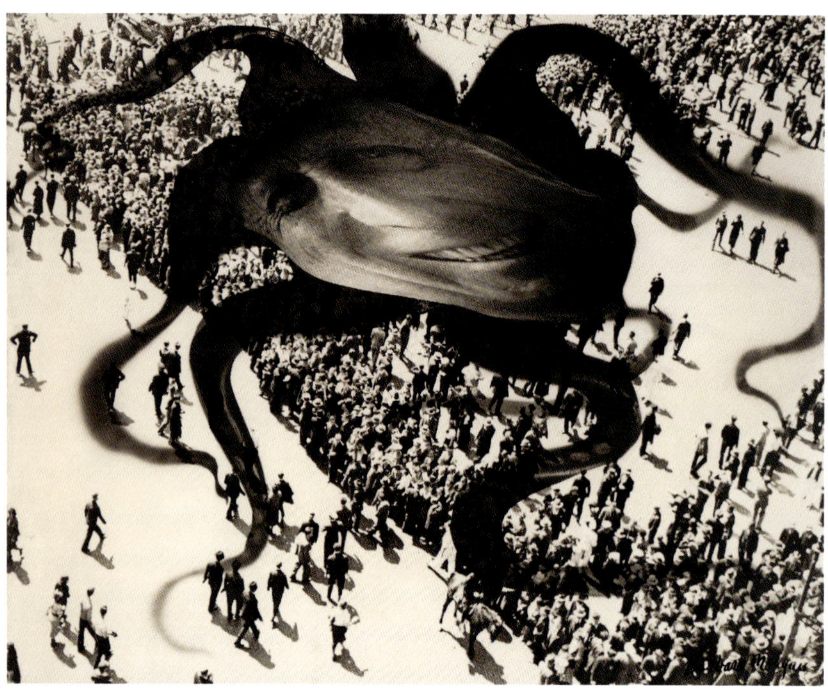

Barbara Morgan
Hearst Over the People, 1939
Gelatin silver photomontage, 38.9 x 49 cm (15⅜ x 19⅜ in.)

Already well known for her photographs of contemporary dance performances, the American photographer Barbara Morgan (1900–1992) took the risk of creating something false in order to convey a truth: the distorted smile of American newspaper magnate William Randolph Hearst no longer looks as friendly as it did before the photo was edited during the printing process.

WHEN FALSEHOOD EXPRESSES TRUTH

While many people are only interested in photography for its ability to create a copy of the world, others prefer when it tells barefaced lies. Since the 1890s, adverts in specialist journals have offered amateurs the chance to buy special lenses that alter proportions, tools for creating double exposures, or photographic paper with a pre-printed pattern – a whole range of tools that could be seen as the antecedents of today's digital photo-editing software. The transformations made possible by these tools were seen as a playful way of engaging with photography. Of course, the official history of this art form prefers to focus on the more 'serious' works of the Dada and Surrealist movements. The Hungarian-born photographer André Kertész (1894–1985) had close links with these groups. But, whether the aim is to create art or simply play around, it is done in the same spirit: using visual games and collage to shatter that transparent window onto the world.

In both of these photographs, the rippling lines don't just have the comic effect of funhouse mirrors. Barbara Morgan's octopus (above)

André Kertész
Pendulum, Distortion,
1938
Glass-plate negative

Here is another shape that has been distorted, in this case to express the difference between real time and how we experience time – and perhaps also the groggy eyes of someone peering at the alarm clock on their bedside table, surprised to find they have slept past 10.00 a.m.

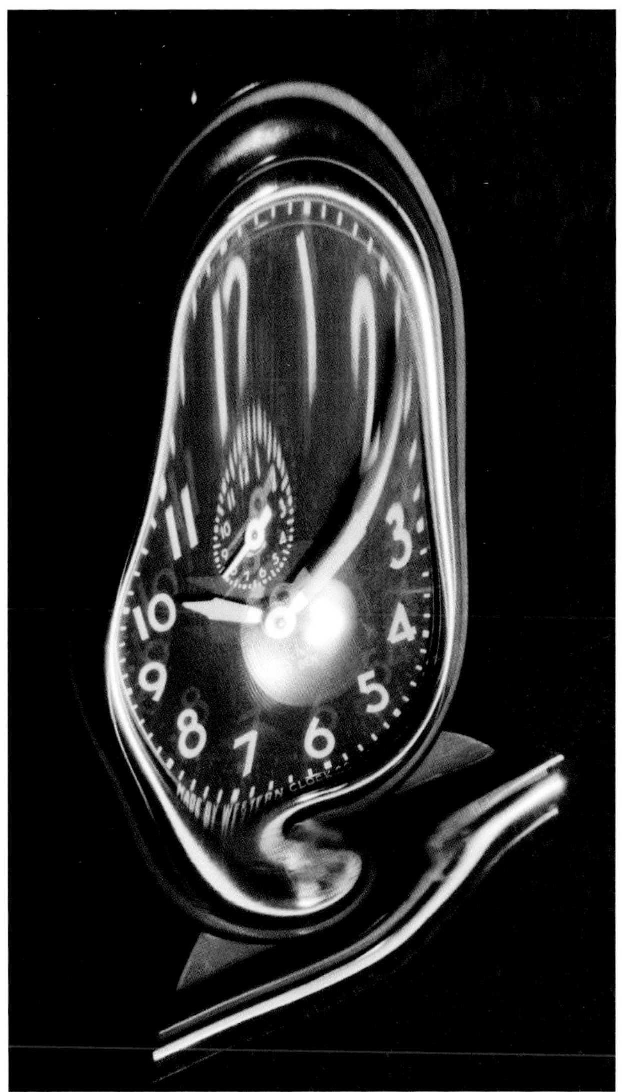

has the face of newspaper magnate William Randolph Hearst; its undulating tentacles represent the way in which journalists disseminate their boss's ideology, cajoling and flattering their readers in order to suck them in. At first we think we are being embraced by a friend, but then realize that we're being manipulated.

As for the photograph of the distorted alarm clock (page 43), it relies on the same visual technique as a Surrealist painting of 1931 by the Spanish artist Salvador Dalí, *The Persistence of Memory*. This painting shows 'melting watches', which mould themselves to the contours of the objects on which they are resting. It is impossible not to think of the expression 'the flow of time', or of grains of sand slipping through an hourglass just as time slips through our fingers. In both photographs, the rippling lines express uncertainty, doubt, a lack of confidence when faced with things that are difficult to pin down – the way in which the media manipulate us, or how time sometimes speeds up without warning. These photographs do not try to hide the fact that they are faked, unbelievable and artificial. They still seek to express a truth, but use different methods to do so, rather than embracing the transparent window model.

Something predatory about the camera lens

Photographs that are clearly doctored engage our knowledge of the technical side of photography. They seem to ask us: 'Do you know how this was achieved? With scissors and glue, or with a computer?' By contrast, when a photograph seems to have been captured from life, our first instinct is to look for the image of the objects that were 'behind the window' at the moment when it was taken. To get the most out of a photograph, whatever its apparent relationship with reality, we must shake off both of these instinctive reactions. They get in our way and are often a waste of time.

Digital technology makes it very easy to edit photos, and these techniques have become both much more advanced and more commonplace. In this photograph (opposite), the British fashion photographer Nick Knight (b.1958) is parodying the hyper-detailed depiction of violence in modern cinema. But in the context of a fashion magazine, such as the one in which the shot was published, this shocking treatment may also prompt the reader to reflect on the articles designed to make them want to

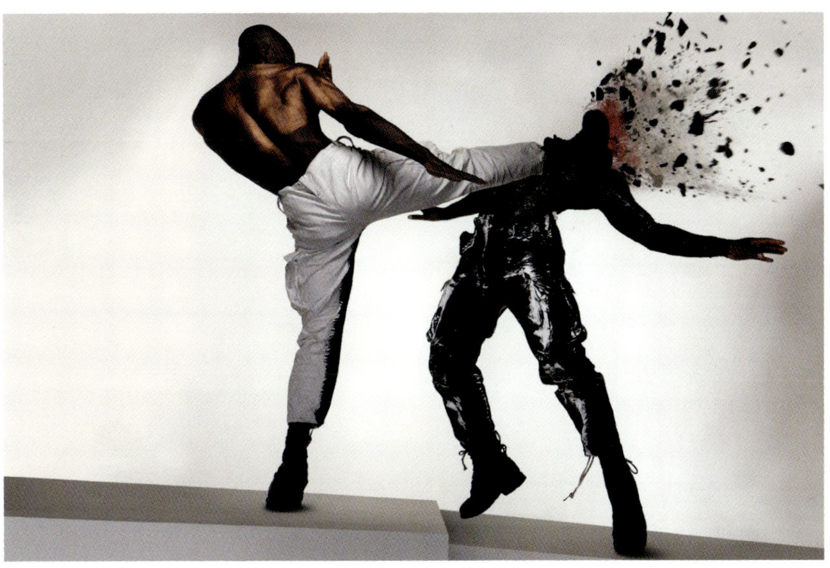

Nick Knight
War, for *Big Magazine*, issue 18, 1997

This photograph shows two fighters, one wearing white trousers and the other in black. But it also brings together elements taken from the real world and ones that have been digitally created (the exploding head). The wall, which looks like a white sheet of paper, also encourages us to view this image as a painting rather than a record of the world.

buy clothes. What if they are full of lies? What if I don't look like the model in the magazine when I wear this outfit?

A significant proportion of photos posted on social media have had one or more filters applied to them. These are used in turn to saturate or desaturate the colours, to make the corners of the frame darker or lighter, to make the lines sharper or more blurred. Filters are everywhere and they play a role in creating a more *attractive* likeness of the world. But digital technology can also be used in a different way. Instead of trying to work out the techniques used to create a photo-collage, we could instead use the photograph as a prompt to reflect on the questions that the photographer seems to pose. That is the case for the two examples we have just seen: *Hearst Over the People* (page 42) asks, 'How can we know what is going on in the world if some media outlets are manipulating us?', and *Pendulum, Distortion* (page 43) asks, 'Why does time not always seem to pass at the same speed?'

Known for his conceptual approach to documentary photography, the Irish photographer Richard Mosse (b.1980) did not use digital technology for his series 'Infra', but instead turned to a technique that predates the digital era: Kodak Aerochrome III Infrared film. Now discontinued, this film, which was sensitive to infrared rays, was put to military use to detect humans or other living creatures in the jungle or any plant-based environment that was dense enough to provide cover. Mosse used it during the civil war in the Democratic Republic of the Congo – a conflict that was difficult to understand for outside observers, in which more than five million people lost their lives. Mosse did not want to take 'sensational' pictures of the conflict, as that would have felt exploitative. 'It's almost like self-loathing, because there's something predatory about the camera lens,' he later said in an interview with the *British Journal of Photography*. The fighters that Mosse photographed were usually camouflaged so that they blended into the dense vegetation, but through the ingenious use of the infrared film, their appearance is transformed, revealing how they are seen by a foreigner incapable of understanding exactly what is at stake in their war.

Richard Mosse
She Brings the Rain, 2011
from the 'Infra' series
Digital c-print,
152.4 x 121.9 cm
(60 x 48 in.)

We would not be surprised to see that the green plants had been changed to pink if this were a fashion shot. However, the fact that the subject is holding a sub-machine gun makes us stop and think. No, this is not a fashion shot, but a war photograph, even though it shows a photogenic young man in a passive pose.

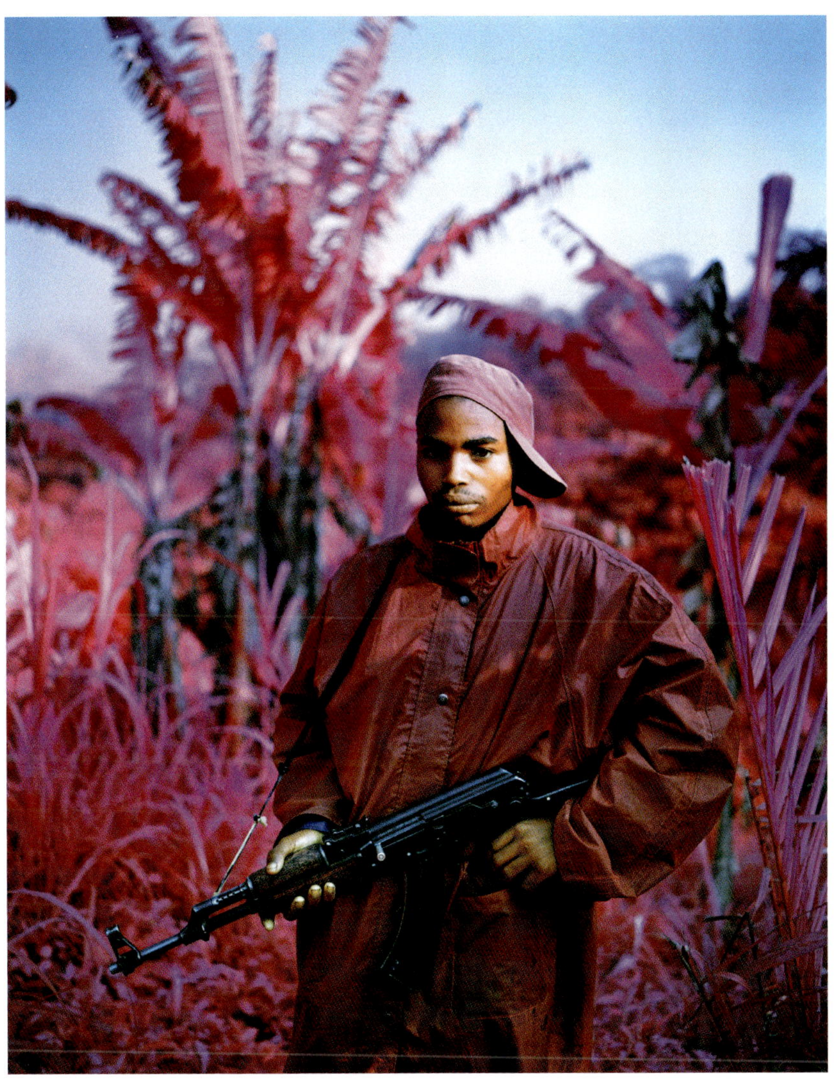

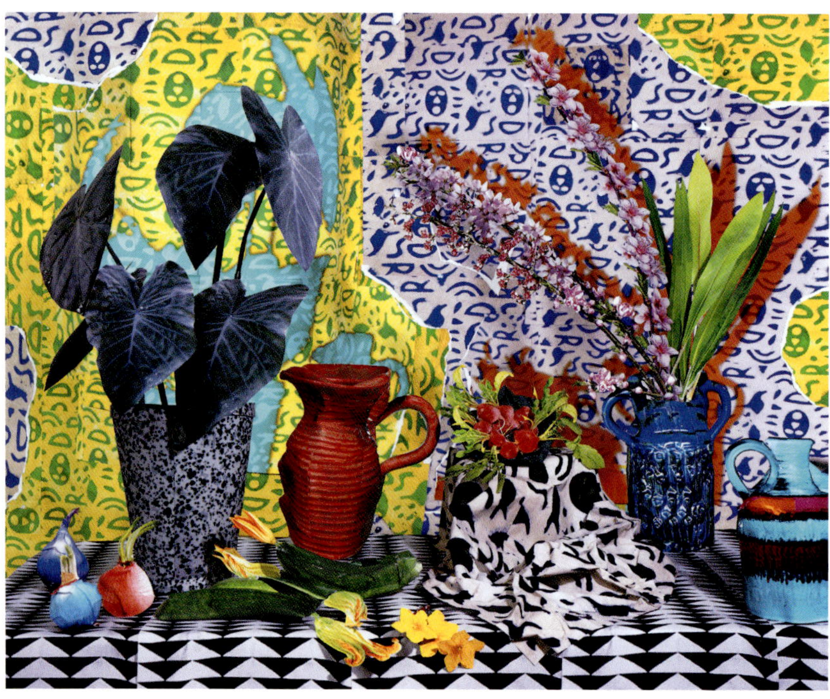

THE ART OF COMBINING ART FORMS

The word 'doctoring' still bothers some people, just like the phrase 'artificial intelligence'. But as long as photographers do not deliberately lie about how they created a picture, why should we not allow them the same freedom as painters? Often, it is less important to understand how a photograph was created than to know whether it connects with us emotionally and makes us think.

The American artist Daniel Gordon (b.1980) prefers the world of pictures to pictures of the world; he is a child of hyperreality, the desire to believe that what is happening on our screens is more true than what is happening in real life. He searches the internet and magazines for images, cuts them out and glues them together or attaches them to objects, then rephotographs them in his studio (above). As in the paintings of French artist Henri Matisse, the vertical surfaces of this still life (the wall in the background) cannot be clearly distinguished from the horizontal surfaces (the table). The jug and the courgettes are also reminiscent of Matisse's 1905 painting *Still Life with Vegetables*. Another similarity is the imperfect joins between the edges of the pieces of paper that have been cut out.

Daniel Gordon
Still Life with Cherry Blossoms and Zucchini, 2013
C-print, 126.4 x 157.9 cm (49⅞ x 62¼ in.)

There are lots of recognizable objects in this photograph, but as in the case of the Cottingley Fairies, we are unsure whether they are physically there: are they two- or three-dimensional? Paintings or sculptures? Here, Gordon embraces a technique adopted by many modern painters, who choose not to 'trick' people by creating an illusion of depth in two-dimensional paintings.

Matisse, who towards the end of his life exclusively used the technique of cutting out paper and sticking it onto a canvas, placed great value on these kinds of deliberate 'mistakes'. In the centre of the photograph, the jagged line that separates the yellow and green wall from the white and blue wall would not be visible if the two parts had been glued together perfectly, or retouched with the help of Photoshop. It is no surprise, then, that Gordon says he is interested in the idea of 'showing my hand and letting people see the imperfection'. Whether these objects really exist or not isn't important. In nature, there are probably no red or blue onions like the ones sitting on this table, but what does that matter?
The photograph depicts a world that has been remade, reorganized, and we are free to choose whether or not to transpose its charm (or its strangeness) onto a 'real' kitchen or 'real' vegetables.

To the naive outrage of the purists

Of course, the line between truth and falsehood is not always as clear as we would like. The work of Edward Sheriff Curtis (1868–1952) is a good example of this. Curtis is best known for his photographs of thousands of Native Americans in the early twentieth century (below). He did not hesitate to scratch his negatives or to erase those elements that did not match the idea he had of 'true Indians' – he thought it was a shame that they had

Edward Sheriff Curtis
Loitering at the Spring, plate 400 from *The North American Indian*, 1921
Photogravure, 29 x 39.1 cm (11⅜ x 15⅜ in.)

Rather than attending to their task of fetching water, six women from the Hopi nation are shown chatting and smiling in elegant poses, while one of them nonchalantly trails her hand in the stream. We can tell that this photograph has been staged, but if its subject is the harmonious relationship between nature and culture, does that matter?

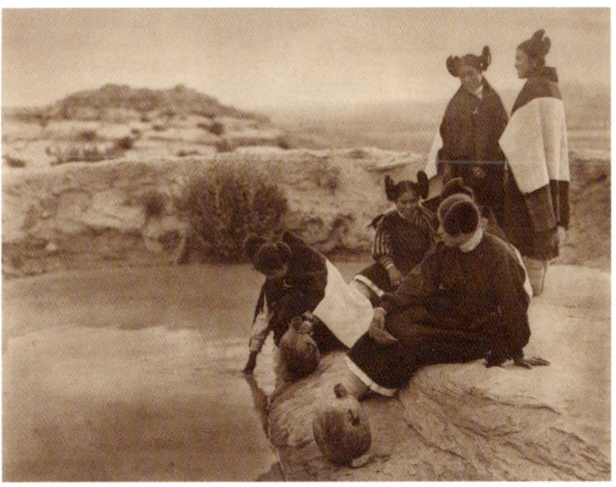

adopted some aspects of white culture. Therefore, he often asked his models to dress and do their hair in styles their grandparents had worn, or to go about their work in ceremonial dress, which they would not usually have done for fear of getting their clothes dirty or damaging them. How we view his photographs depends on our interpretation. Some people criticize Curtis for deliberately erasing traces of the destruction of indigenous culture by white colonists. Others praise him for creating striking, dignified images of Native Americans, which served as inspiration for those who didn't want to see this civilization disappear. Curtis's subjects nicknamed him 'Shadow Catcher': they could not have put it better, because trying to piece together an accurate picture of Native American culture before colonization truly does involve rescuing these remnants from the shadows.

In his book *Message from the Darkroom* (1949), the extravagant Italian designer and photographer Carlo Mollino (1905–1973) wrote that the art of photography does not begin until after we have pressed the button. For him, the only thing that matters is the end result. 'All is permitted,' he wrote, 'even abolishing entire disturbing parts of the image, right down, to the naive outrage of the purists, to dangerous and interfering retouching of the negative or positive, superimpression and photomontage.' When we are trying to express something that has no visual form, such as feelings or ideas, doctoring and retouching are valuable resources, even though they have a bad reputation because they are often used to spread lies and fake news.

If doctored images and politics usually make for an explosive combination, there is at least one way to use them to make people think. Instead of pretending that a photograph is a window onto the world, the photographer can be open about incorporating unreal elements into their picture. That is the approach taken by the German artist Thomas Demand (b.1964). Unlike the cardboard cut-outs used in cinema and theatre to trick the audience into believing that the things they are imitating are really there, the objects used by Demand proclaim loud and clear that they are fakes.

'Embassy', the series in which this picture (opposite) appears, takes its inspiration from the Nigergate scandal. After Niger's embassy in Rome was burgled in 2001, documents detailing the sale of uranium to dictator Saddam Hussein were leaked. These documents were a key factor in US president George W. Bush's decision to invade Iraq, but it later emerged that they were fakes, forged by Italian military intelligence. Demand's work makes us stop and think: everything is made of paper. The so-called important documents, the printer, the chair, the CD, and even the

Thomas Demand
Detail XI, from the series 'Embassy', 2007
C-print/Diasec,
94 x 90 cm
(37⅛ x 35½ in.)

Reality has been altered so much that it has become a sculpture. These objects only look like the things that they represent; they are not functional. It is no use trying to print anything on this printer.

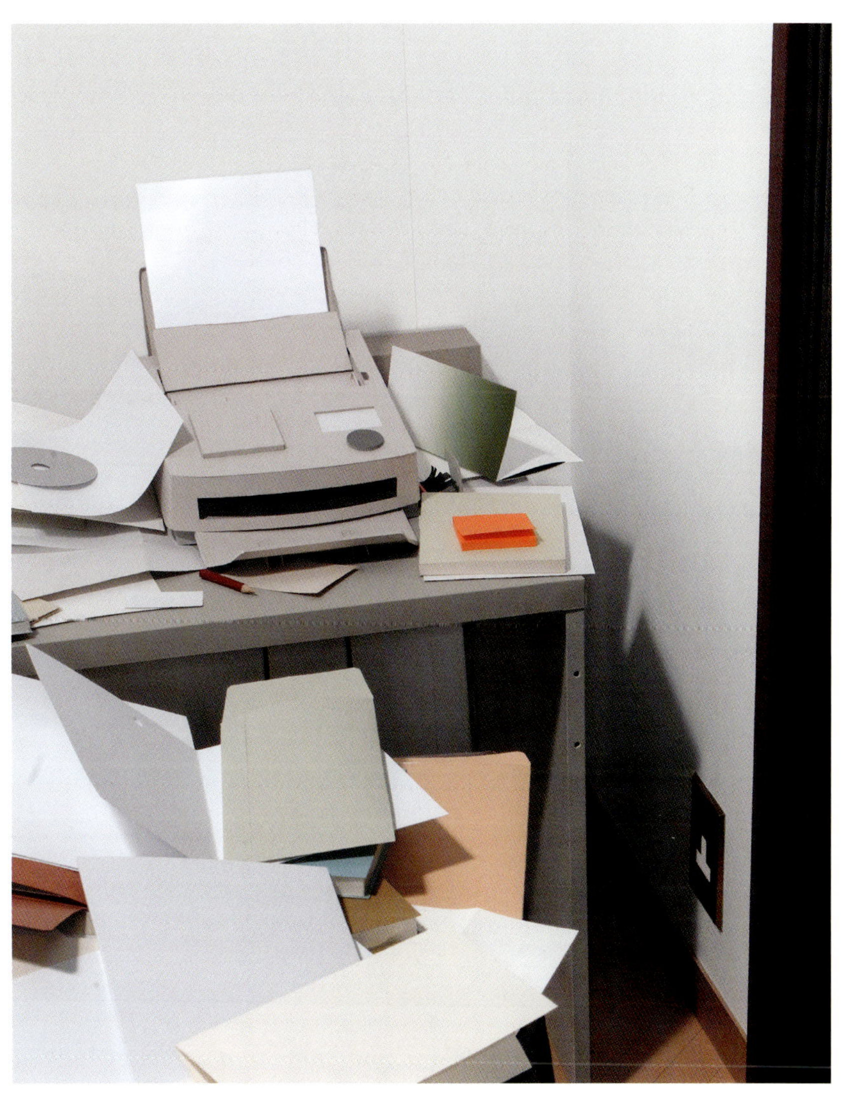

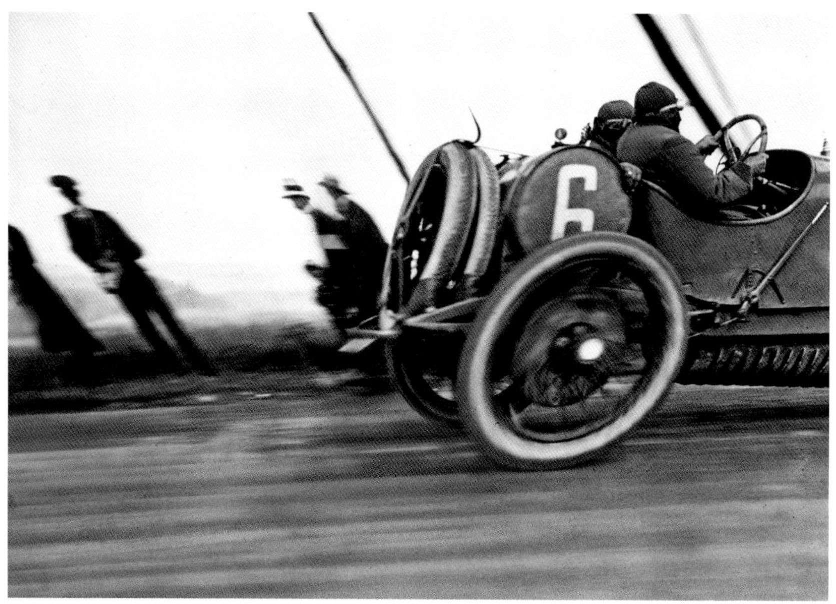

Jacques Henri Lartigue
Grand Prix de l'Automobile Club de France (Grand Prix of the Automobile Club of France), 1912
Positive scan of glass negative, 9 x 12 cm (3⅝ x 4¾ in.)

This picture is both false (a wheel cannot be an oval shape, even if it is spinning fast) and truer than true. The overall impression is one of speed. The car is travelling so fast that it is already halfway out of the field of view.

photograph in which all of these objects are captured. Furthermore, the framing is a little strange. There is a black vertical stripe on the right, but it does not seem to have a function, and the desk is cut off on the left. We might say that the photographer was in a rush when he pressed the button, so he didn't stop to line up the camera properly or centre the shot. Looking at this photograph, it is impossible not to imagine how the story fabricated by the Italian agents would have played out: one night in Rome, 'burglars' broke into the embassy and discovered the mysterious 'documents' there. There is an entire universe of false pretences lurking here.

MAKING STRANGE

In the mid-nineteenth century, artists and intellectuals celebrated photography for its ability to create an archive record of things that were destined to disappear. But they were more sceptical when it tried to compete with painting. In 1857, the British art historian Elizabeth Eastlake wrote in the *London Quarterly Review* that photography is 'as detrimental to art as it is complimentary to science'. Despite the efforts of the Pictorialists, this opposition persisted; it was the Russian Formalists, in the 1910s, who finally defeated it.

At first the Formalist movement was made up of linguists and poets. Rather than studying how a work was shaped by the historical and social context in which it was created, they thought it was more important to examine the way in which art can, by its very nature, shape the world, or at least how we perceive it. The essayist Viktor Shklovsky introduced the concept of defamiliarization, which he defined as 'making strange'. He argued that the role of the artist is to make us see the world differently. To achieve this aim, Shklovsky wrote in his *Theory of Prose* (1925), 'it is necessary to detach the object from the domain of life, to wrest it out from the web of familiar associations, to turn over the object as one would turn a log in the fire'. And of course, photography is well suited to this role.

All techniques were permitted in the name of defamiliarization; shaking the camera, doctoring pictures, superimposing them on top of each other, bringing together elements that shouldn't appear together, testing the limits of good taste. Simple defamiliarizing effects can be created 'by hand', as the French photographer Jacques Henri Lartigue (1894–1986) did when trying to capture a racing car driving past him at high speed (opposite).

No, in reality, wheels cannot become oval-shaped; no, the spectators are not being buffeted by such a strong wind that they

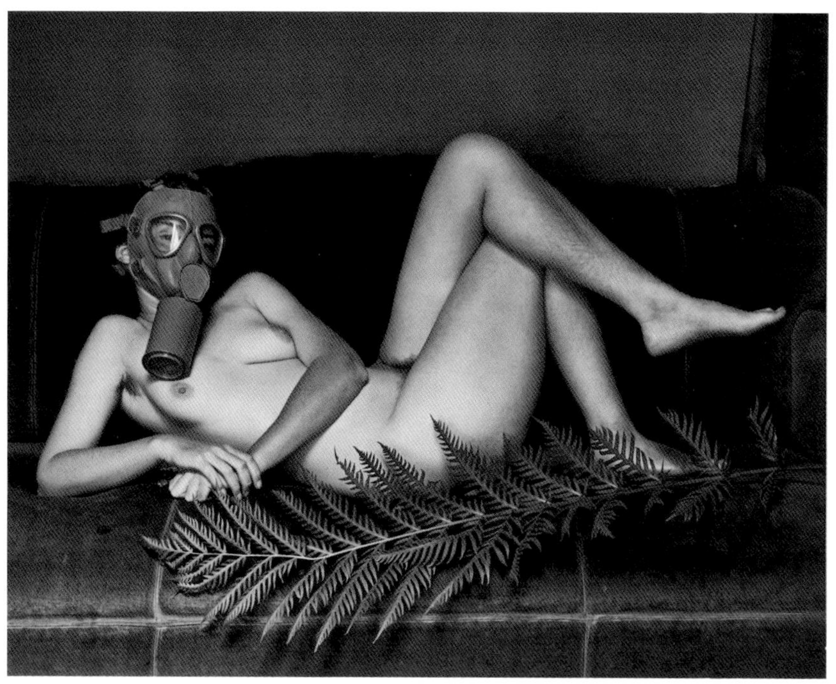

Edward Weston
Civilian Defense, 1942
Gelatin silver print

This encounter between a gas mask and the tradition of the nude is just as striking as the one between a sewing machine and an umbrella. Especially as the subject's carefree, relaxed pose implies that it is unremarkable.

lean at a 45-degree angle as the car speeds past them with a deafening roar. All of that is defamiliarization. Here it relies on the distortion of familiar objects – and why shouldn't the photographer be allowed the same freedom as a comic-strip artist, who would not hesitate to draw oval wheels in order to convey a sense of speed?

In 'The Paths of Modern Photography', an article published in 1928, Alexander Rodchenko (1891–1956), a Russian multidisciplinary artist who co-founded the Constructivist movement, argued that defamiliarization was a kind of wake-up call for our minds. Because we see the same things every day, we no longer look at them as closely as we should and, as a result, all our judgements – including our political judgements – are skewed. Today, digital filters allow us to change the age or gender of the person being photographed, in a way that is both defamiliarizing and playful. But there is another way to make us see something afresh when our perception has been dulled by seeing the same thing over and over again: combining objects that usually don't go together.

The absurd distinction between beauty and ugliness

It must be said that changes in the way we live have made this less unusual. When photography was first invented, the world was more static than it is today. It was not common for people to travel to foreign countries. As images were not yet being circulated in huge numbers, unexpected combinations of objects were rarer. The 'chance encounter, on a dissecting table, of a sewing machine and an umbrella', imagined by the French poet Lautréamont in his work *Les Chants de Maldoror* (1868–69), therefore had an explosive effect. The Surrealist movement, born from the wreckage of the First World War, came to worship this phrase. Then, life changed radically for large swathes of the planet. Machines invaded daily life, the wave of urbanization intensified, people began to travel a lot more and visual culture was transformed. We needed a new lens through which to see the world. In 1930, French writer André Breton's *Second Manifesto of Surrealism* proposed to abandon 'the absurd distinction between beauty and ugliness, truth and falsehood, good and bad.'

When he took this photo (opposite), the American photographer Edward Weston (1886–1958) was working as an air raid plane spotter for the US Defense, and the gas mask was part of his equipment. The fact that Charis Wilson, the photographer's wife, is wearing it is even more ironic because there was no enemy attack on mainland US territory, let alone a gas attack. Other ironic elements are Wilson's relaxed pose, crossing her legs, and the fern branch, which seems to mimic the vine leaves so often used to prudishly cover private parts, while here it is not hiding anything. But the mask also reminds us of Cubist painters' interest in African art – in 1907, Pablo Picasso gave his *Demoiselles d'Avignon* faces inspired by the sculptures he had seen for the first time in the Ethnographic Museum of the Trocadero, Paris.

The British photographer Juno Calypso (b.1989) allows us even more freedom to let our thoughts run wild (opposite). This time, the mask is attached to a strange box, and if the scene takes place in a hotel room on a couple's wedding night, the husband seems to have run away on seeing what his new wife has brought along (including, on the sofa, a dish and a bottle of baby oil). When asked, 'Would you say there's a comic nature to your photographs?', Calypso replied, 'Definitely. I love comedy. I love making people laugh.'

In these examples, the photographer takes on the role of a theatre or film director. But, as we will see, there are plenty of other ways to turn a photograph into something other than a mere copy of reality.

KEY IDEAS

A photograph is not a questionnaire with precise, right answers.

Photography sometimes reveals things that are not visible to the naked eye.

Learning how to look means first thinking about the relationships between the objects within the frame.

Making people see the world in a new light is an important function of photography.

KEY QUESTIONS

Can we find something in a photograph other than what the photographer wanted to show?

Is seeing something with our own eyes necessarily better than imagining it based on a photograph?

Can we allow fakery if it is used to convey a truth?

Should we expect photographers to tell us if their photo has been retouched?

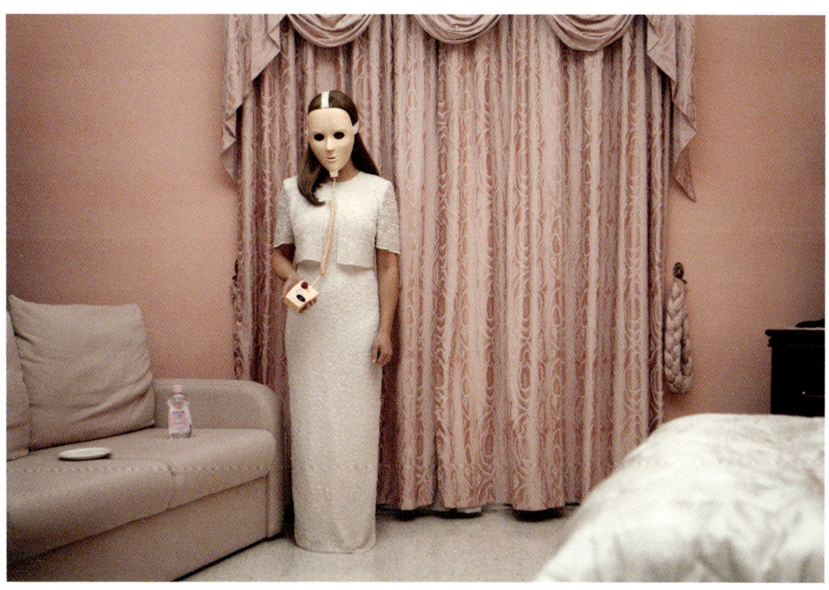

Juno Calypso
12 Reasons You're Tired All the Time, 2013
Photographic C-type print

The curtains are closed, so that the neighbours cannot see what is going to happen here. But what should we expect? A mix of kitsch, everyday and bizarre elements, while the viewer tires themselves out (that is perhaps what the photograph's title is referring to) trying to work out what is happening in this room.

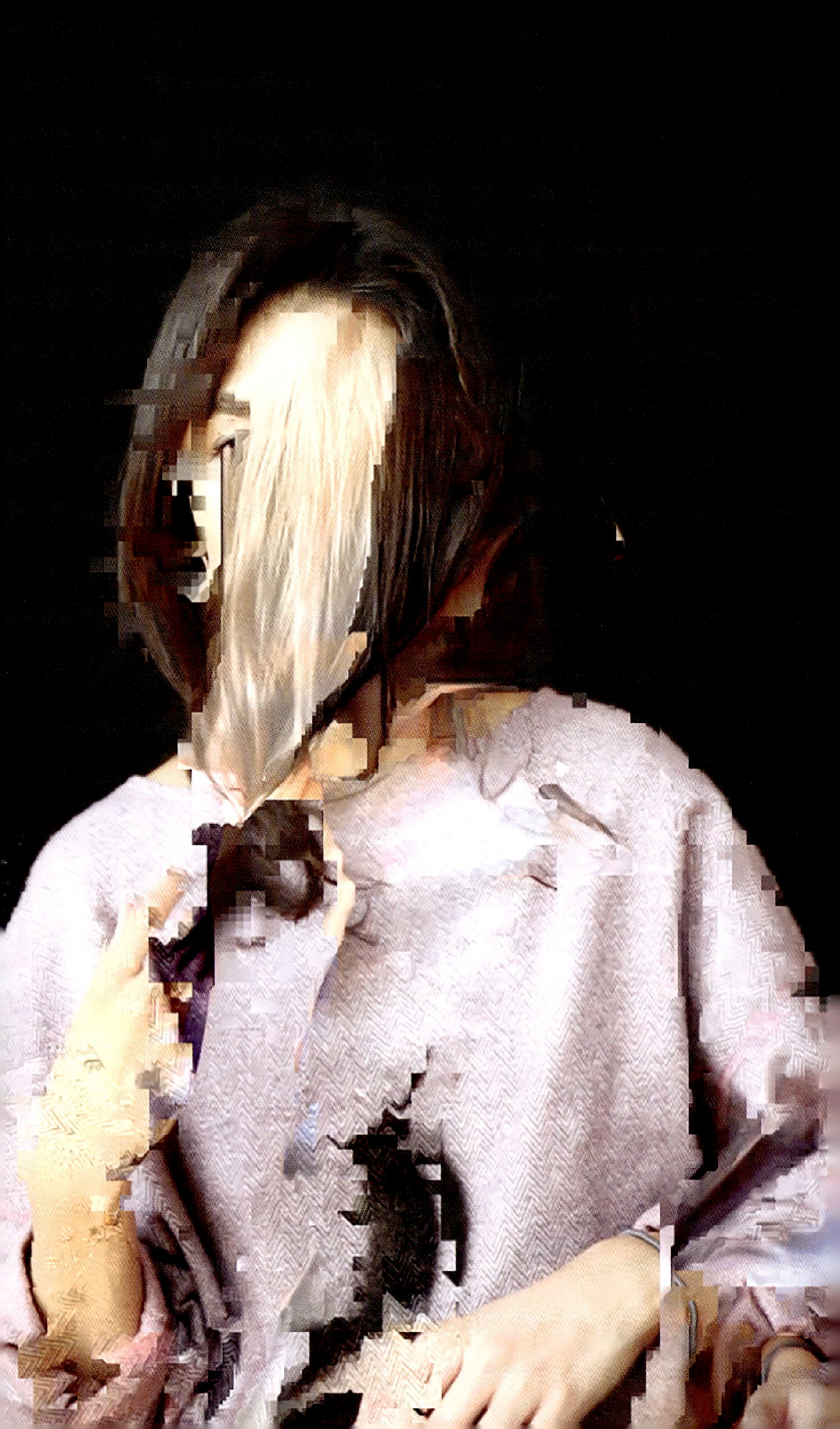

AREAS OF UNCERTAINTY

-

The imperfect medium of the digital image is always at risk of degrading, introducing glitches and errors, as though interrogating the perfection we have tried to preserve

-

Susana Moyaho

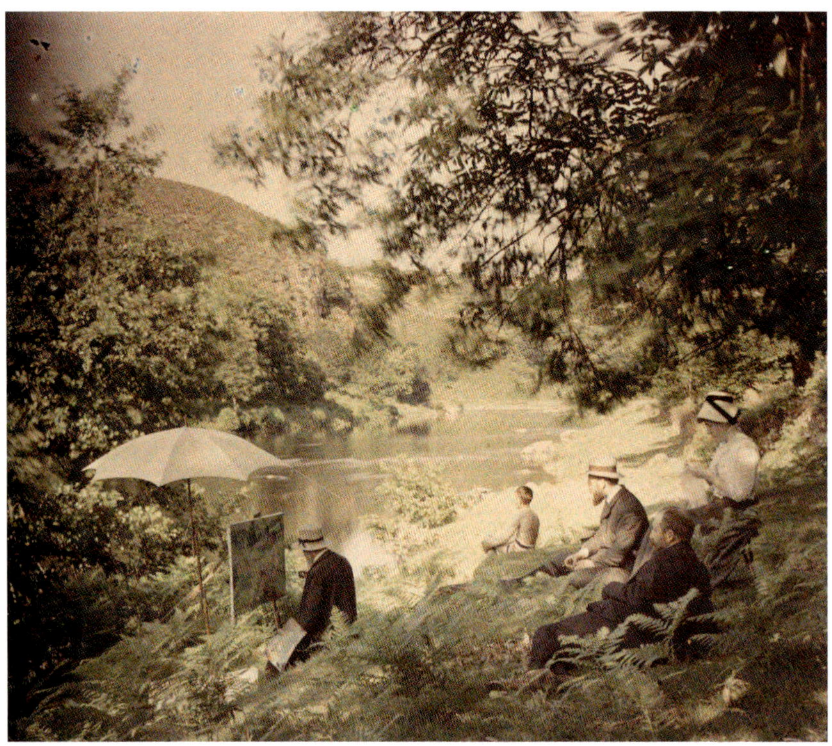

Antonin Personnaz
Le peintre Armand Guillaumin peignant 'Baigneurs à Crozant' (The Painter Armand Guillaumin painting 'Bathers at Crozant'), c. 1907
Autochrome, 9 x 12 cm (3⅝ x 4¾ in.)

'What an artist's brush does, the autochrome glass automatically achieves the same thing,' Personnaz wrote to his friend the French painter Claude Monet, one of the founders of the Impressionist movement.

The pioneers of photography saw this new invention as a kind of magic mirror that allowed them to preserve images instead of watching them slip away. In other words, they were seeking precision, accuracy, a perfect depiction. They were trying to create an exact copy of reality. Of course, photographs erased one of the three dimensions of the real world, as a print is always flat, but aside from that, a photograph had to be perfectly accurate. However, this accuracy was not well received by many people. In 1857, Elizabeth Eastlake reported the disappointment experienced by the early clients of photography studios when they received their portraits and saw that 'the eyes were decidedly contracted, the mouths expanded, and the lines and wrinkles intensified'. Eastlake therefore agreed with the Royal Photographic Society, founded four years earlier in London, that: 'Pictures taken slightly out of focus, that is, with slightly uncertain and undefined forms, though less *chemically*, would be found more *artistically* beautiful.' The public simply had to be made to comprehend 'the possible beauty of a slight *burr*'.

Many poets and painters also criticized the unwavering accuracy of photographs. It has often been argued that it was no coincidence that the Impressionist movement emerged shortly after the invention of photography, that a number of painters chose to adopt a softer, more hazy approach in response to the sharpness of photographs. It is certainly safe to say that both emerged around the same time. At first photography was admired for its clarity, but soon some photographers began to embrace an 'artistic haziness' in a deliberate attempt to soften the image. They envied painters their freedom to use the bristles of their brushes to press and smear paint onto the canvas in a chaotic way, and tried different approaches to create photographs that were less sharp and clinical.

SOFTENING EDGES

As we saw in the previous chapter, it was not long before the first photographers began retouching photographs to make their clients look more beautiful. But the public needed more time before they started to appreciate the areas of uncertainty in photographs, places where we are unsure exactly what we are looking at, other than blurriness, stains or darkness.

Autochrome photography is one early example of the move away from photographic precision. Patented in 1903 by the Lumière brothers, this process was the first technique used to create colour photographs, using a glass plate covered in grains of potato starch dyed green, purple or orangey red. Although this was not the main aim, it softened the edges of the objects that had been photographed. When the photograph was developed, the grains of starch gave it the feel of a Pointillist painting, as they blurred together: the red generally contained traces of green, and the white, created by additive colour mixing, truly looked like a mixture of all the other colours.

The French art collector Antonin Personnaz (1854–1936), who was one of the first photographers to work in colour, decided to portray a painter at work (opposite). The painter's two friends watch him in respectful silence, a woman sits absorbed in her needlework, and a young man poses for him; they are spending a pleasant Sunday afternoon together. The difference between the painting that the artist is working on and Personnaz's photograph is most obvious at the top of the frame, in the trees, where the slightly blurred branches are being stirred by a light breeze. That is precisely where we can see 'the beauty of a slight burr' – the leaves carried on moving during the few seconds in which the light came into contact with the film.

We might excuse the blurriness of the very first photograph in history, the *View from the Window at Le Gras* by the French photographer Nicéphore Niépce (1765–1833), taken in 1826 or 1827, but only because it was the first. Today, thanks to technical advances, the vast majority of photographs taken on smartphones are highly sharp and precise. Perhaps that is why no one spends very long looking at them. As the American photographer Sally Mann (b.1951) noted: 'If there's no ambiguity, why bother?' You really have to make an effort – shake the phone when you press the button, for example – to create a blurry photo.

Over the years, a number of photographic techniques have been developed that do not follow the model of the magic mirror, that in fact even run contrary to it. Today, amateurs who want to move away from the ideal of accuracy and precision can use a whole array of digital filters: these allow them, for example, to recreate the soft focus that was so highly valued by the Pictorialists, making the light dimmer and softening edges, to make a part of the image completely blurry, or even to recreate the mistakes that often occurred in the age of analogue photography (stripes, stains, dog-eared or torn paper). These charming imperfections also appealed to, among other artists, Andy Warhol, who took many Polaroids throughout his career when he would only have had to say the word and someone would have come rushing in with the latest high-tech camera.

The soft focus that some people sought in photography sometimes occurs naturally, when it is created by two things: reflections and distance. This work (opposite) by Korean photographer Byung-Hun Min (b.1955) shows the surface of a river covered in perfectly sharp water lilies, but also offers an indirect view of the sky and the trees reflected in the water; these not only appear upside down, but their reflection is also subtly distorted by the ripples. A watery surface is not as smooth as a real mirror, which perhaps explains why, in Greek mythology, the youth Narcissus spent hours staring at his reflection in a pool.

In the distance, everything blurs together

The softening effect of distance is related to a phenomenon called the 'texture gradient'. If I walk through a meadow, for example, as I look at parts of the field that are further away, I will be less able to pick out each individual blade of grass; they will

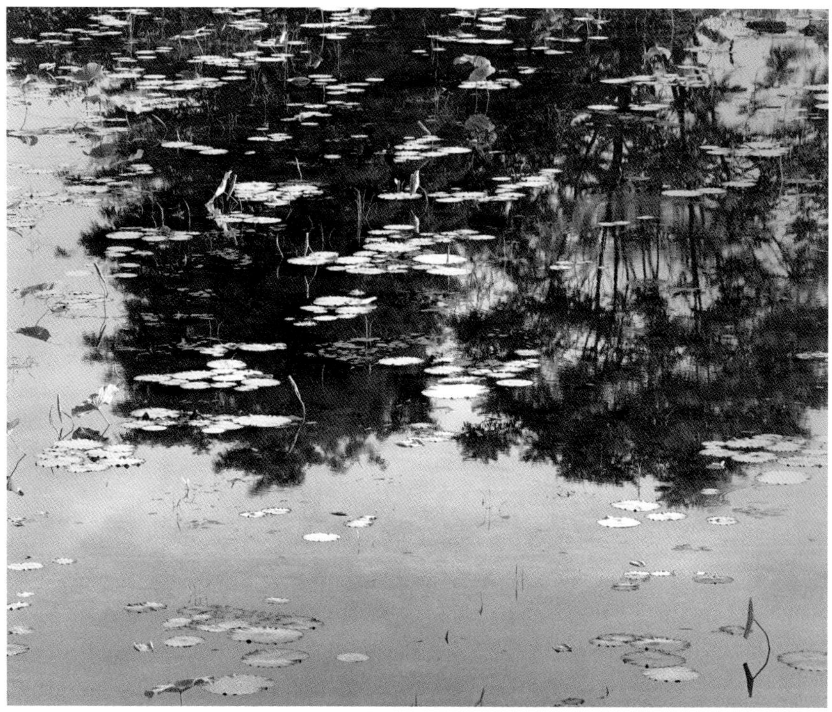

Byung-Hun Min
River (RT029), 2011
Gelatin silver print

A century after Antonin Personnaz's autochromes and Claude Monet's *Water Lilies* series, Byung-Hun Min never retouches his photographs; if there is an area of visual uncertainty, it already existed with no editing.

merge into an indistinct mass. And if I look at the horizon, another phenomenon, called 'atmospheric perspective', comes into play: in the distance, everything blurs together and takes on the bluish hue of the earth's atmosphere.

In this photograph (overleaf), beyond the four boats that form a straight line in the distance, the waves are indistinguishable from one another; all we can see is an expanse of blue. A non-professional photographer would probably have moved to avoid having this incongruous wooden post in the frame, but the Italian Luigi Ghirri (1943–1992) decided to make it into a sort of screen onto which the shadows of objects with vague outlines are projected – perhaps the pieces of straw or leaves that make up the beach hut this post is supporting. Ghirri never forgot his background as a land surveyor, but the cartographic aspect of his works often serves to show that nature does not have the same desire for regularity and perfect symmetry that is so prized by us.

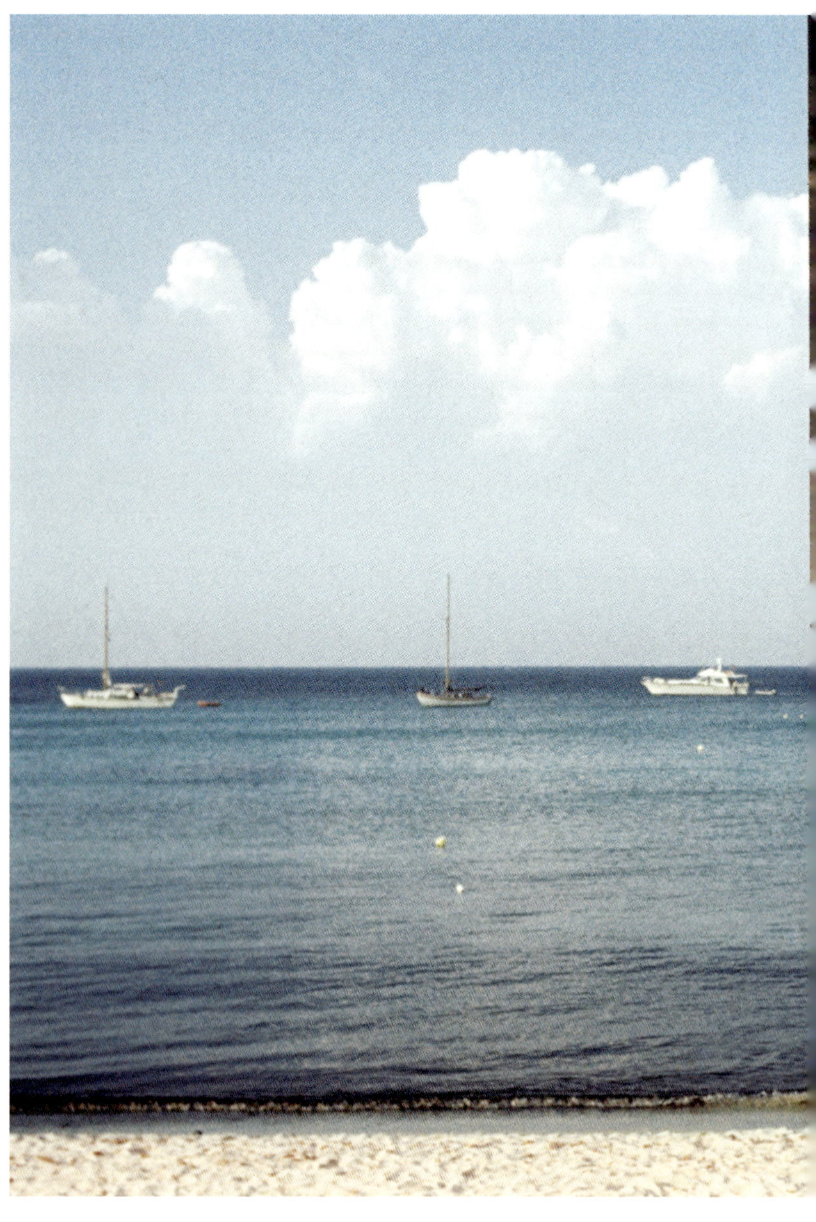

Luigi Ghirri
L'Île Rousse, 1976

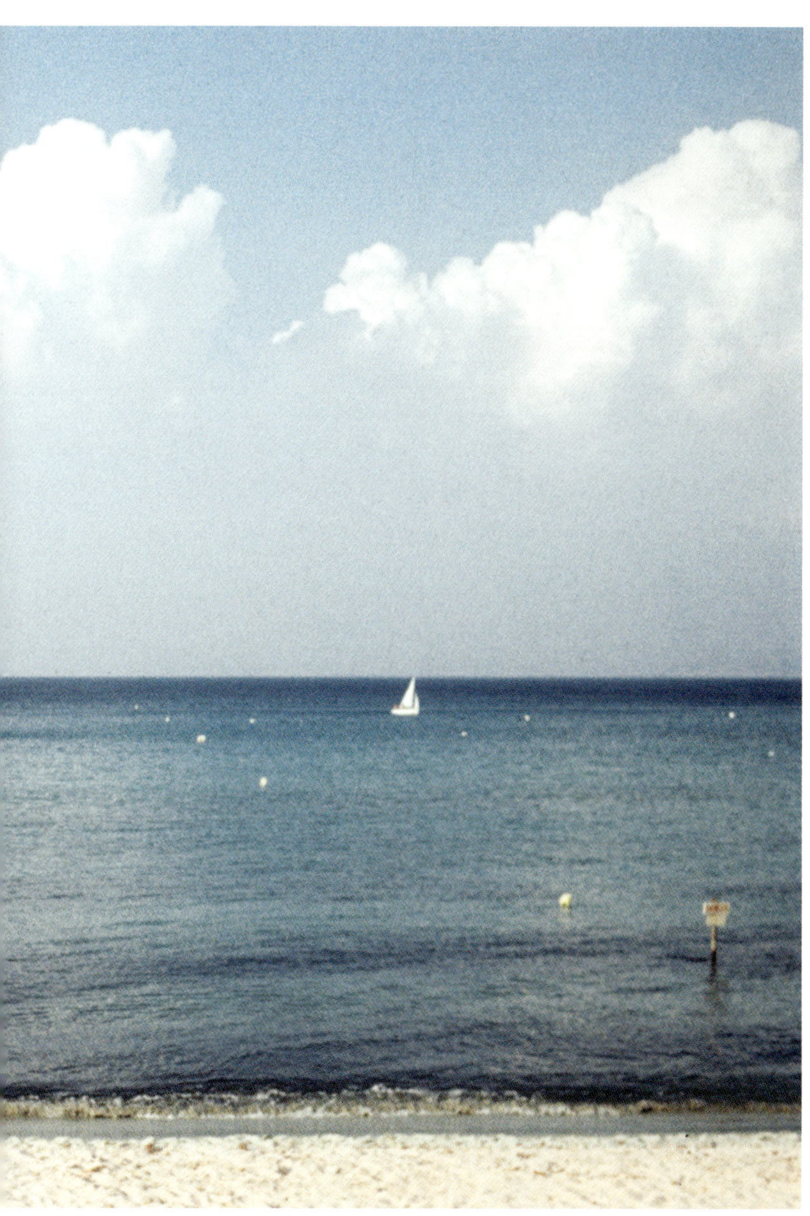

The frame is cut in half twice: horizontally by the horizon and vertically by a wooden post. There is something ironic about this vertical division, because it separates two almost identical parts of the landscape, whereas the horizontal division separates the sky from the sea.

SEEING IN THE FIRST PERSON SINGULAR

Blurriness cannot always be attributed to the object being photographed or to technical concerns: it can also be due to the eyesight of the person looking at a photograph. Nowadays, people are experimenting with the subjectivity of vision, for example, exploring how we squint when looking at the sun, how we see when we have a fever, when we look at the world through tears or simply feel our vision growing weaker with age. Of course, the verb 'to see' does not only have a sensory meaning. It also has a cognitive aspect, in the sense that our desires and political and religious convictions affect the way in which we interpret visual information. Here are two artists whose autobiographical work highlights the phenomenon of cultural influence.

Ming Smith (b.1950) was the first woman to become a member of the Kamoinge Workshop, a collective of Black photographers founded in Harlem in 1963, and the first Black woman whose work was featured in the permanent collection of the Museum of Modern Art in New York. She valued the ability of street photography to document life: 'You have to catch a moment that would never ever return again, and do it justice.' But in reality, her way of 'doing justice' to isolated moments is to recognize that we only briefly glimpse the strangers whose paths cross with ours. We only see a vague trace of these fleeting figures, and it quickly vanishes from our memory, leaving only an impression – it is this impression that is captured in *First Sunday I* (opposite). Here, the camera does not correct the imprecise nature of our perceptions; it makes us appreciate this imprecision as proof of our humanity.

By contrast, the South African artist Mohau Modisakeng (b.1986) aims for a high degree of precision in his pictures, which merge his personal history with that of his country of origin (overleaf). 'In my photographs,' he says, 'I am in control of how I want the viewer to relate to me, and therefore I become autonomous, in control in ways that my ancestors never were. In this way, I am seen, so that they, too, may be seen, anew.' In this photograph, the light comes from above and falls on the artist as he steps forward, wearing an elegant outfit. The series title (*Qhatha,* meaning 'let's fight') has connotations of violence, but it is a symbolic violence. The leather apron traditionally worn by manual labourers contrasts with the bowler hat of the middle classes, a hat that is even more incongruous because it looks like it is floating in mid-air rather than sitting on his head. And, under the apron, a faux leopard skin singlet suggests that ancient beliefs survive in some form even after the steamroller of Westernization has tried to crush them.

Ming Smith
First Sunday I (Grandmother's Pocketbook), 1980
Archival silver gelatin print, 35.6 x 27.9 cm (14 x 11 in.)

A quick glance at this grandmother walking out of a hotel in her Sunday best. What is she doing with her pocketbook, which appears as if it is floating in front of her? What are the little girl and her mother looking at? As we will never know the answers to these questions, the appeal of this photograph lies in the uncertainties it leaves unresolved.

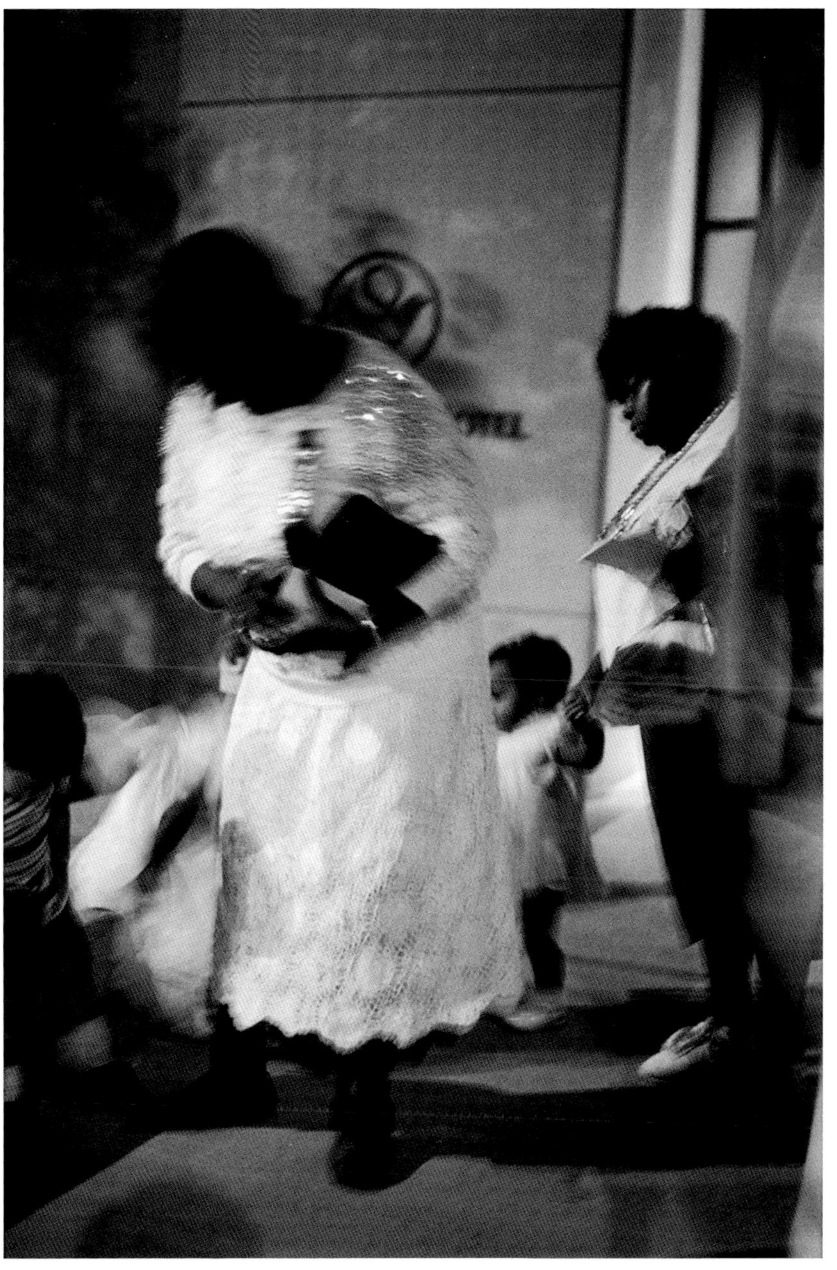

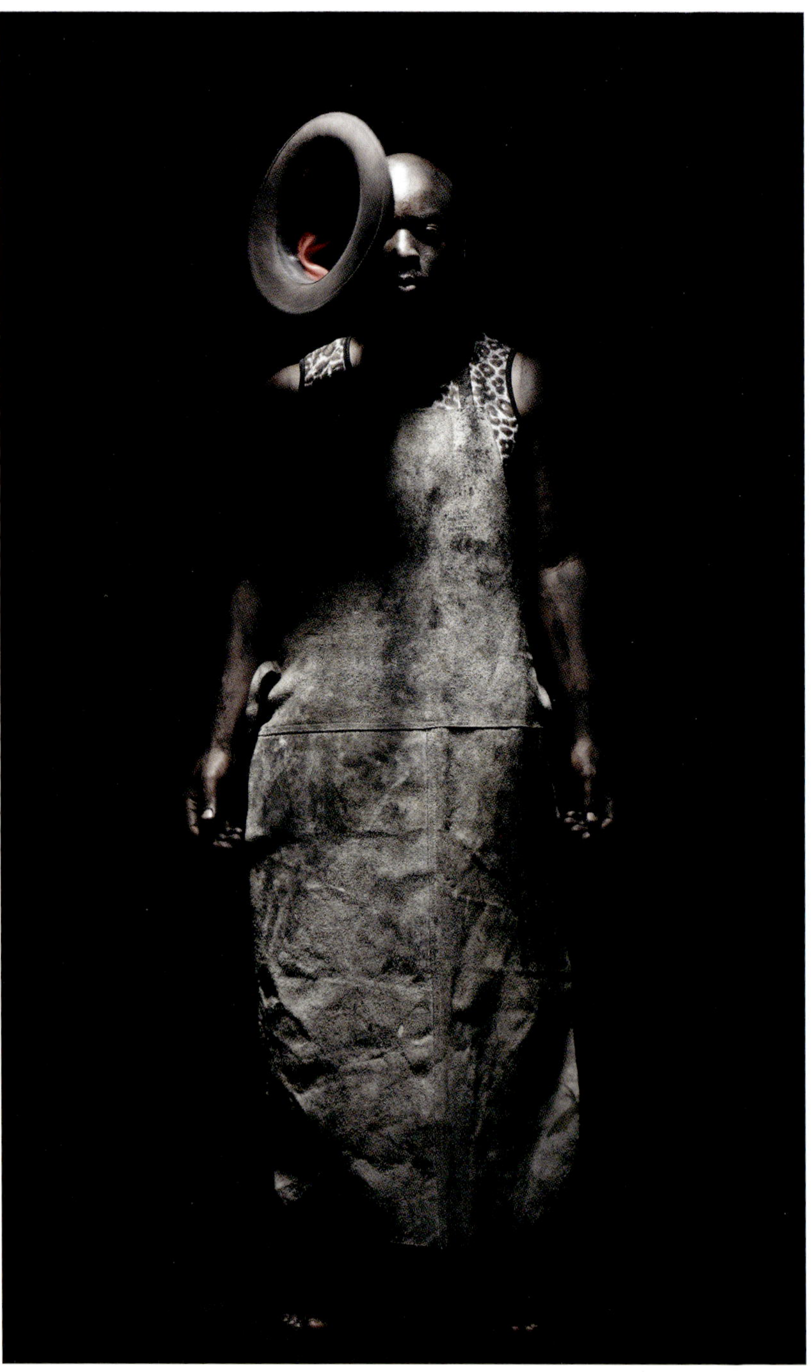

Mohau Modisakeng
Untitled (Man with a Hat), from the series 'Qhatha', 2011
Inkjet on watercolour paper, 170 x 108 cm (67 x 42⅝ in.)

Shot from a slightly low angle, the subject steps out from the shadow, seeming to challenge us to make him return to the void that swallowed him up just a moment ago. This photograph is sharp, but that does not mean it answers all our questions – this floating hat is no less strange than the grandmother's pocketbook.

SELECTIVE ATTENTION

The earliest photographers aimed for absolute stillness. Resting on its tripod, the camera was not supposed to move, and neither was the subject, because the slightest movement from one or the other would result in a blurry photograph. Furthermore, until the late 1880s, the exposure time was very long. For portraits, photographers sometimes used metallic headrests that were more or less well hidden, or asked the subject to rest their head on one hand. That is why, as the photography historian Clément Chéroux suggests, photographs from this period always evoke a certain sense of melancholy. It is not because the photos are old, but because the sitters often adopt this listless, gloomy pose.

The haziness that is a common feature in the works of British photographer Julia Margaret Cameron (1815–1879) is caused by the long exposure time that she imposed on her subjects (below), although technical advances meant it was only necessary for them to hold their pose for a few seconds. She liked this game of stillness, of 'playing dead', which not only gave the individuals she

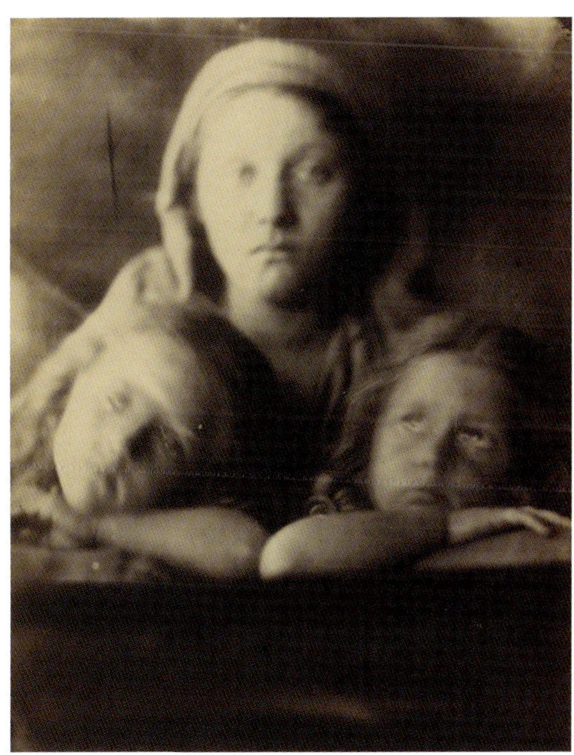

Julia Margaret Cameron
Mary Hillier and Two Children, 1864
Albumen print, 26.6 x 21.1 cm (10½ x 8$^{5}/_{16}$ in.)

What are the children looking at? Are they wondering what they are doing there, or are they gazing at the heavens? The little girl on the left has shifted more than the girl on the right, and her face is also more brightly lit. A small mistake with the chemicals while developing the photograph has also created a line across her left eye, which makes her look half-ecstatic, half-blind.

photographed a melancholy air, but also blurred their features. The soft, indistinct faces suited her purpose, which was to evoke stories and myths rather than represent her sitters accurately. Here, Mary Ann Hillier, who was Cameron's maid, is transformed into the Virgin Mary, and the two children adopt the same pose as the famous cherubs in the *Sistine Madonna* painted by Raphael in around 1514. The blurriness makes all the insignificant details disappear and creates a kind of halo; the Madonna and her cherubim seem to prompt us to reflect on our own relationship with religion.

A world to inhabit

Blurriness can also be used to express how things escape our attention: when we focus on something, everything around it fades away. In reality, two types of blurriness impact our perception of the world. The first concerns the edges of our field of vision, which are very sensitive to movement but don't pick up details. The second concerns our line of vision: when we focus on an object, everything between us and the object becomes hazier, as do its surroundings. In photography, this second kind of blurriness is what we mean when we speak of the 'depth of field': this expression refers to the area in line with the lens within which objects appear sharp. This area is limited in *Red Umbrella* by Saul Leiter (page 100), since the snow in the foreground is blurry, and in *Christina in a Red Cloak* by Mervyn O'Gorman (page 118), where we can barely make out the sea in the background. But in this example (opposite) by British photographer Roger Mayne (1929–2014), the depth of field is very large, and the subjects stand out clearly from their surroundings because of the strong contrast between light and dark, rather than because they are sharper.

The little girl on the left has spotted Roger Mayne's camera – and she is the only one of several children to have noticed it. In this way, she continues a tradition begun by Renaissance artists, whose paintings often featured a person who was aware of the presence of an onlooker, watching them and sometimes beckoning to them, inviting them to see the painting as a kind of window opening onto a three-dimensional world, a *world to inhabit*. This little girl looks thoughtfully at us, her hands in her pockets. She is also the only child not playing, the only one who is on her own.

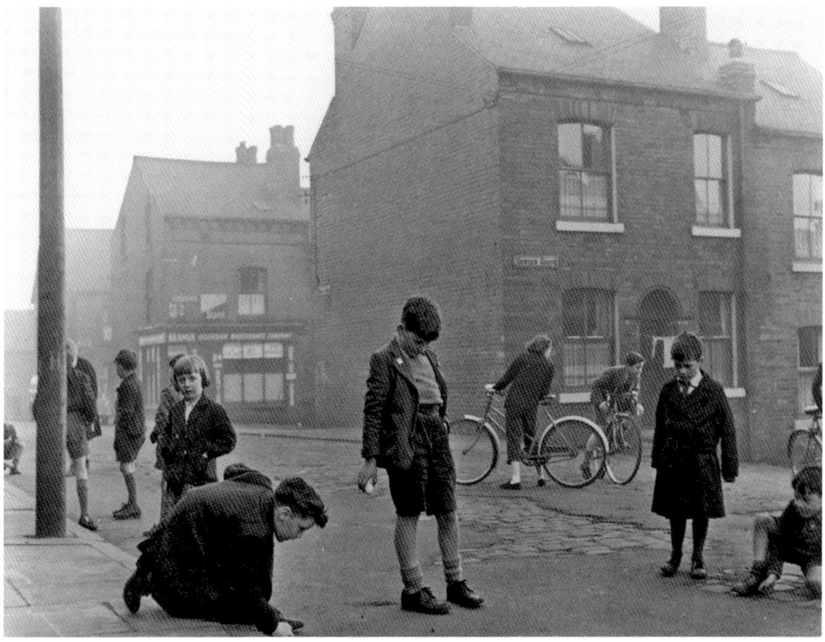

Roger Mayne
Street Scene, Leeds, 1957

The striking contrast between the grey city, which looks like it is swathed in fog, and the dark black clothes worn by these children makes them stand out from their surroundings, as if to show that they could be playing anywhere in exactly the same way as they are doing in this street in Leeds.

DIFFERENT TYPES OF BLURRINESS

In general life, the verb 'to focus' means to concentrate our interest or activity on something. In photography, it has a slightly different meaning: adjusting the lens to make sure there are no blurred areas within the image, or at least that the main subject is sharp. In both cases, however, the word has the same basic meaning: selecting what is important and giving it our full attention. And, as a consequence, leaving the rest blurry.

Blurriness is often seen as a sign of a bad photo, or as an effect used by photographers who consider aesthetic considerations more important than conveying a message or information. However, just because a photograph is unfocused does not mean it has no message, even (and particularly) if the blurriness is taken to the extreme. A picture can express something very precise even if the outlines of the shapes within it are indistinct. The following two works, created by editing existing images, make use of blurriness to highlight the importance of remembrance.

This installation (overleaf) by the French artist Christian Boltanski (1944–2021) focuses on a group who are at even greater risk of being forgotten, because we do not know who these people are or what became of them. Their faces have been cut out from a

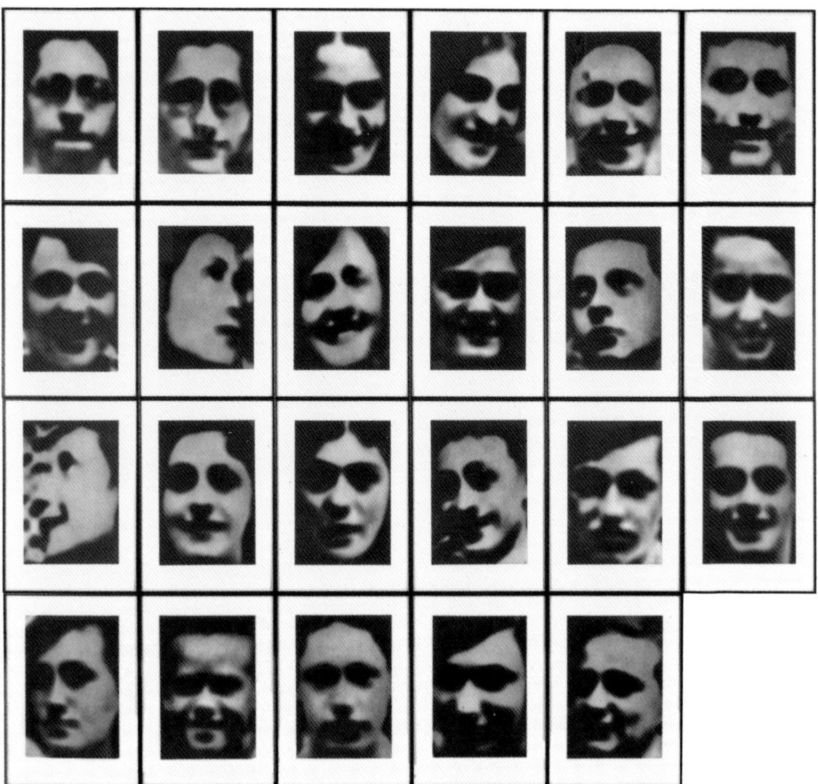

Christian Boltanski
Gymnasium Chases, 1991
Portfolio of 24
photogravures,
each 48.3 x 33 cm
(19⅛ x 13 in.)

The blurriness that renders these teenagers anonymous is a sinister reminder of the reason why they were killed: Nazi racial ideology. In the eyes of their executioners, it didn't matter who they were as individuals. The blurriness of their faces also reminds us of how details are lost when we make physical copies As the subjects and the original photographs have both disappeared, we are reduced to copying these pictures again and again, losing more detail each time, so that in the end we no longer recognize anyone, and so forget them.

class photo taken at the Jewish Chajes School in Vienna, dated 1931, then blown up, made blurry by adding more contrast, and stuck onto metal boxes laid out as if in a funeral home. The name of the school has been changed to 'Chases' – playing on the double meaning of pursuing someone and embossing metal – referring to the Nazis hunting down the Jews in Austria from 1938 onwards and Boltanski creating the metal boxes years later. The fact that the boxes are empty plays into the same sense of loss as the blurred faces. The only way to remember what took place is to rely on human memory; all the traces have vanished or are in the process of vanishing. The 23 tins are laid out in rows of six, which highlights the sense that something is missing – the square that they form is incomplete.

What does a disaster look like?

The move to digital does not mean that ultra-sharp photos now reign supreme. Nor does it spell the end for blurriness. Photos are also blurry when they are taken quickly, during an emergency, when there is no time to aim the camera, as in this example (overleaf) by the British photographer Alison Jackson (b.1970), known for her faked photos of celebrities.

In her series 'Disaster', Jackson imagines people in emergencies – their building is on fire, their ship is sinking, their plane is going to crash – taking out their phones to record the moment. There is a lot of camera shake, enough to create a sense of panic, but not so much that we are unable to recognize details. However, the artist's aim is not to castigate us for our obsession with photographing everything and filming all the time, but more to highlight the 'industry of fear' cultivated by the media through 'sensationalist' photographs and video clips. On her official website, Jackson says that, in her work, she 'depicts our fantasies of fear, as we live in a world of constant, impending dread, raising questions about the media's premise of creating bad news'.

Even when nothing is moving – not the photographer nor the subject – the simple fact of storing files can lead to them becoming damaged. Because you have to store them somewhere: even digital files have some kind of physical existence. When she discovered that some of the self-portraits she had taken a few years earlier had been damaged in this way, the Mexican photographer Susana Moyaho (b.1983) decided to make the most of it (page 77). 'I couldn't help

Alison Jackson
Plane, from the series
'Disaster', 2010
C-type archival print

Despite the technical advances in digital photography, camera shake can still create blurriness at the moment of taking a photo. Therefore, why not make use of it, especially if you want to highlight the sensationalism of some unscrupulous media outlets that seek to show us *everything*.

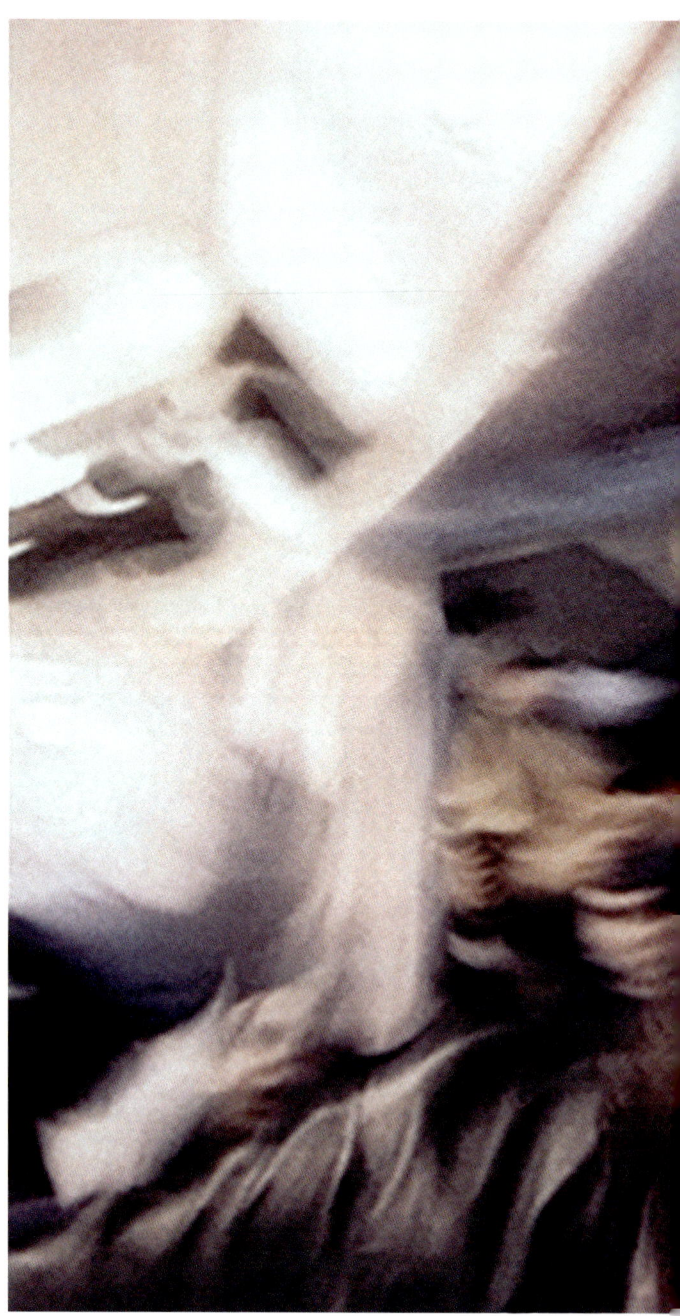

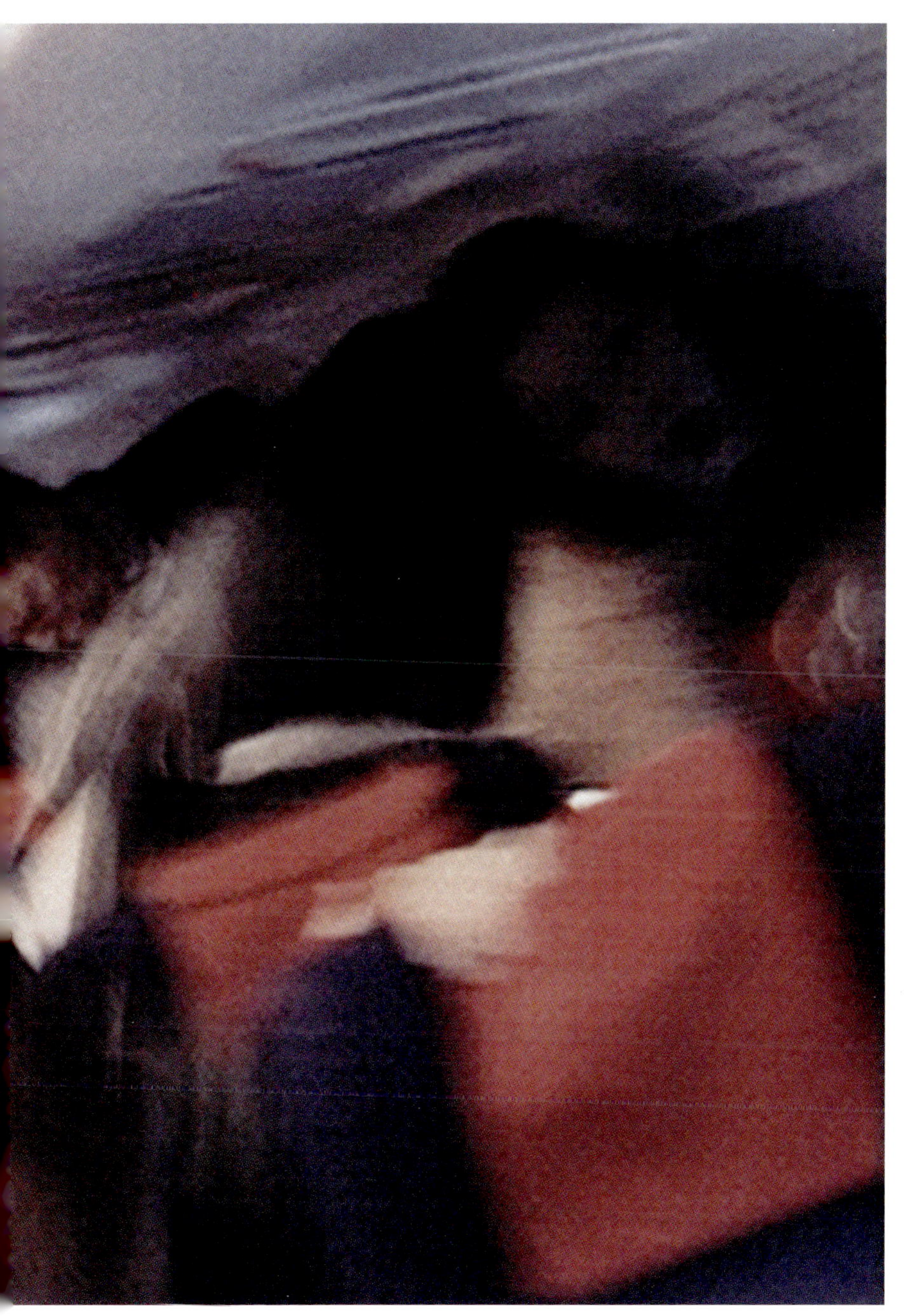

reflecting on the fact that while I was looking for perfection in the way I wanted to be remembered, the very medium I had chosen was undermining my desire.' Here, technical imperfections and the loss of detail do not diminish the photograph's ability to represent its subject. On the contrary, while these glitches show failures of technology, they also expose the vanity of trying to make yourself beautiful, of always trying to present the best image of yourself to the camera.

Susana Moyaho
Debris 20, from the series 'Misremember Me Correctly', 2020
Video screenshot

Digital archives are supposed to be reliable. Translated into millions of 0s and 1s, the pixels that make up each photograph are supposed to stay exactly where they are. However, sometimes there are unexpected accidents, which remind us that nothing lasts forever.

KEY IDEAS

A photograph does not necessarily have to be in focus in order to be considered technically proficient.

Blurriness is not always accidental.

When we are unsure what is depicted in a photo, that is a chance to see it as something other than a window opening onto the world.

Blurriness can lead us to reflect on our doubts, our fleeting impressions or the things we fail to notice.

KEY QUESTIONS

Should sharpness be considered an ideal to strive for?

Does it make sense to spend a long time looking at a blurry photograph?

Should a photographer always prefer light to shadow?

Are areas of uncertainty in photographs always a sign that something is being concealed from us?

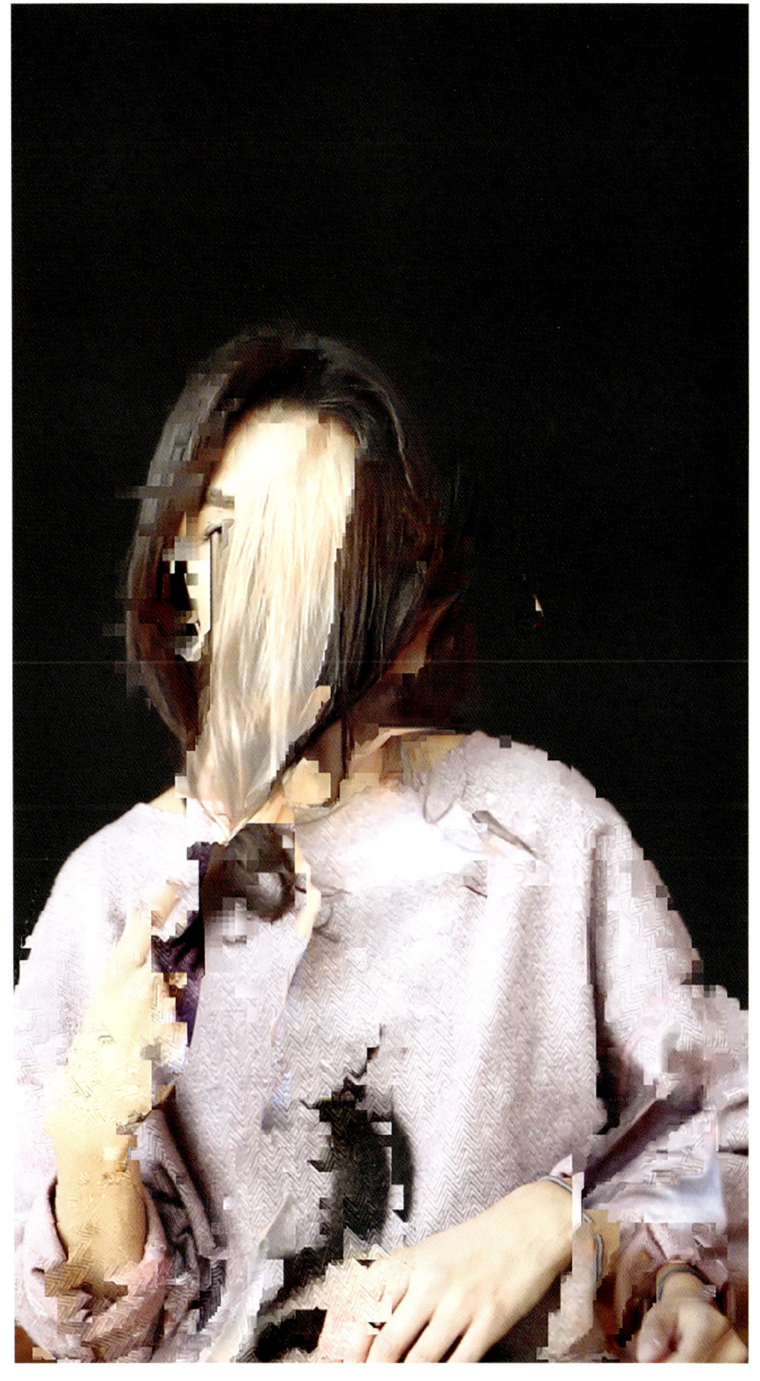

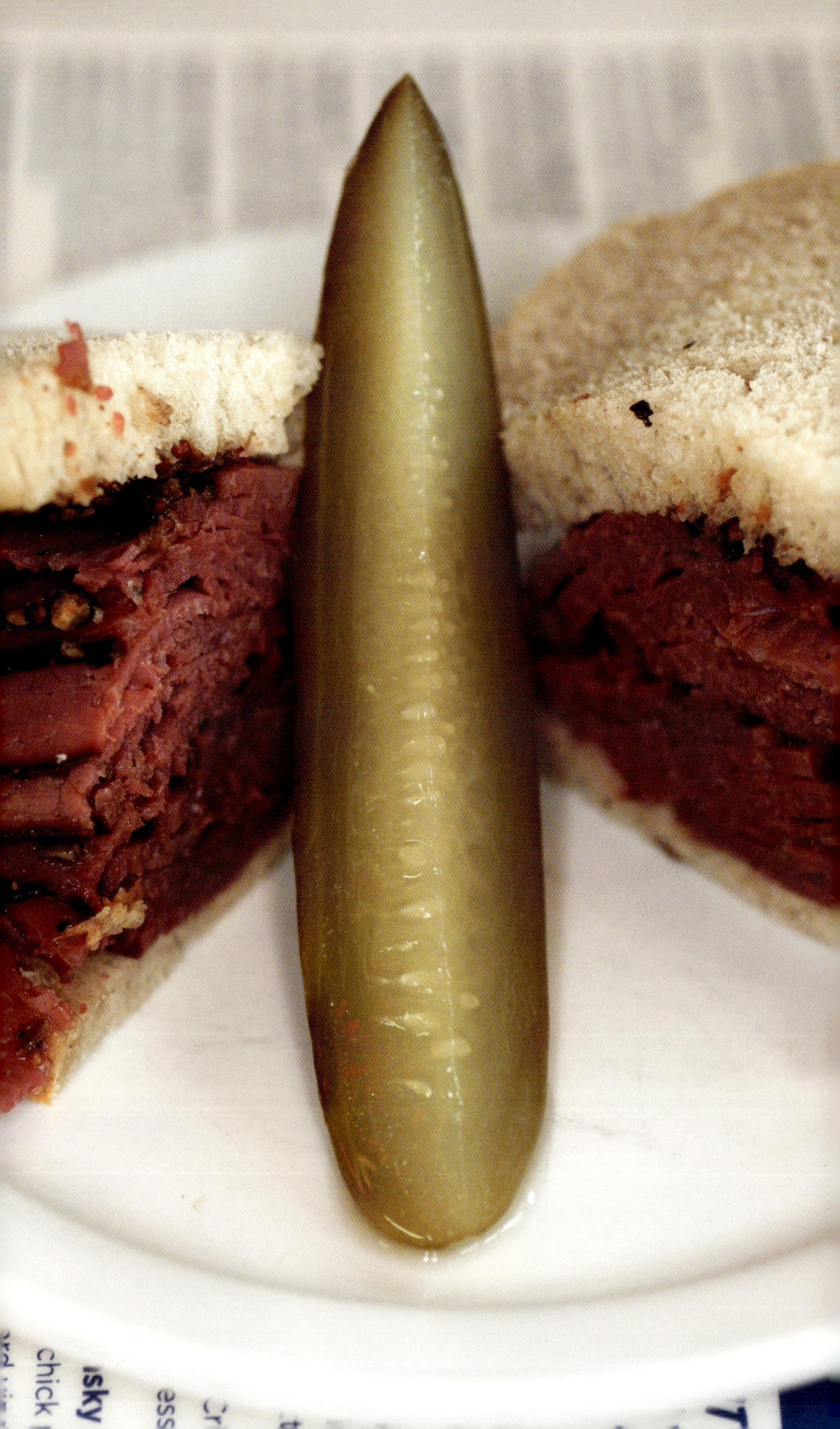

THE RIGHT ANGLE, THE RIGHT DISTANCE

-

The photographs that I take simply reflect my point of view, and through them, I try to illustrate the contradictions in our society

-

Martin Parr

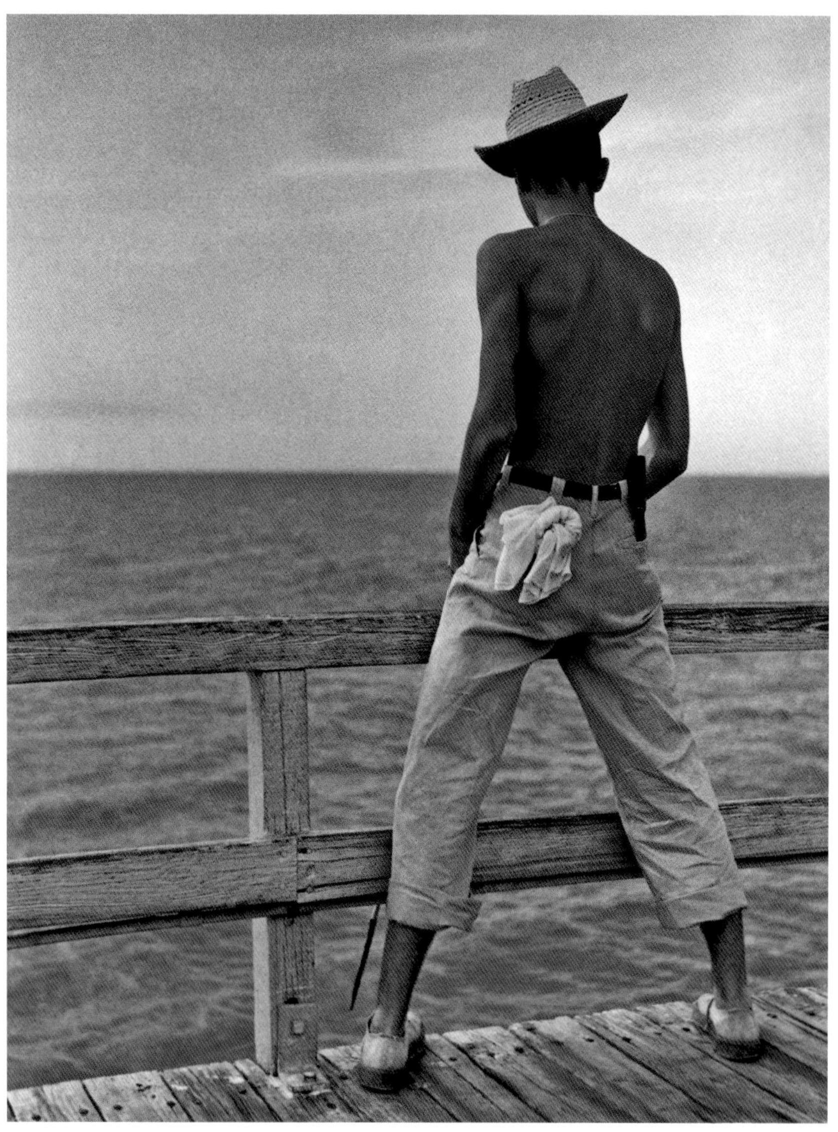

Berenice Abbott
Boy Fishing, Daytona Beach, Florida, 1954

The straight line of the horizon is at the same height as the boy's slightly curved belt. The line separating the sky from the sea merges with the line separating the boy's bare torso from his clothed lower half.

Everyone knows the tired old joke about the tourist taking a photo of his friends or family on the harbour, with his back to the sea. Trying to find the best distance from which to take the photo, he takes one step backwards, then another...and falls into the water. Professionals are more careful, but all photographers are looking for the same thing: the *right point of view* – a visual perspective that, they hope, will also convey their moral, emotional or ideological perspective on the scene that they have captured. There is a subtle combination of aesthetics and ethics at play in the choice of where to stand in order to take a photo, perhaps more so than in any other technical consideration.

The difference in how classic cameras and smartphones work also plays a role here. When we place our eye against the viewfinder, we may be using the lens to change how we see, but we are still looking directly at the world; whereas looking at the photo that we are trying to take on a screen means that we are no longer focusing on the world itself, but on an image of it.

APPROACH / AVOID

Animal behaviour is governed by two contrasting kinds of movement that are both vital to survival: *approach/avoid*. That is, drawing closer to prey or getting away from a predator. Humans are not exempt from this rule, although photographers subvert it to some extent. Like binoculars and telescopes, cameras belong to the family of optical instruments that allow us to see something up close when we are physically far away. A photograph is like a protective pane of glass. Like the wall of an aquarium tank or the bars of an enclosure in a zoo, it offers us a glimpse of a hostile environment. The photographer has taken all the risks on our behalf, sometimes even risking their life to present these pictures for us to enjoy. Some photographers did not survive, like the Swedish-Argentinian photojournalist Leonardo Henrichsen, who filmed his own murder by the soldiers who carried out the military coup in Santiago, Chile, in 1973.

-

A false sense of ubiquity

-

Of course, drawing closer to get a better view of something beautiful doesn't raise so many issues. Sometimes a camera plays a similar role to a microscope or a telescope, allowing us to discover those parts of the world that are invisible to the naked eye. This kind of exploration is enjoyable but, as Susan Sontag suggests, it can be dangerous in the long term: 'Photography's ultra-mobile gaze flatters the viewer, creating a false sense of ubiquity, a deceptive mastery of experience.' We end up seeing everything as a spectacle and no longer truly engaging with what we are looking at.

Fortunately, there are some photographers who show us how to engage with the world. Their work is not always spectacular, or even political. It is simply a celebration of humanity, as in the case of the American photographer Berenice Abbott (1898–1991).

What could be simpler than immortalizing a young man while he is fishing (page 80)? It is truly a dream for a photographer, as he is not moving. Abbott chose to photograph her subject from behind so as not to disturb the peace of the moment. Because this is not just any fisherman; in fact, if we didn't know the title of the photograph, we might wonder what the young man is doing. There is no fishing gear at his feet, not even a fishing rod in sight – the angle from which the photograph was taken has obscured it, but you can just make out the tip in front of the boy's left calf. With his feet planted wide apart, adopting a relaxed pose with one hand in his pocket, the young man looks like the *paisanos* (peasants) described by John Steinbeck in his novel *Tortilla Flat* (1935). Steinbeck writes that these men 'merge with their habitat. In men this is called philosophy, and it is a fine thing.' Abbott felt it: she drew near but also showed respect; she did not disturb the harmony of the moment, a man at one with his environment.

The opposite is true of this photograph (opposite) depicting the horrors of war. The horrors depicted here are twofold. On one hand, the Biafran War (1967–1970) sparked a famine in Nigeria that claimed more than a million lives; on the other hand, sensationalist photojournalism fed off the spectacle created by the symptoms of *kwashiorkor*, a terrible illness that afflicted children suffering from malnutrition. When he arrived on the scene, the Iranian photographer Abbas (1944–2018), a member of the Magnum agency, was troubled by what he saw. He chose to use a reverse angle to capture four of his fellow photographers snapping away at a trembling child in torn clothes. Is this truly a turning of the tables? From a visual perspective, it is certainly a reversal, but is it an ethical one? It doesn't matter whether this poor lonely child is shown from behind or face on, because it is clear that no one asked his permission before pressing the button.

The protection offered by photography encourages us to look at sights that we would turn away from if a photographer hadn't recorded them for us. We find violence less disturbing when it is

Abbas
End of Biafra, Owerri, Nigeria, 1970

Abbas remained standing; he did not want to play the game of getting down to the child's level.

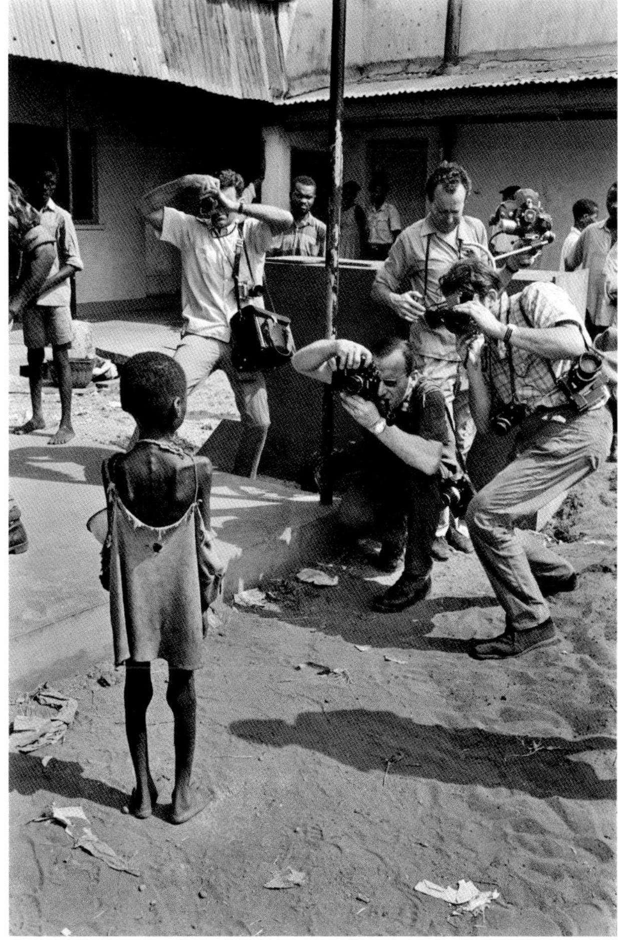

enclosed within a rectangular frame and stripped of one of its three dimensions, when we are no longer witnessing it in the flesh. We can look at it in a more detached way, even appreciate it from an aesthetic perspective, our moral scruples forgotten. That is why war photographers are always playing with fire to some extent. What are the ethics of showing the ravaged corpses of ill-fated young men, when the person looking at the photograph already knows that war is a terrible thing and has to fight against *schadenfreude*, the secret satisfaction of seeing another person who is suffering more than us? When faced with such a scene, a good photographer does not allow us to become a voyeur: instead, they prompt us to reflect, to go beyond our instinctive reaction.

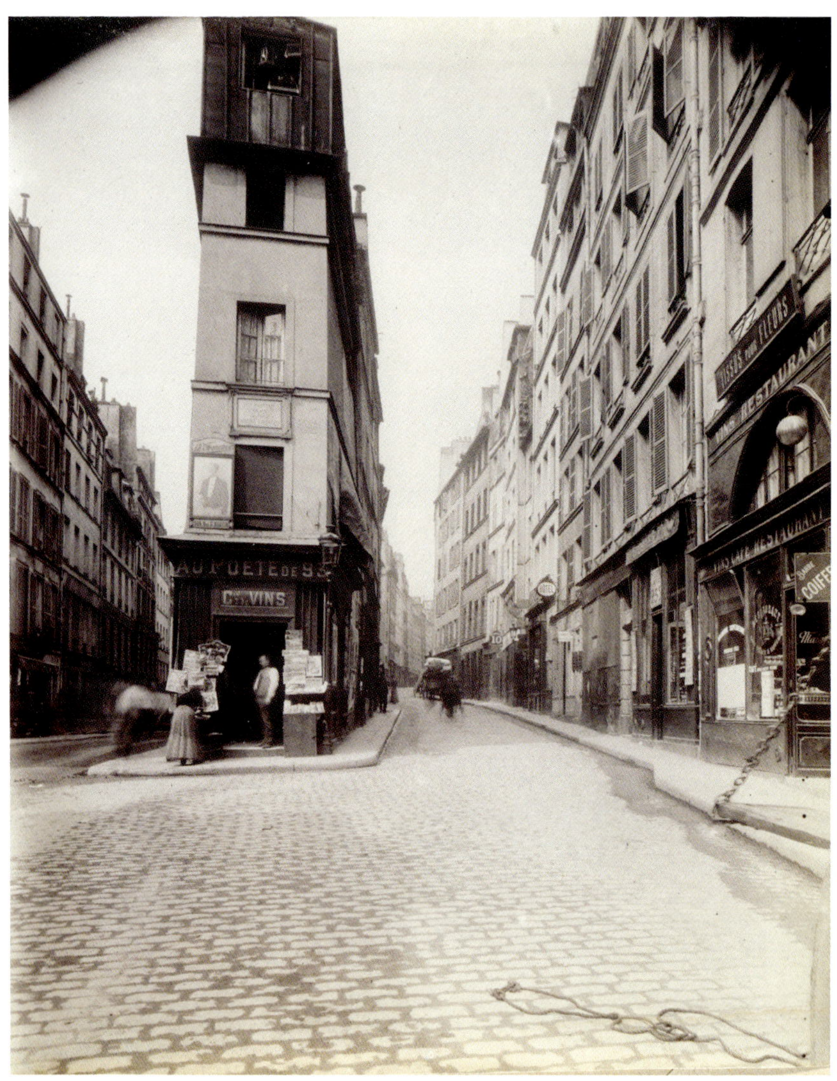

Eugène Atget
André Chénier's house, corner of the rue de Cléry and rue d'Aboukir, Paris, 1907
Albumen print, 21.5 x 17.8 cm (8½ x 7⅛ in.)

Like other pioneering photographers, Eugène Atget worked without a viewfinder; this may explain why the ridge of the building's roof touches the edge of the frame, while there is a vast stretch of paved road at the bottom.

EYES LIKE SCISSORS

Tourists taking pictures on safari and photojournalists covering a football match cannot get up close to their subject: therefore they use a telephoto lens or long-focus lens. To explain how this works, imagine that the width of the field of view is like a pair of scissors. When the scissors are open wide, the two blades are very far away from each other. In the same way, with a short-focus lens, the space being observed spreads out on either side of our eyes. By contrast, when the two blades are brought closer together, they form a more acute angle: with a long-focus lens, the field of view becomes narrower, but it is completely filled by what was previously small and far away.

While the focal distance of our eyes is fixed, the focal distance of a camera or smartphone can vary. Armed with these gadgets and using a short focal distance, an object that is nearby will seem to be far away. Alternatively, with a long focal distance, we can look at a remote object and see it close-up.

It goes without saying that the possibilities offered by varying the focal distance only serve to exacerbate the moral issues around voyeurism. Looking at people from far away, using a telephoto lens, is a bit like being a spy. The photographer needs to have a good reason for doing so or risk being banished from the ranks of reputable photojournalists. We might think of the Hungarian-born American photographer Robert Capa's (1913–1954) famous saying: 'If your pictures aren't good enough, you aren't close enough.'

However, photographers often use a wide-angle lens, or a short-focus lens, when they want to draw attention to the relationship between different elements in a scene. It allows the photographer to *put things into perspective*, in both the literal and the figurative sense, instead of isolating the subject by stripping it of all context. However, this perspective also distorts the vanishing lines which create a sense of depth in the picture: the result therefore looks slightly different from how we perceive the world. The French photographer Eugène Atget's (1857–1927) photographs of the streets of Paris (opposite) often rely on this phenomenon. Taken around the time that the metro was being built and the capital was being transformed by sweeping grand boulevards, they make use of the distancing effect created by the wide-angle lens to convey the sense that the former Paris is now very far away, lost in the depths of time.

The wine merchant on the ground floor of this narrow Parisian building disappeared a long time ago, and the building itself no longer appears the same as it used to. However, no one walking along this street has ever seen the façades taper as sharply as they

Luca Campigotto
Gulf of Bothnia, Lapland, 2003
Archival pigment print, 101.6 x 127 cm (40 x 50 in.)

Because the ship was trapped in the ice and therefore couldn't move, Luca Campigotto was able to leave the shutter open for a long period, just as the pioneers of photography did. The result is that the people who carried on moving on the bottom right are blurred.

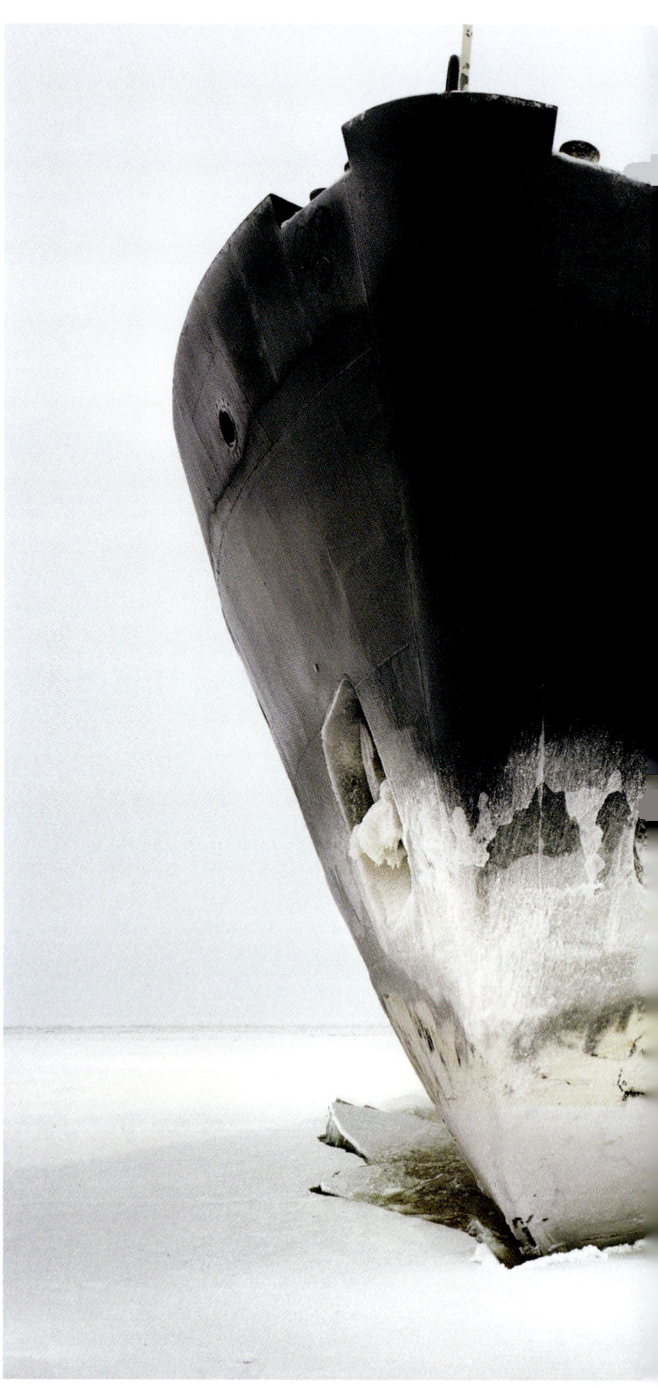

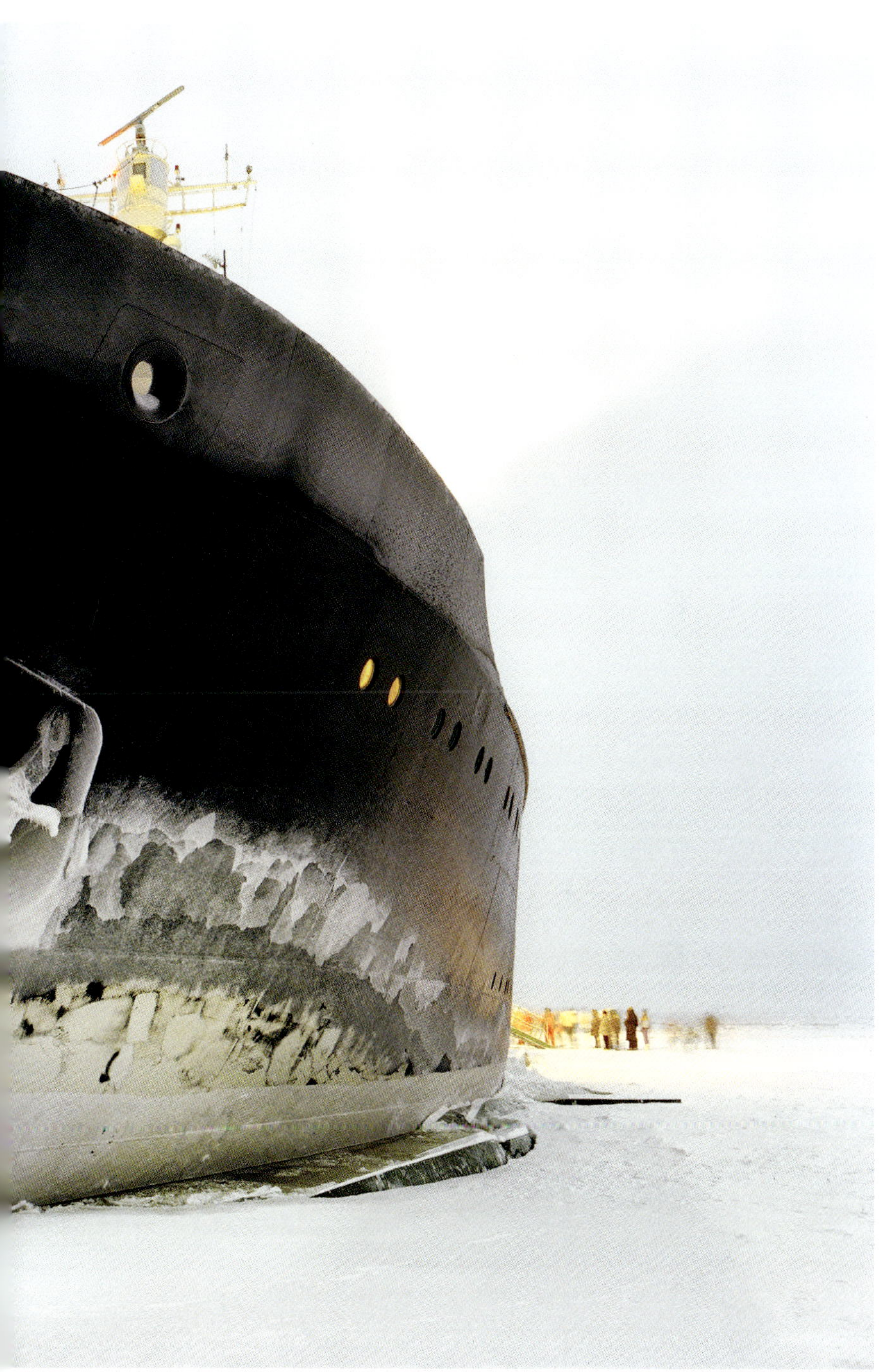

do in this photograph. The distortion of the vanishing lines is also emphasized by the rounded corners of the frame.

To avoid these effects, many photographers simply prefer to use lenses with a focal distance similar to that of our eyes, and to get physically closer to or further away from their subject. But we can also use distortions to express ideas or feelings. That is what the Italian photographer Luca Campigotto (b.1962) is doing in one of his projects inspired by his travels (pages 86–87).

The wide-angle lens makes the ship's bow look even more like the face of a monstrous shark. The two circular openings of the bulwark look like eyes, the anchors make one think of nostrils, and the patches of ice at the bottom of the hull resemble teeth. The scene is also imbued with irony: humans have copied nature by building a ship in the shape of a fish, and now they are being punished, with the ice preventing them from going any further.

THE RIGHT PLACE

At around seven years old, children reach what psychologists call the 'age of reason' and begin to develop a greater capacity for empathy. They start to understand how people around them are feeling and to make the connection between thoughts and actions. Photography offers a concrete manifestation of this capacity, enabling us to see through someone else's eyes. At times this perspective even allows us to understand a situation better than if we had been there ourselves, in the photographer's place. It is interesting to note that the expression 'point of view' refers to both vision and judgement. Physically changing our position in space to look at something can also lead to a change in our moral or political position – some newspapers even feature a section that provides an overview of what the foreign press is writing about the national news. As well as making it possible for us to change our minds, this different perspective sometimes allows us to discover beauty in unexpected places.

Let's take, for example, a primary school (opposite). It doesn't matter what country it is in, or what time period. There are only two things we need in order to appreciate its beauty: the right moment and the right position. Ten children are getting ready to play musical chairs. The long shadows suggest that it is early morning or late afternoon. They are captured in a moment of hesitation; the game is about to begin, unless the adult on the left is turning their head to console a child who has already been eliminated. The Indian

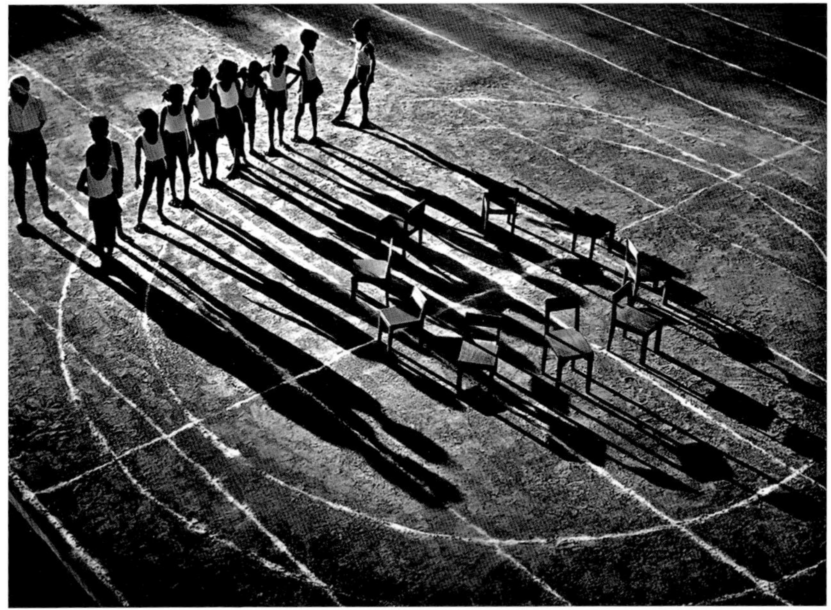

Vidyavrata
Music, Pondicherry, 1962
120mm black & white film negative

To capture the graphic beauty of the moment, with the chairs and shadows forming the quavers and sharps of an imaginary score, the photographer had to stand in that exact position.

photographer Vidyavrata (1920–1999) climbed up onto a rooftop or a balcony. He saw the straight lines on the playground and the chairs set out in a circle.

A photographer can also find the right position by visualizing what the scene will look like as a flat image – because, unlike the real world, photographs are only two-dimensional. This flattening effect is not a drawback when we abandon the idea that photography should produce a copy, or even a clone of the world. In fact, it allows us to directly link things that, in reality, are too far away from each other for us to see the relationship between them.

The Ethiopian artist Aïda Muluneh (b.1974) aims to 'advocate through art' about the 'plight of water access' in her country (overleaf). There is plenty of water in Ethiopia, but it is in underground reservoirs and can only be accessed using expensive equipment. In the upper half of the photograph, blue is the dominant colour: the sky, the umbrella, the head-wrap and the woman's make-up. This colour is entirely absent from the lower half, although all the water is concentrated in that section. The heroine's pose draws attention to this: the jerry cans she trails nonchalantly behind her are empty, and the umbrella is useless. The composition aims to give visible expression to a problem that, if it is not resolved, will claim the lives of many Ethiopians.

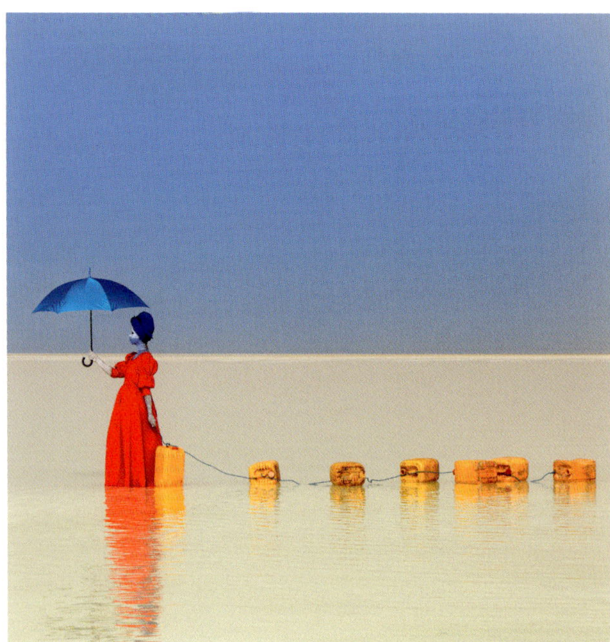

Aïda Muluneh
The Shackles of Limitations, from the series 'Water Life', 2018
Inkjet print on paper, 80 × 80 cm (31½ x 31½ in.)

The horizon that cuts across the centre of the frame separates the woman's head from her body. At the heart of the composition, this line functions as a symbol of the fundamental divide between the world of ideas (how we should address the water crisis) and the world of concrete actions (what is happening in reality).

The camera's eye goes where the human eye cannot

Driven by a similar desire to inform, the photographers and filmmakers of the Soviet avant-garde in the 1920s believed it was their duty to show farmers, factory workers and miners what they looked like when they were working, to help them see themselves from a different perspective. They aimed to convince them that they were doing something noble and beautiful. Perhaps it worked, sometimes.

Seeing themselves through the eyes of Arkady Shaikhet (1898–1959), these two manual labourers (opposite) might have realized that their work assembling a globe on the pediment of the Telegraph Central Station was in fact symbolic of the institution's mission. The composition is also influenced by the Constructivist movement, which sought to break away from the gratuitous intricacies of fine art and instead focus on geometric shapes that were more suited to representing the new world brought about by the Russian Revolution. Embracing this approach, the thick lines that form the internal structure of the globe are overlaid with fine ones that trace its outer shape. This network of lines represents the connections that are forged between people on opposite sides of the world, including those who are fundamentally opposed to each other – and it is therefore apt that our two workmen are standing back to back.

MAPPING THE WORLD

The most fascinating perspective is perhaps an extreme high-angle shot. This is often called a God's eye view, as it shows an overhead angle that we cannot usually access. In photography, its origins can be traced back to 1858, when the pioneering French photographer Nadar (1820–1910), who was one of the first to use artificial lighting, applied for a patent for 'aerostatic' photography,

Arkady Shaikhet
Assembling the Globe at Moscow Telegraph Central Station, 1928
Vintage gelatin silver print, 24 x 17.8 cm (9⅜ x 7 in.)

This photograph appeared on the cover of *Ogoniok*, a weekly magazine featuring photoessays, which was the USSR's equivalent of *Life* magazine in the United States. By chance, the worker on the left is wearing the same kind of cap as Trotsky, while the man on the right is sporting one in a similar style to those worn by Lenin.

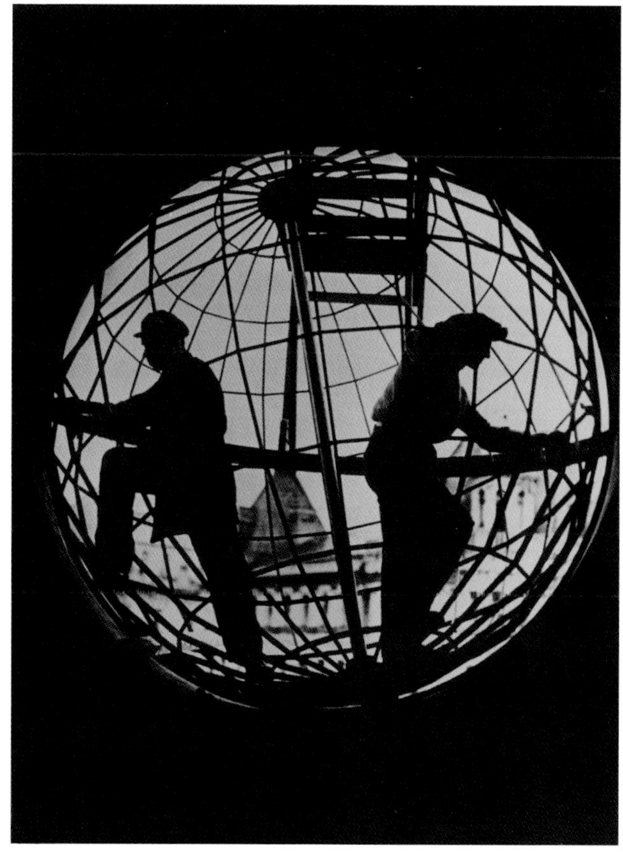

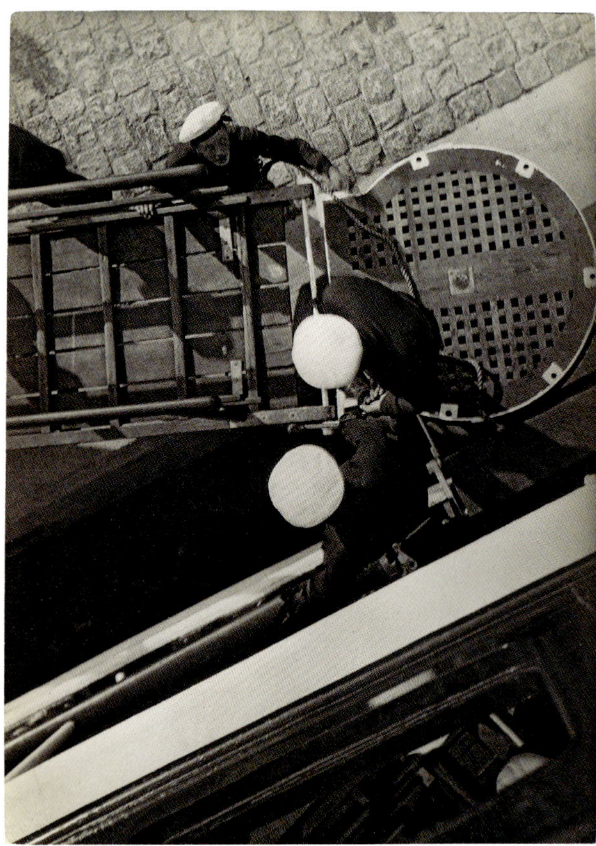

László Moholy-Nagy
Scandinavia, 1930
Gelatin silver print,
23.5 x 17.1 cm
(9¼ x 6¾ in.)

The God's eye view creates the impression of being *above it all*, of breathing a purer air, freed from all the material concerns of life below. The hashtag #fromwhereistand has been doing the rounds on the internet for some years now, used to tag countless photographs taken from high angles, including those from a God's eye view.

meaning photographs taken from a hot-air balloon. Although today Nadar is widely known for the emotional power of his photographic portraits, his aim in flying 200 metres above the earth was not to create art, but to draw accurate maps and take measurements. Nothing more, nothing less. In the end, he failed in this endeavour. The photographs, which he eventually managed to take ten years after filing for the patent, are at a diagonal angle – it wasn't until satellites and drones were invented that we were able to take photographs at an angle exactly perpendicular to the ground. But that doesn't matter: these extraordinary images inspired Nadar's contemporaries to adopt a radically different perspective, one that would later reach its full potential when the first planes were invented.

To describe this radical new perspective, we could borrow a term from the vocabulary of cinema: the reverse angle, when the camera operator turns around, sometimes 180 degrees, to film from the opposite point of view to the initial shot. Throughout time, the myths and beliefs of many cultures and religions have been built around the simple gesture of lifting our eyes to the sky; now photography could offer the reverse angle to this gaze, so everyone could see it. This fundamentally transformed visual culture.

What does the photograph on the left show? Three sailors disembarking onto the docks? No. It shows the gaze of someone observing them from the upper deck of a ship. This gaze takes in geometric patterns: the grid of the paving stones echoes the pattern on the end of the gangway, which has a circular shape resembling that of the sailors' hats. In turn, the light-coloured strip that marks the edge of the dock echoes the railing. What is even more captivating to the eye is that none of the lines within the field of view are parallel or perpendicular to the edges of the frame. 'In the photographic camera we have the most reliable aid to a beginning of objective vision,' said the Hungarian artist László Moholy-Nagy (1895–1946). Here, rather than sailors in a port, he wanted us to see a pure combination of lines, patterns and geometric shapes. Paul Klee, his colleague at the Bauhaus, used the phrase 'cow's eye' to describe this non-analytical gaze. But it isn't as simple as that: one of the sailors is looking up, straight at us. Therefore it is impossible to maintain the impassive gaze of a cow.

Ernst Haas
Park Avenue Taxis,
New York, 1958

The high-angle perspective emphasizes the fact that each category of object has its own specific colours, as if there is no space for individuality in this kind of environment: the plants are naturally green, but cultural convention means that yellow and brown are the colours assigned to the cars, while black and white are for people.

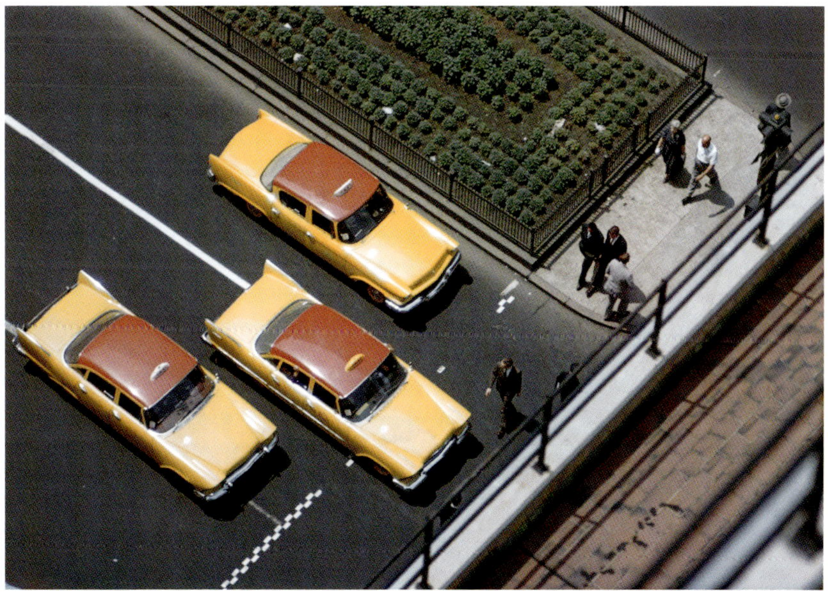

We are led to wonder what he thinks of this oddball photographing him from on high.

The picture on page 93 was taken by another photographer who was known for transforming the world into abstract shapes, the Austrian-American Ernst Haas (1921–1986). Like Moholy-Nagy's *Scandinavia*, this photograph does not contain any lines that are parallel or perpendicular to the edges of the frame. But the composition, which creates a 45-degree angle, is harsher, stricter. It presents a world of geometric shapes, a space shared by living beings (people, plants) and inanimate objects (cars) that have to follow the straight lines marked out for them in order to avoid getting into danger. Everything is aligned or intersects at right angles. One of the three taxis has crept a bit too far forward, immediately drawing the – most likely disapproving – gaze of the pedestrian in the suit and tie.

Look what I'm going to eat!

Playing around with perspective in this way has its roots in popular culture. In the early twentieth century, a movement of amateur photographers had already sprung up, practising photography as a hobby. They wanted to play with their cameras, with all the implications of childlike wonder that the word evokes. While they enjoyed experimenting with the distortions and doctoring explored in the previous chapter, they were even more drawn to unusual perspectives. High-angle and low-angle shots testified to the agility of amateurs, who were determined to climb up as high as possible or crouch down low, to the point that in 1907 the popular amateur photography magazine *Photo pêle-mêle* ran the headline 'Risking life and limb to entertain readers'.

There is a humbler kind of high-angle shot, with no divine connotations, as seen in the photos taken by people in restaurants before they drink their latte or devour their sandwich. The British photographer Martin Parr (b.1952) chose a more complex process for this picture (opposite): it was taken using a ring flash, a camera surrounded by a ring of light that means there are no shadows in the photograph – an effect that, as Parr says, 'strips it of all romanticism'.

We are sitting in a delicatessen (the menu lists kishke and gefilte fish among its offerings) and getting ready to wolf down a pastrami sandwich garnished with a slice of pickle. By we, I mean both the imaginary customer who took the photograph and the person

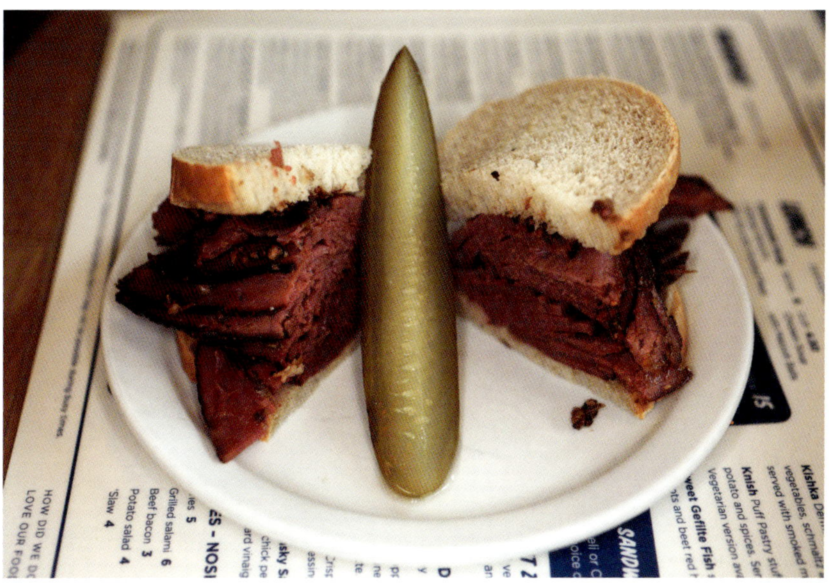

Martin Parr
Food, Toronto, 2012

The composition is governed by a kind of bilateral symmetry in the shape of the sandwich. But neither the photographer nor the chef pushed this regularity to its extreme: the meat and the bread do not look exactly the same on both sides, and the subject is not precisely centred (the space between the plate and the edge of the frame is slightly larger on the left than on the right).

looking at it. We are one and the same. The surroundings have disappeared. Parr's photographs are often close-ups that explore, as he puts it, 'the idea of saying more by showing less, by getting closer'. Saying more, in this photograph, means emphasizing the hunger, using the picture to say: I'm going to gobble this sandwich up in a single bite. Then, of course, there is the pickle, placed in the centre like some kind of trophy. Parr is often accused of mocking the simple pleasures of the working classes, but he leaves the interpretation up to us. If we think it is ridiculous to present an unrefined sandwich in the shape of a butterfly, or if we think that the pickle has phallic overtones, that is coming from us, not the photographer. 'If you want to see it, you will see it,' said Parr. Other people looking at the same photograph might be content simply to drool over it.

SHOWING BY HIDING

Photographers using wide-angle lenses and aerial photography seek to capture the largest possible amount of space within a single shot. But there are also those who prefer stripping the scene back rather than including as much as possible. What fascinates them is what we don't see. What we sense, feel, imagine – starting with what is outside the picture, beyond the rectangular edges of the frame, the mysterious and enticing world that is just out of shot.

Let's start with what is on either side of the frame (opposite), what we would usually be able to see simply by turning our head or moving our eyes. There are six children looking at us. Two of them are tucked away behind the window, two are only half in shot, and two are standing with their feet planted in front of the camera, in the middle. The latter are the main characters, who give the photograph its title, and they represent its 'official' subject – the shameless exploitation of children who are taken out of school and forced to work. A sociologist by training, the American photographer Lewis W. Hine (1874–1940) was hired by the National Child Labor Committee to document this practice. There is something poignant about these children, who are adopting the expressions, poses and clothes of adults. But they are also troubled by adult concerns, although here their brows are furrowed because they are squinting into the sun.

Did Hine know that he had cut off their friends on either side? Probably not. At the time, the reflex finder – a viewfinder that used mirrors to show photographers exactly what would be in the frame – had not yet been invented. Photographs were taken by removing the lens cap to allow light in, and the framing was mostly guesswork.

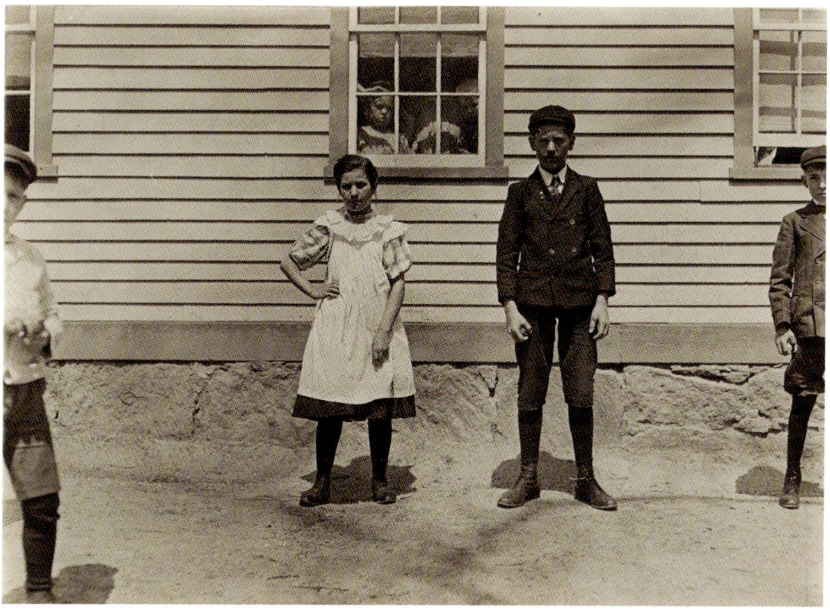

Lewis W. Hine
Edward St. Germain and His Sister Delia, Mill Workers, Phoenix, Rhode Island, April 1909
Gelatin silver print, 11.8 x 16.9 cm (4⅝ x 6⅝ in.)

The composition is arranged around a central line of symmetry: there are the same number of children on the left-hand side as on the right, and the four bodies are divided in the middle by the horizontal line that runs along the bottom of the building.

When he developed the film and saw the shot, perhaps Hine decided to keep the two children cropped by the edge of the frame because they convey the same message as their companions: half of their childhood is being stolen as they are being forced into the factories at the age of eight or nine. The two little rascals behind the window are more fortunate – but they also seem sad. Perhaps they already know what is lying in wait for them.

Drawing attention to what is not in the frame

One particularly intriguing area outside of the frame is what is on the other side of the fourth wall. This expression originally comes from the world of theatre. Set designers only build three of the four walls of the room in which the action takes place, otherwise it would be hidden from the audience. However, this fourth wall exists in our imagination, separating the spectator from the world of the story. In photography, the surface of the image constitutes the fourth wall. To imagine what is in front of it, we have to turn around, to ask ourselves where the photographer was and perhaps what they were thinking when they pressed the button. That is one

of the questions raised by the American photographer Francesca Woodman (1958–1981) in this image (above). We do not have a lot of information about her work. For example, we do not know whether she used a timer to take this photograph or whether she asked someone else to press the button. Since it is probably a self-portrait, did she know that her head would be out of shot? Here, it is not only the fourth wall that is mysterious, but also what exists above the top of the frame.

This photograph is reminiscent of the French painter Yves Klein's 'Anthropometries', which he created by asking women slathered in blue paint to lie down on his canvases. But we interpret this photograph differently when we know what it cannot tell us itself: suffering from depression, Francesca Woodman committed suicide by jumping from a window shortly before her twenty-third birthday. It is no longer just the outline of the figure on the floor and the

Francesca Woodman
Providence, Rhode Island,
1976
Gelatin silver print

The young woman has left behind an outline of her body, by lying down naked on a floor covered in flour. This incomplete, imperfect outline echoes the photograph itself, as the framing cuts off the subject's face.

seated young woman that are incomplete; the photographer's life itself was cut short.

Cuts and cut-outs

The New York School of Photography was an informal movement active from the 1930s to the 1950s. It brought together very different artists who all sought to create an honest portrait of this city where not everyone can be happy all the time – a portrait that did not romanticize it but was not pessimistic either. The American Saul Leiter (1923–2013) was one of these artists. When taking this photograph of a wintry street scene (overleaf), he would have known that he was cutting off the passerby with the red umbrella – or perhaps he chose to do so when developing the photograph, which amounts to the same thing. The only glimpse we get of this stranger braving the falling snow is the hem of her coat and part of her umbrella.

We sense that she is hurrying home, wanting to escape this environment that is mainly designed for cars, where the tyre tracks take up most of the frame. They have made the snow dirty and we are grateful to the passerby for adding a touch of warmth to this grey cityscape, with the flash of bright red.

Rather than cutting off objects within the frame, the German–Canadian photographer Fred Herzog (1930–2019), celebrated for his pioneering street photography shot in colour, chose to use a very tight framing that removes all context (page 101). This allows him to play around with three elements that would have been lost in the surroundings if he opted for a wide shot. The first element is the balance between the two most striking colours in the photograph, green and red. Red is the complementary colour to green, which is made up of yellow and blue, the two other primary colours. Secondly, the window frame becomes like the frame of a painting, transforming the dress into an object worth looking at, rather than a piece of clothing to slip on without thinking. Thirdly, we are close enough to make out the shadow of a cable that draws a line across the building's façade, like a touch of *wabi-sabi* in a Zen garden, adding a little disorder into the symmetry. Without this shadow, the composition would be too precise. The cherry on the cake – but Herzog could not have predicted this – is that, in this book, the line connects the red dress to Saul Leiter's red umbrella.

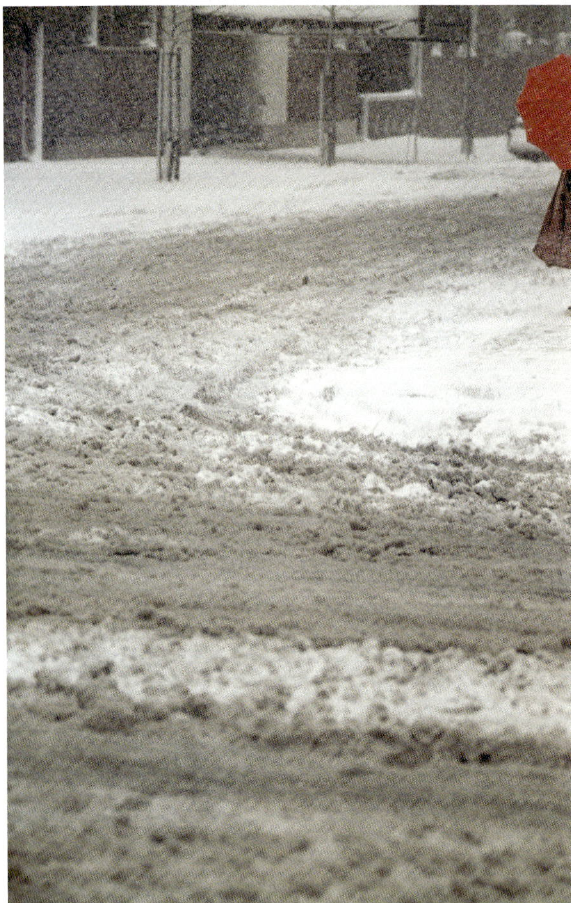

Saul Leiter
Red Umbrella, 1957

Being in the right place sometimes means accepting that we cannot see everything. At first we think this is a study of snow in black and white, but that is not the case: it is a slice of city life in colour. If the passerby had taken up the whole frame, she would have become the main subject, rather than this contrast between the dirt of the city and the almost-summery cheerfulness of the umbrella.

KEY IDEAS

Being interested in the subject of a photograph doesn't stop us from wondering what is out of shot beyond the frame.

A photographer doesn't have to be physically close to their subject in order to take a close-up shot.

It is always worth asking where the photographer was when they pressed the button.

There is no single perspective that would be the best way to look at a subject: the photographer chooses a visual perspective to express their moral, emotional or ideological perspective.

Fred Herzog
Dress in Window, 1986
Archival pigment print

Has this dress been positioned especially for the photograph, or was it hung up to dry by a stranger who never suspected that it would add a touch of poetry to the city? That doesn't matter; what matters is the end result.

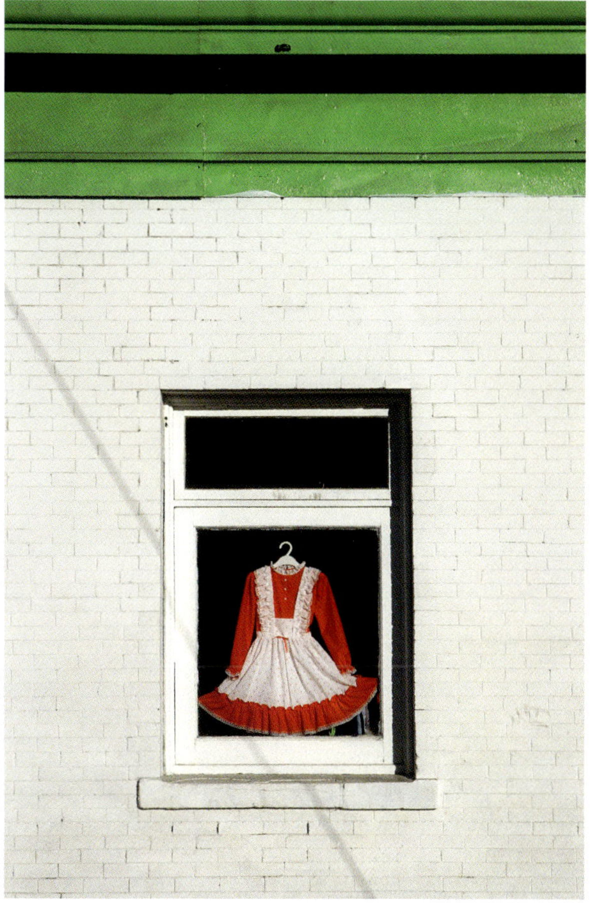

KEY QUESTIONS

... to ask with a photograph in front of you:

Does the perspective look similar to the way our eyes perceive reality, or does it appear as if the scene is being viewed through an optical instrument?

How do the angle and distance influence my feelings about this scene?

Would I have the same response if the perspective were different, if it were closer to or further away from the scene?

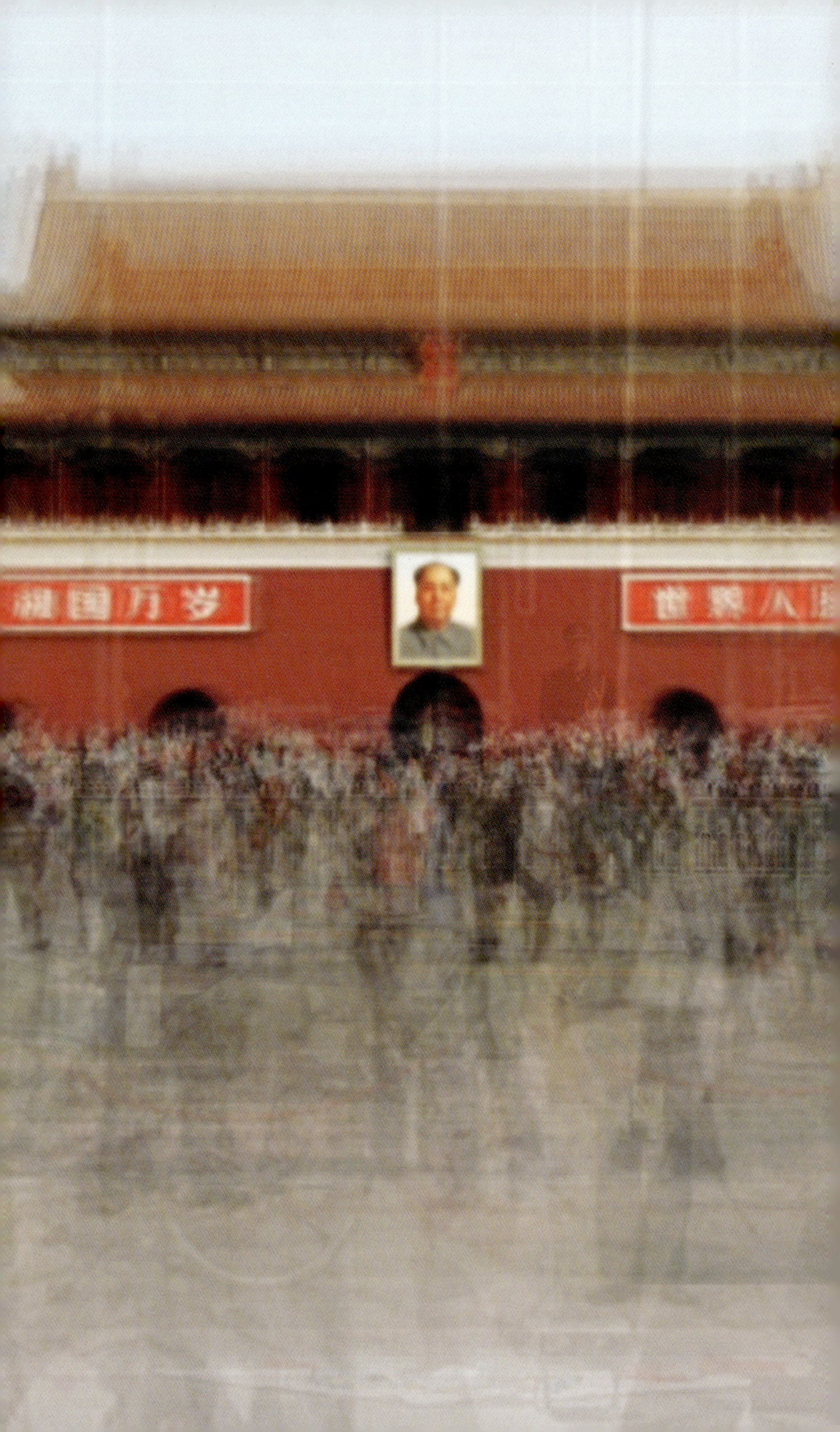
国万岁
世界人

SUSPENDED TIME

-

When we take a picture of famous monuments such as the Leaning Tower of Pisa or the Eiffel Tower, do we refer to an image that we already know? Do we try to reproduce an image of an image?

-

Corinne Vionnet

Certain art forms, such as music, dance and cinema, have an obvious relationship with time, because their works only come to life over a period. That is not the case for painting and sculpture, but we can always sense the passing of time in them. Everyone knows that it takes a long time, sometimes years, to paint a canvas or carve a statue. By contrast, a photographic masterpiece can be created in a millisecond. However, if we look more closely, we can see that photography also has a direct relationship with time.

Let's take for example the context surrounding the birth of photography, during the golden age of Romanticism. The poets and writers who belonged to this movement were fascinated by ruins and the sense of melancholy that was evoked when contemplating them, thinking about the beauty of the buildings that used to stand in their place. These ruins were a visual representation of the sinister warning engraved in Latin on certain old tombstones: '*Eram quod es, eris quod sum*' ('I was what you are, you will be what I am'). Photography often has the same effect, but by very different means: it immortalizes beauty, capturing its image and inviting us to compare *what was* with *what is* now.

Susan Sontag confidently declared that 'every photograph is a *memento mori*'. It is true that the people in photographs are unmoving, and in living beings – except for plants – stillness is usually a sign of death. But, fortunately, these melancholy reflections are not the only relationship between photography and time.

Paulette Tavormina
Cabbage and Melon, After J.S.C, 2010
Archival pigment print

This photograph is a recreation of a *bodegón*, a still-life painting of food, by the Spanish painter Juan Sánchez Cotán in the early seventeenth century. The frame and the black background give it the feel of a death notice – fruit decays quickly.

AN IMITATION OF LIFE

It was not only the accuracy of photography that made it unpopular with many artists and intellectuals in its early days. They were also wary of it because it seemed to rely more on machines than human beings. As a result, it was relegated to the realm of what was disdainfully termed *mechanical arts*. In some ways, photography imitates the human body: the lens of a camera, whether film or digital, follows a similar process as our eyes. But in other ways, it was considered fundamentally inhuman. And what made it most inhuman, in their eyes, was its relationship with time. No individual, however hard they concentrate, can make time stand still, but a photograph can.

The camera freezes what is happening – we lose all the movement, of course, but what we gain is a chance to look again at details that escaped us in the moment.

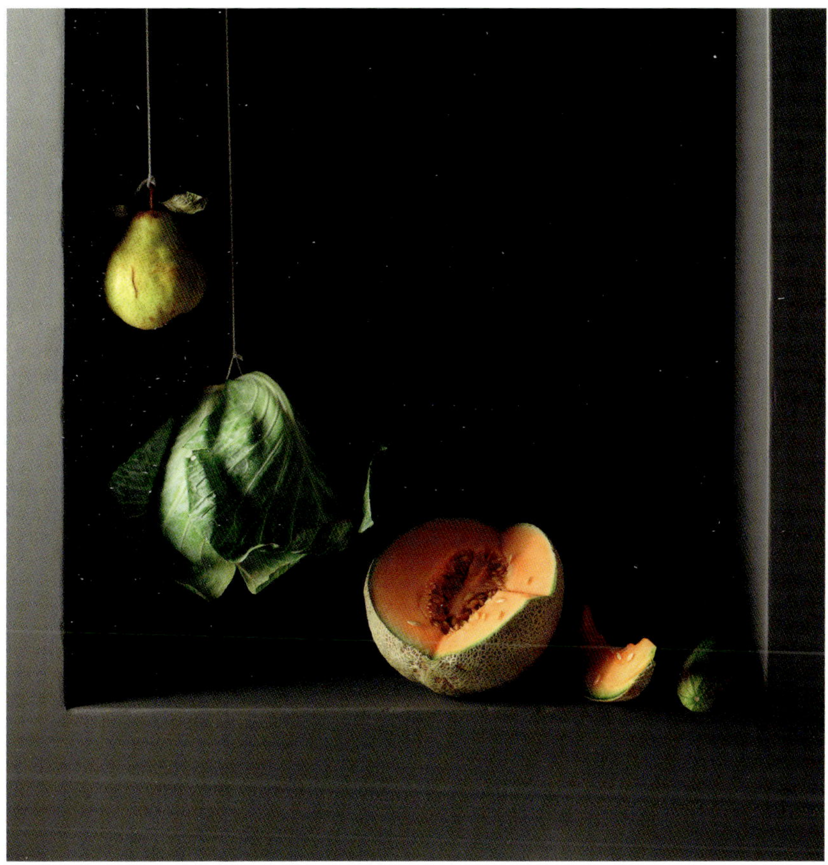

This still life (above) by the American photographer Paulette Tavormina (b.1949) is not entirely tragic: there is something a little childlike in the act of hanging the fruits and vegetables on strings to 'make them look pretty', and the melon does look very appetizing – as if, once the photograph had been taken, the photographer and her assistant were going to gobble it up! The painter would have needed a very long time to finish the *bodegón* on which this photograph is based, far longer than the fruits would have remained ripe. Therefore, even more than the painting, this photograph reminds us of the delicate and ephemeral nature of beautiful things. A photograph does not just show what *was*; often, it also shows what *is* going to happen. Of course, to return to Susan Sontag's gloomy pronouncement, this predictive power has a more light-hearted feel when looking at a photograph of a melon than when looking at a

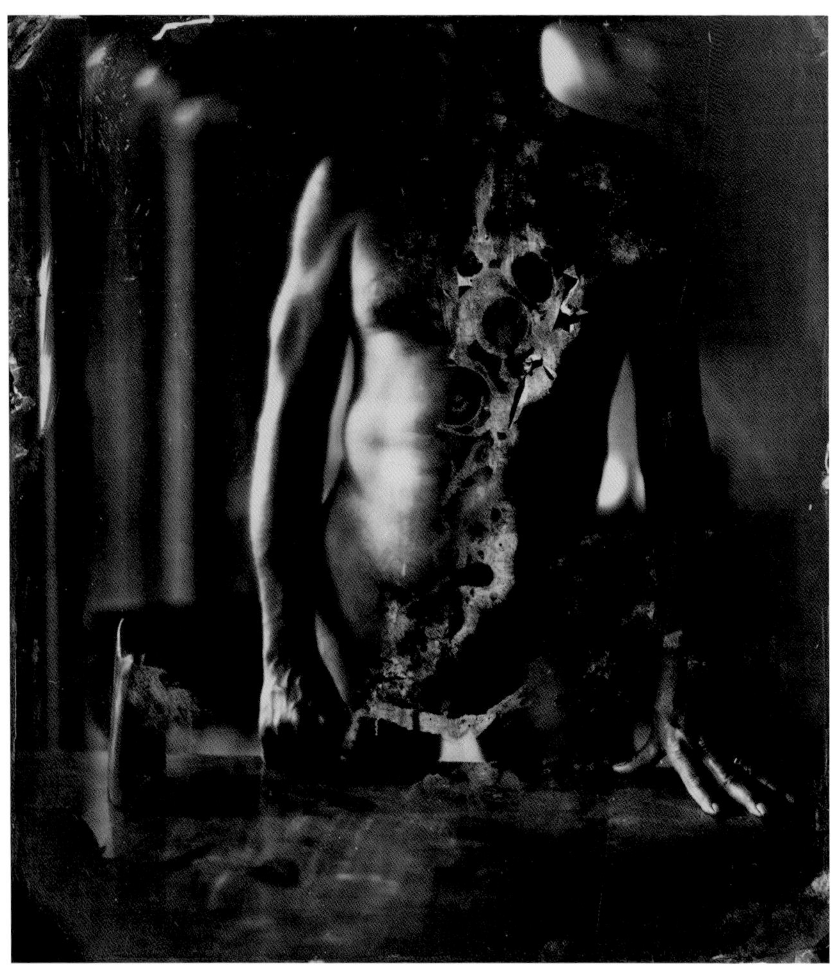

Sally Mann
Hephaestus, from the series 'Proud Flesh', 2008
Gelatin silver print, 38.1 x 34.3 cm (15 x 13½ in.)

It is tempting to equate the marks *on* the photograph with the marks *in* the photograph: these technical imperfections feel like signs of his illness. We even get the impression that the photograph will continue to deteriorate at the same pace as the illness takes over its subject's body.

picture of a loved one. But it is useless to avert our eyes, as the art of photography has more sophisticated ways of making us reflect on death than simply showing the differences between two portraits of the same person taken years apart, as we can see in the work of American photographer Sally Mann (b.1951).

Mann's work (opposite) is a far cry from the perfect accuracy of digital photography. She uses collodion and silver nitrate, like the pioneers of the nineteenth century, and embraces the unpredictability of this chemical process. The result is that her photographs often come back from the laboratory damaged in some way. For her series 'Proud Flesh', to which this picture belongs, Mann photographed her husband Larry. He was suffering from muscular dystrophy, a genetic disease that progressively replaces the muscles with fatty tissue. Sufferers grow gradually weaker, until they can no longer even stand up on their own.

The degenerative condition from which Mann's husband suffered attacks the body while leaving the mind unaffected: perhaps that is why she positioned his head out of shot at the top of the frame. Her choice of title also has a certain tenderness: the god Hephaestus, a blacksmith in Greek mythology, gained the favour of the most beautiful women in Olympus despite his proverbial ugliness and physical deformity.

Recapturing lost time

The aim of photography is not only to help us remember what was, or to provide a record of rare and extraordinary things. It can also capture trivial moments, or rather moments that we have perhaps too hastily dismissed as trivial. In this way, it is a means of recapturing lost time. Once they have been 'rewritten' by photographs, the most insignificant moments, which seemed meaningless when we were living through them, are imbued with charm, interest and colour that they didn't possess previously, or that we could not see before.

The Dutch photographer Erwin Olaf (1959–2023) drew inspiration for the series 'Grief' from Jacqueline Kennedy's period of mourning after her husband was assassinated (overleaf). Here, one of the two armchairs is empty and only one of the two sockets, at the bottom left of the picture, is in use. The woman has drunk her whisky after pouring out a glass for someone who is no longer there – unthinkingly, out of habit, or perhaps deliberately, because she

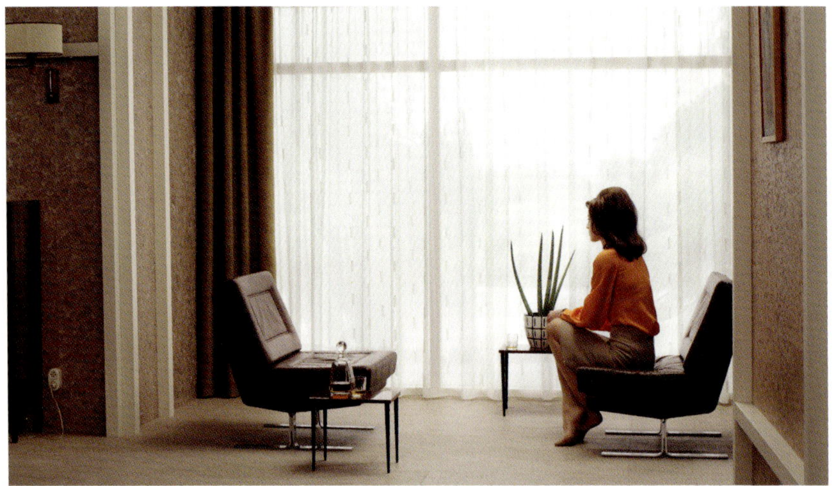

Erwin Olaf
Caroline, from the series 'Grief', 2007
Chromogenic print

'"Grief" is a series about the choreography of emotion, and what you can create in the studio,' Olaf said. 'So I wanted to ask the question: how does grief really look? What is the aesthetic of grieving?'

doesn't want to give up these small daily rituals quite yet. Her feet are bare, so she is not going anywhere, but is sitting on the edge of her armchair, as we do when we are having a lively conversation. If this is the 'choreography of emotion', it is a choreography of denial: let's pretend he's still here. The reference to president John F. Kennedy's assassination seems to justify the fact that this photograph is staged, as we still don't know exactly what happened in Dallas on that day. In the absence of historical truth, the fictions of art have free rein.

TRAVELLING WITHOUT MOVING

When he was threatening to quit the Magnum Agency in 1966, the French photographer Henri Cartier-Bresson (1908–2004) sent its directors a rather curt letter that signed off with these words: 'On that note, I will go out into the street to see what is happening...' For him, a photographer's most important responsibility was to be on the ground, to show what was going on in the world to those who are not there to see it. The problem is that the world carries on changing when the camera has been packed up and put away.

In 1913, the invention of the belinograph offered a solution to this problem. Created by the French engineer Édouard Belin, it made it possible to send photographs across great distances, before the invention of faxes or the internet. Almost as soon as an event had taken place, photographs of it started to appear in the daily newspapers. For readers, it was as if time and space were collapsing in on themselves: 'The Earth has shrunk. We laugh in the face of distance,' boasted one editorial writer.

Today this enthusiasm seems somewhat quaint, as news bulletins feature pictures of events happening in far-off places that scroll across our screens 'in real time'. If we add in the photos we send our 'friends' on social networks, we are so constantly bombarded with images that we hardly have time to do more than glance at them. In this world of snap and share, photographs are often used to illustrate, embellish or replace a message hastily typed on a keyboard, and they have perhaps lost their meaning as a memento mori.

We live in a world that is bursting with images. What is the point of taking a photograph when we visit Tiananmen Square? It has already been photographed thousands of times, almost always from the same spot. The work of French–Swiss artist Corinne Vionnet (b.1969) shows that we tend to take pictures of pictures (below). Even if I resist the urge to take out my camera, will I truly be able to see what is before my eyes? Can my brain, packed full of thousands of identical pictures of the square, dismiss all of these archive images and allow me to look at the place I am in as if I were discovering it for the first time? Even when we are, in fact, on our first-ever visit to a famous site, it is very difficult to see things with fresh eyes.

Corinne Vionnet
Beijing, 2007, from the series 'Photo Opportunities', 2005–present
Archival pigment print

Corinne Vionnet searched the internet for photos taken by tourists and superimposed them on top of one another, so that we notice their similarities. All of these amateur photographers travelling to Beijing chose to centre the portrait of Mao Zedong that hangs on the gate of Tiananmen Square.

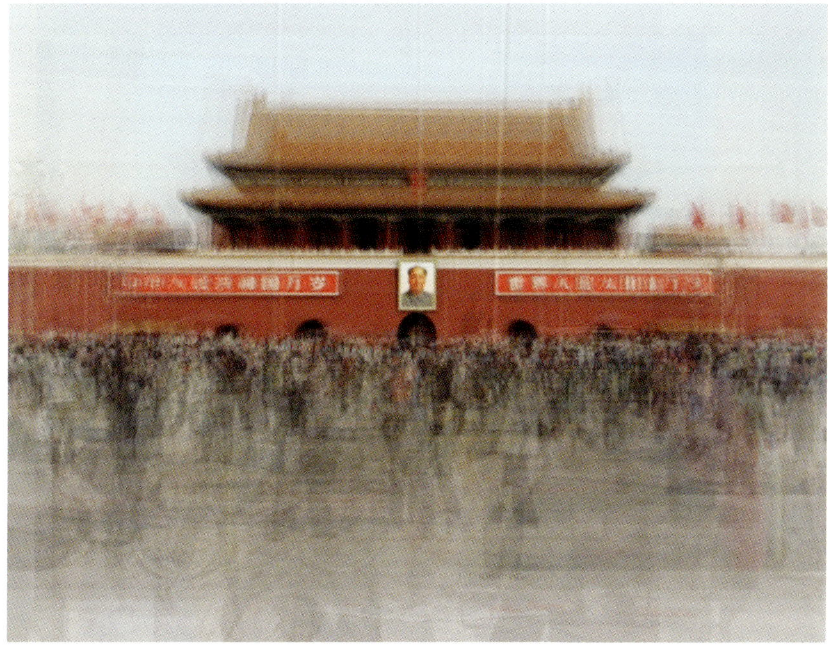

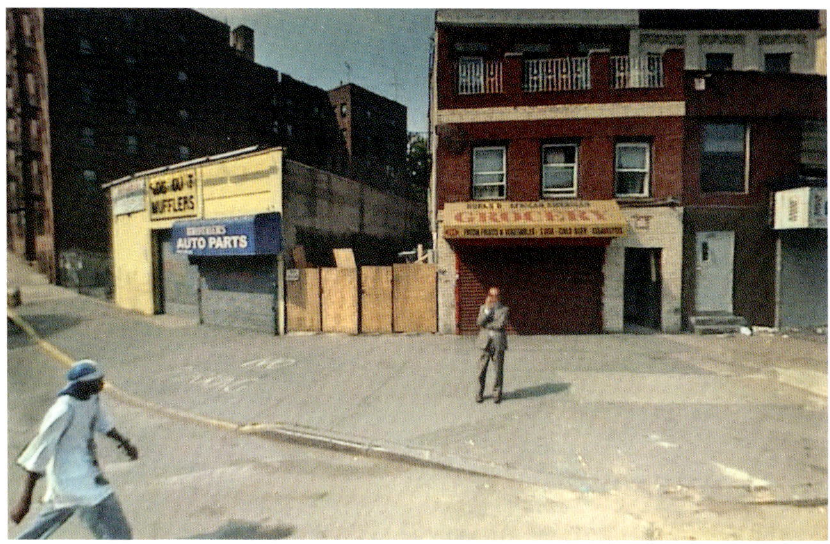

Doug Rickard
#40.805716, The Bronx, New York N.Y., 2009, from the series 'A New American Picture', 2011

Since 2007, the robots of Google Street View have been driving along every street in the world, taking nine photos every 10 metres. But sometimes it makes mistakes, like on this day in the heart of the Bronx.

As the American artist Doug Rickard (1968–2021) said, our screens are flooded with pictures 24 hours a day, and the effect is that 'we are on a road to "know" more but experience less'. Rickard tried to make some sense of this glut of pictures, or at least restore some of the humanity in photography, by patiently pointing out mistakes on Google Street View (above). The Street View algorithm erases passersby by merging successive images together. Here, the short-focus lens distorts the figure of a young Black man, wearing his cap backwards, while a white man in a suit stands talking on his phone. It is up to us to imagine what they may be thinking when they see each other, and therefore the picture prompts us to reflect on the relationships between the different communities that live in the Bronx.

THE DECISIVE MOMENT

No one creates a painting by accident, or a symphony, a film or a novel; but anyone can take a good photograph by accident. All you need is to be 'where it's happening' and to press the button at the right moment. This is the *decisive moment*, to use the phrase coined by Henri Cartier-Bresson – the exact freeze frame in which the scene has a clarity or richness that it did not possess a second before and will not possess a second later.

Henri Cartier-Bresson
Gold Rush. At the end of the day, a crush in front of a bank to buy gold. The Last Days of Kuomintang, Shanghai, 1948

The decisive moment: when the impatient customers' arms tangle together in this complex choreography, halfway between a rugby scrum and a human caterpillar. But also the moment when some of them are looking at the lens – and therefore at us. Perhaps they are angry with themselves for showing such an undignified side to humanity; or perhaps they are thinking that, in their place, we would do the same.

In the case of the image below, the city is Shanghai and the date is 23 December 1948. Cartier-Bresson was on a commission for the American magazine *Life*, roaming the streets to capture the final days of the Kuomintang government as the Communist Party got ready to proclaim the People's Republic of China. Anticipating a currency crisis, people who had savings stormed the bank counters to change their money into gold. All the photographer had to do was find the best place to stand and press the button at the right moment.

Of course, today, anyone could find themselves 'where it's happening'. Phones transform us into tourists visiting our own lives, always ready to press the button. The mark of a good photographer is no longer just about choosing the right moment. The humblest digital camera can take many photographs in the space of a second, and all we need to do is choose the best one to keep. But there are still some artists who want to create something beautiful without relying on cameras that snap away like high-tech submachine guns, although that doesn't mean they want to relinquish the task of capturing daily life to the thousands of amateur photographers walking around with their phone in their hand.

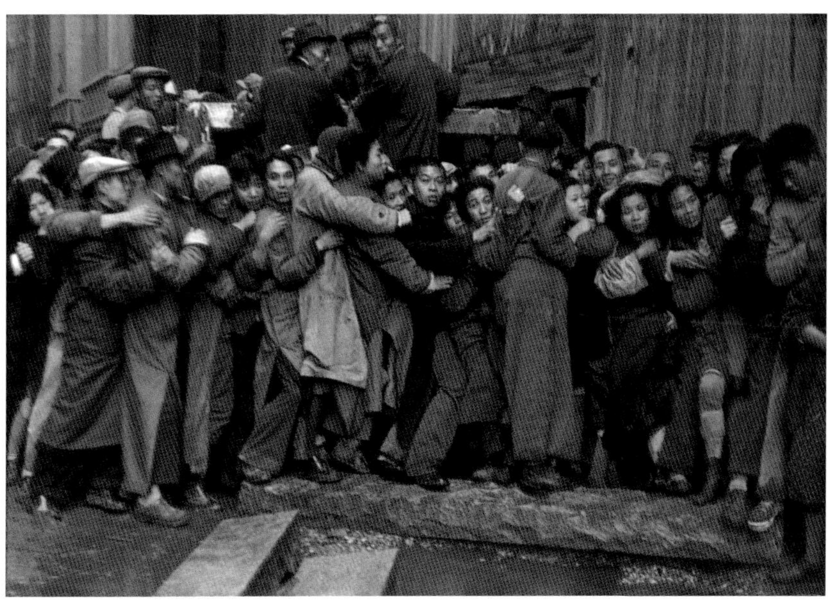

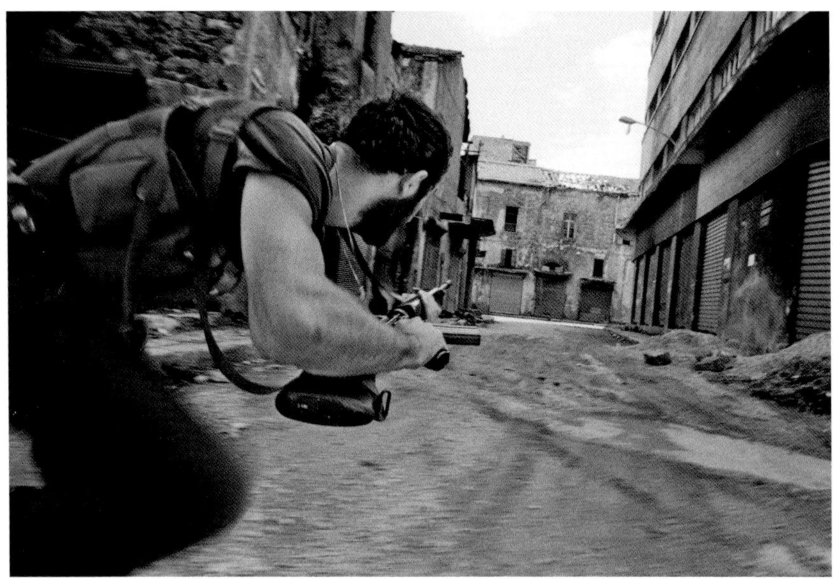

Raymond Depardon
A Christian Falangist,
Beirut, 1978

The fighter's leg is blurry because he is running fast, and he is running fast because he is afraid. The framing, at a slight angle, conveys the photographer's fear, as he is also in danger of being shot. He is standing right behind the man: the man's right elbow looks larger than his head, which shows the photographer is using a short-focus lens.

Stopping time?

Photography's relationship with time is similar to a telescope's relationship with space: we use it to satisfy our curiosity by enhancing our eye's ability to examine something. But 'stopping time' is a misleading expression. The world keeps on moving during the period when light is passing through the shutter. Therefore, a photograph does not capture a single moment, it captures time passing. Even scientific photographs taken in a millionth of a second record a period of time. That is why we shouldn't laugh when we read that in 1839 people thought that daguerreotypes, the precursor to photographs, were an 'almost instantaneous' way of obtaining mirror images, although the average exposure time was almost quarter of an hour! All photographs are 'almost instantaneous': time needs to pass in order for the light to enter the camera and hit the sensors, otherwise we would end up with nothing more than a black rectangle.

The time that passes sometimes leaves a direct trace on the image, called motion blur. The pioneers of photography sought to eliminate this from their work, but for many years now their successors have used it to convey a sense of speed.

Commissioned to report on the Lebanese Civil War (1975–1990) by the German magazine *Stern*, the French photographer and documentary maker Raymond Depardon (b.1942) captured the daily life of Christian Falangist fighters (opposite). In this photograph, he sets up a stark contrast between foreground and background by including a compositional line that runs in the direction the camera is pointing. This draws the eye from the background to the foreground (the enemy might shoot at the Falangist) and from the foreground to the background (the Falangist might shoot at the enemy). The fighter's head, turned to the side to watch for hidden snipers, and his crouched stance define the foreground as a place of safety (as long as he is running, he is alive) and at the same time define the background as a place of danger (it's too far away to see clearly). Here, space and time work hand in hand to make us feel as if we are experiencing this moment alongside the fighter.

-

What we would not be able to see with our naked eye

-

Motion blur is not vital for conveying the passing of time. Simply freezing someone or something that is moving very fast can also make the person looking at a photograph feel the presence of both the moment *before* and the moment *after*. We can see this in the below image by the Kenyan-born British photographer Anup Shah (b.1949) where, as in painting, expressiveness takes precedence over

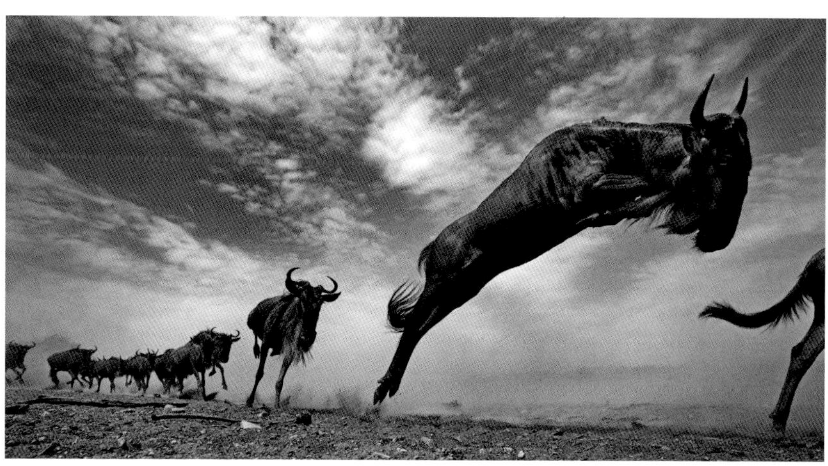

Anup Shah
The Seekers, from the series 'The Mara', 2013
Photographic print, 50.8 x 76.2 cm (20 x 30 in.)

This photograph freezes a running wildebeest, its shape distorted by the short-focus lens. The photographer is not in any danger, as he is activating a camouflaged camera from a long way away.

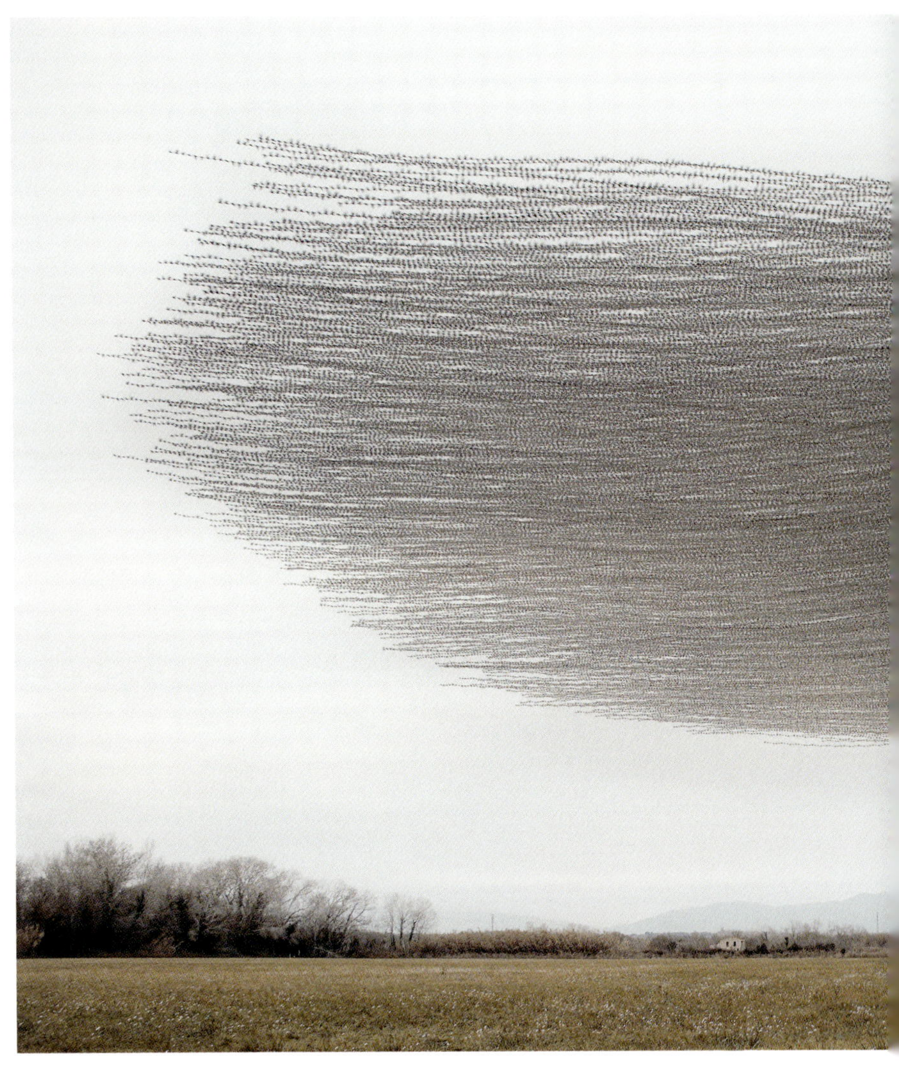

Xavi Bou
Ornithography #171, 2019

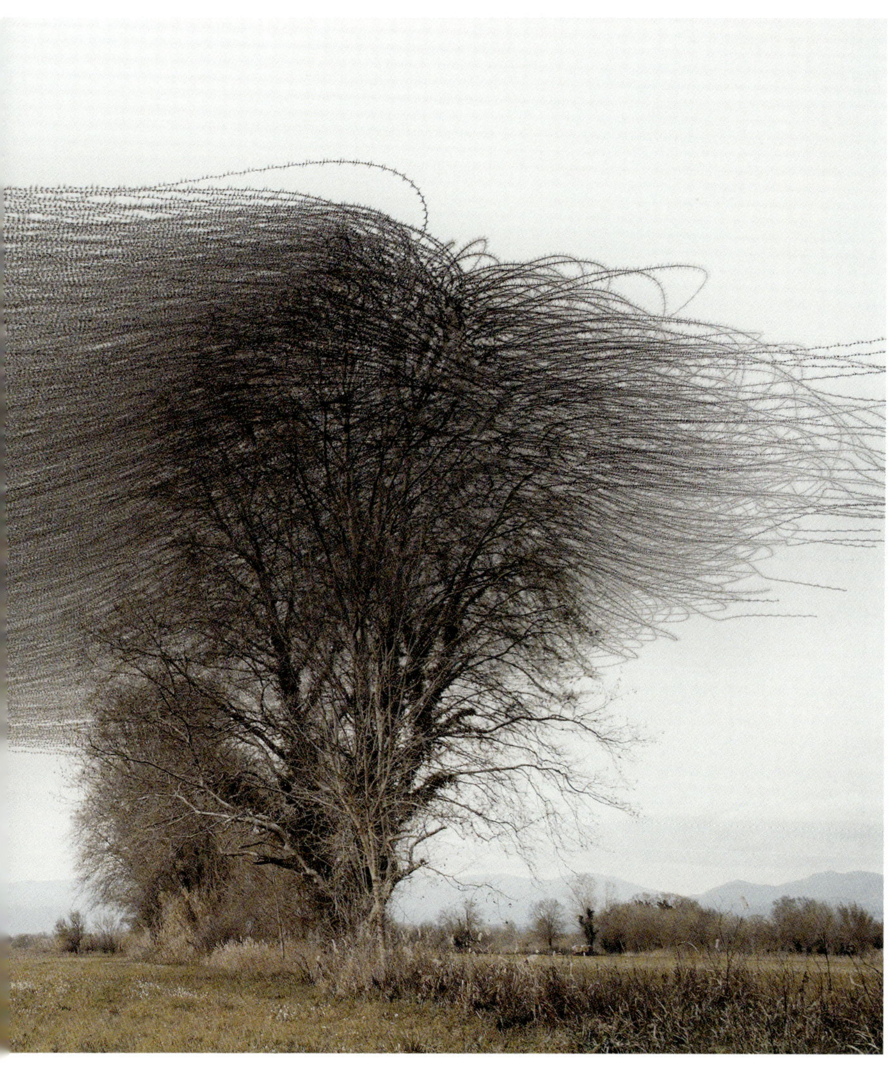

This goes far beyond Muybridge's 24 consecutive shots. Digital chronophotography only requires the use of a single camera, which snaps away taking pictures of the scene for as long as we want. Then, all that remains is to use a computer to superimpose the images on top of each other; here we can see all the different positions of the birds flying around the tree at the same time.

anatomical accuracy. Then there is the Spanish photographer Xavi Bou (b.1979), who breathed new life into chronophotography, also taking animals as his subject (pages 114–115).

The digital era did not originate this opposition between truth and falsehood, or rather between realism and expressiveness. In the late nineteenth century, thousands of amateur photographers made the most of this new technology and amused themselves by capturing human bodies in movement, freezing them in positions that we would not be able to see with our naked eye. Photography magazines were overflowing with these kinds of shots.

At the same time, photography also made it possible to resolve an argument that had arisen between artists and scientists about the movement of animals, notably the flight of birds and the galloping of horses. In paintings, horses often looked as if they were flying above the ground, probably because the artists were mainly trying to portray the animal's sheer effort as it responded to its master's desire for speed. The French physiologist Étienne-Jules Marey's book *Animal Mechanism* (1873) gave the British photographer Eadweard Muybridge (1830–1904) the idea to line up 24 cameras along a race track in order to capture the consecutive movements of a galloping horse, which he later did in front of journalists in 1878. Chronophotography was born, and painters realized that they had lost the fight when it came to realism.

TRACES OF THE PASSAGE OF TIME

Time as experienced by the photographer moves forwards, from the present to the future (they think about *what will be*, meaning how the shot will look once it has been developed). In contrast, when we look at the photograph, for us time moves backwards, from the present to the past (we imagine *what was*). We recognize the objects, animals and people in the scene as *symbols of the past*, whether that is the recent past or the distant past. Our general knowledge naturally plays a role in interpreting these, but because fashions, to take one example, change so quickly, we are usually able to identify them quite easily. Photographs age more quickly than books, because visual appearances change much faster than words.

In his book *Schottenfreude* (2013), described as 'a collection of newly created German words for the contemporary world', the British writer Ben Schott coins the neologism *Rolleirückblende*. Created by combining 'Rollei', the name of a famous German brand of cameras, with the word for 'flashback', this term is defined as 'the flood of memory released when looking at old photos'. But perhaps

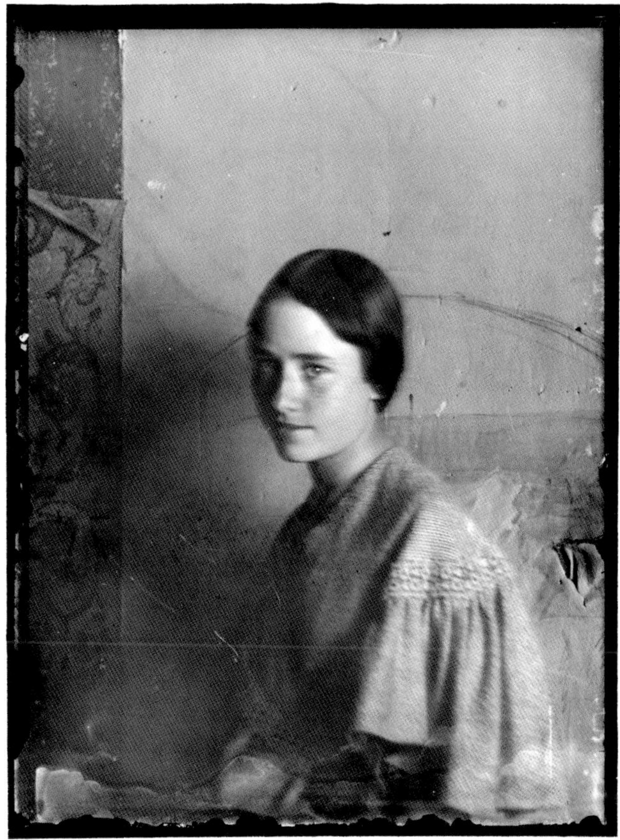

Gertrude Käsebier
Portrait of Gertrude Elizabeth Käsebier at Crécy-en-Brie, 1894
Dry-plate glass negative, 20.3 x 25.4 cm (8 x 10 in.)

Photography is sometimes a battle against the ticking clock, at the end of which we draw our camera like a cowboy draws his revolver (we use the verb *to shoot* for both actions). But we can also refuse to rush – as the photographer did here – and instead create a visual depiction of the passing of time.

we should draw a distinction between memories of a time that we personally lived through and what we imagine about times before we were born. Some of the most popular filters commonly applied to photos on picture-sharing sites allow users to give their photographs a '1960s tint' – or 1970s, 1980s, whatever they prefer. But people who lived through those decades saw them in their true colours, and these filters simply recreate what photographs looked like at a certain stage in the ongoing development of technology.

The American photographer Gertrude Käsebier (1852–1934) believed that photography as a medium was well suited to making time stand still (above). 'Art is long and childhood is fleeting, I soon discovered, and the children were losing their baby faces before I learned to paint portraits, so I chose a quicker medium.' This portrait of her daughter, however, contains many traces of the passage of time. Käsebier could have asked her to pose in front of

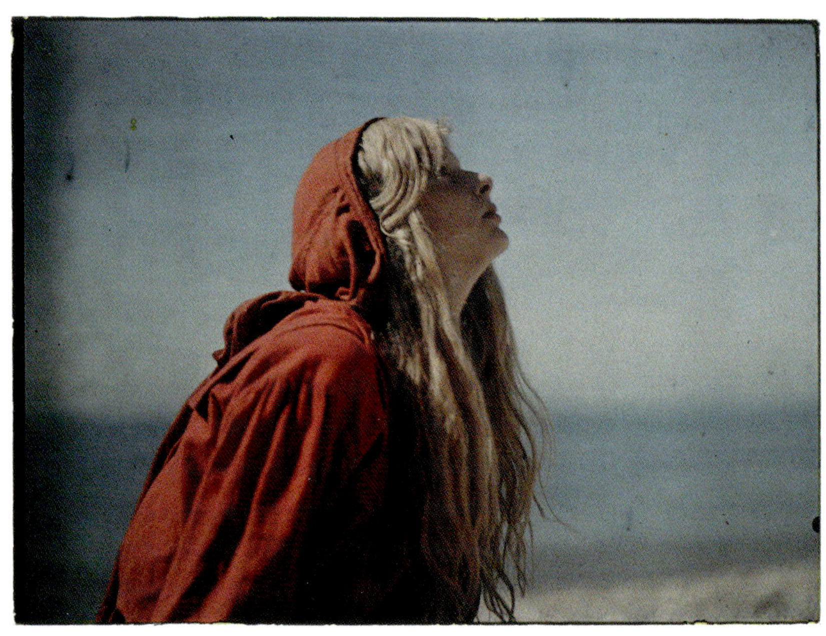

Mervyn O'Gorman
Christina in a Red Cloak, 1913
Autochrome, 12 x 16.4 cm (4¾ x 6½ in.)

We would not be surprised to learn that this photograph was taken last month for *Vogue*: the shallow depth of field is characteristic of fashion photographs, as their creators rarely want the background to overshadow the main subject. The young girl's loose hair, pose and style of clothing all give the same impression. And yet, this picture was taken more than a century ago!

Louis Daguerre
View of the boulevard du Temple, Paris, 1838
Daguerreotype

This is the opposite of a photograph taken in a split second: the exposure time of 5–6 minutes makes this scene look different from how it would have done if we had been there. Leaning on the windowsill, we would have seen a crowd passing along the 'boulevard of crime', as this place was nicknamed because of the crime melodramas performed in the theatres there.

a painted background, as was common practice then, or in front of a white sheet or a blank wall. However, she chose a dilapidated wall, covered in ridges and small dents; on the right, the plaster is even flaking off. And now the negative of this picture is in the same state. It is an old photograph. However, it captures forever that small smile, reminiscent of Leonardo da Vinci's *Mona Lisa*. The girl's gaze is especially bright because of two small white dots, perhaps a reflection, in her left eye. But as the photograph is covered with many similar marks, due to its age, we do not know whether this is in fact a reflection or a sign of the photograph's physical degradation. It doesn't matter, because the effect is still magical.

However, there is no need to be a professional in order to take photographs that convey the passing of time – any class photograph or family album has the same effect on us. But it is not always a sense of melancholy that dominates, as we can see from the work of engineer Mervyn O'Gorman (1871–1958), one of the pioneers of military aviation in Britain, who was also interested in autochrome photography (see page 61). The handful of photographs that he took of his neighbour's daughter (opposite) challenge our assumption that the past was radically different from what we experience today. Generally, we do not imagine that in the 1910s, a young girl would laze around on the beach with her hair down, wrapped in a simple

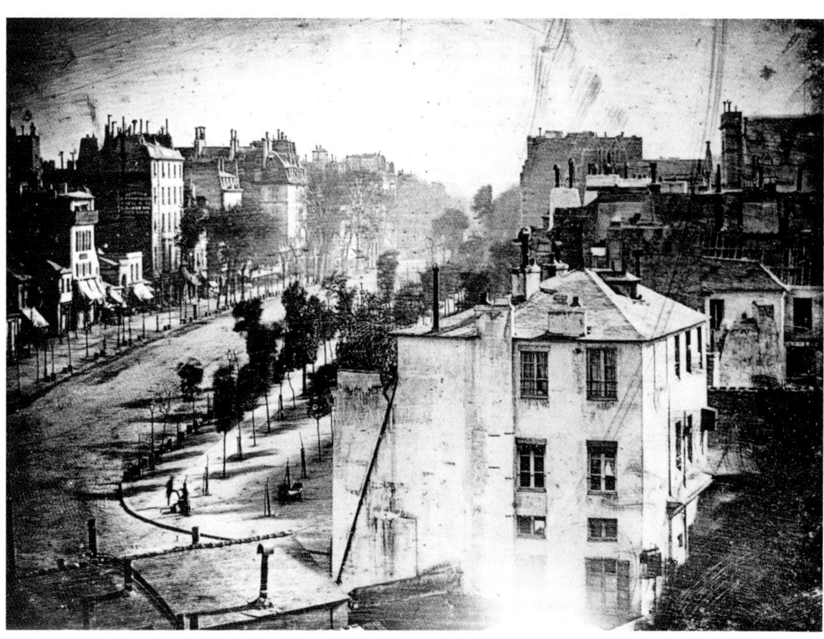

hooded cloak. The red of the cloak is vivid and saturated, but also a little faded; it adds to the difficulty of pinning this photograph down in time, as it evokes the technicolour era of Hollywood in the 1950s.

Hiroshi Sugimoto
Regency, San Francisco,
1992
Gelatin silver print,
41.9 x 54 cm
(16½ x 21¼ in.)

If we had been in the photographer's place, we would have seen a film instead of this blank screen. Over the course of two hours, the room was faintly lit by the projector, then plunged into darkness again when it stopped – a foretaste of its own disappearance, as no one builds cinemas with such elaborate interiors any more.

Capturing the image of time itself

All the people who were walking along the boulevard du Temple in Paris on this spring day in 1838 are now long dead, and this daguerreotype (page 119) – the precursor to photography, named after its French inventor, Louis Daguerre (1787–1851) – can no longer spark memories in the people who look at it. It can only evoke a series of impressions and mental images that are possible answers to the question: 'What was it like?'

Did the passers-by really all disappear from the boulevard du Temple because they were moving too fast to leave a trace on the plate? No. At the bottom left of the picture, we can make out the figure of a man. Experts are divided over whether he is the first human being whose likeness is recorded on a photosensitive surface. The reason why he has not evaporated like the other passers-by is that he was the only one who didn't move during the exposure time. And for a good reason: he was having his shoes polished. We can also make out the figure of the shoeshiner, at least the part of his body that moved the least.

This photograph (opposite) by the Japanese architect and photographer Hiroshi Sugimoto (b.1948) also explores the themes of presence and disappearance. He left the shutter of his camera open for the entire duration of a film being projected in an empty room. Faced with a screen showing 24 images per second, the camera captured only a white light: the film itself disappeared. What remains is, paradoxically, the room itself, which the audience, absorbed by the film, are usually supposed to forget about. Furthermore, such rooms would soon be a thing of the past: for his series 'Theatres', Sugimoto chose old picture palaces that were soon to be demolished or had already fallen into disrepair. The perfectly geometric composition of his photographs gives these rooms a sense of balance and stability that they were denied in the real world.

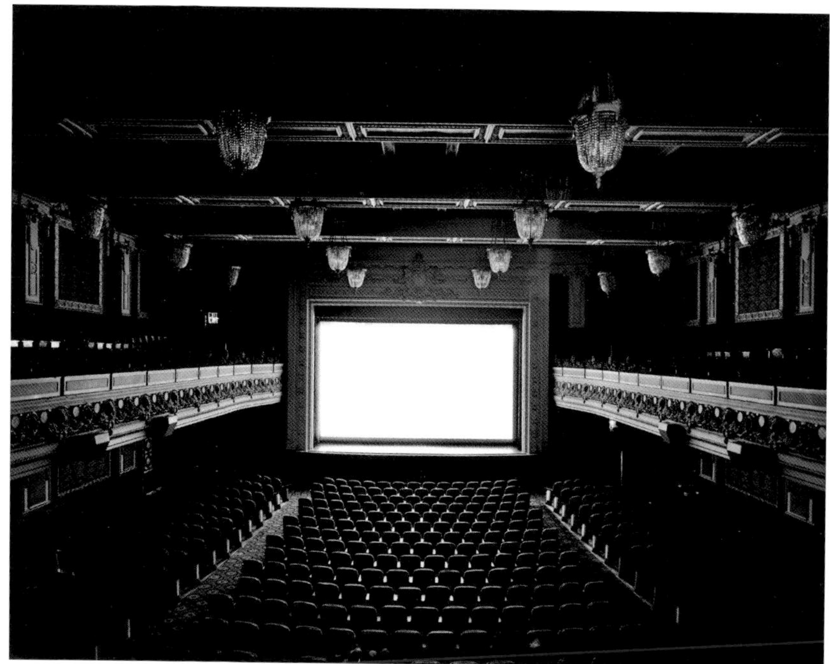

KEY IDEAS

Time can leave its mark on a photograph through the movement of the objects depicted in it.

Every photograph allows us to form a certain idea of a present that has now become the past.

By freezing things that are usually in motion, photography gives us the time we need to study them.

KEY QUESTIONS

... to ask with a photograph in front of you:

Am I looking at a photograph that was taken in a split second, or is this photograph the product of a long exposure time?

What are the symbols that I can use to date this photograph? Are they reliable?

Would this picture be as interesting if the photographer had pressed the button a moment earlier or a moment later?

Has the passage of time left its mark on this photograph? If it has, why did the photographer choose to preserve this trace?

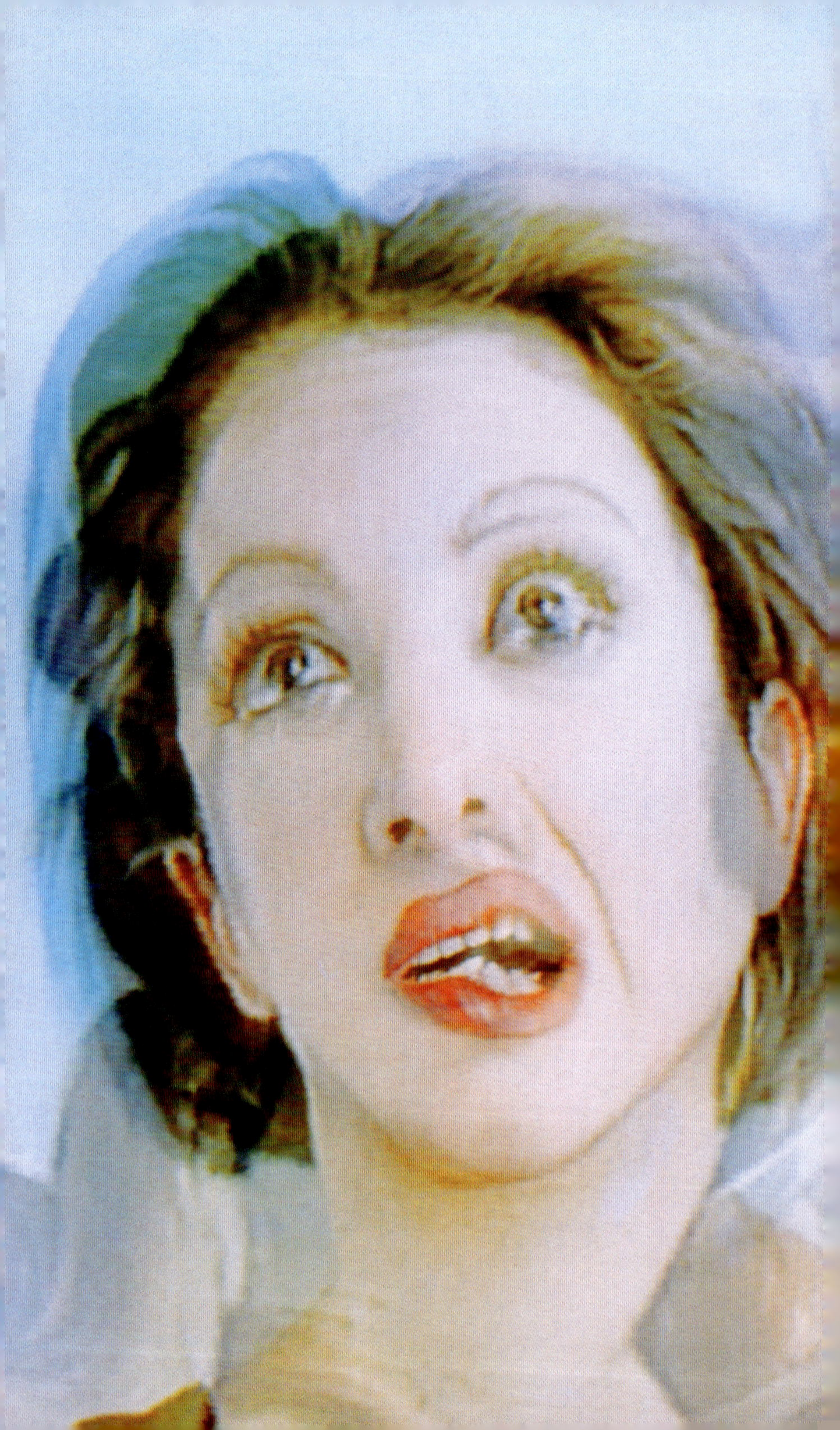

FROM PORTRAITS TO SELFIES

-

Every depiction is insufficient, but not creating one would be worse. That would mean being without a face, without an image, with no way of representing yourself

-

ORLAN

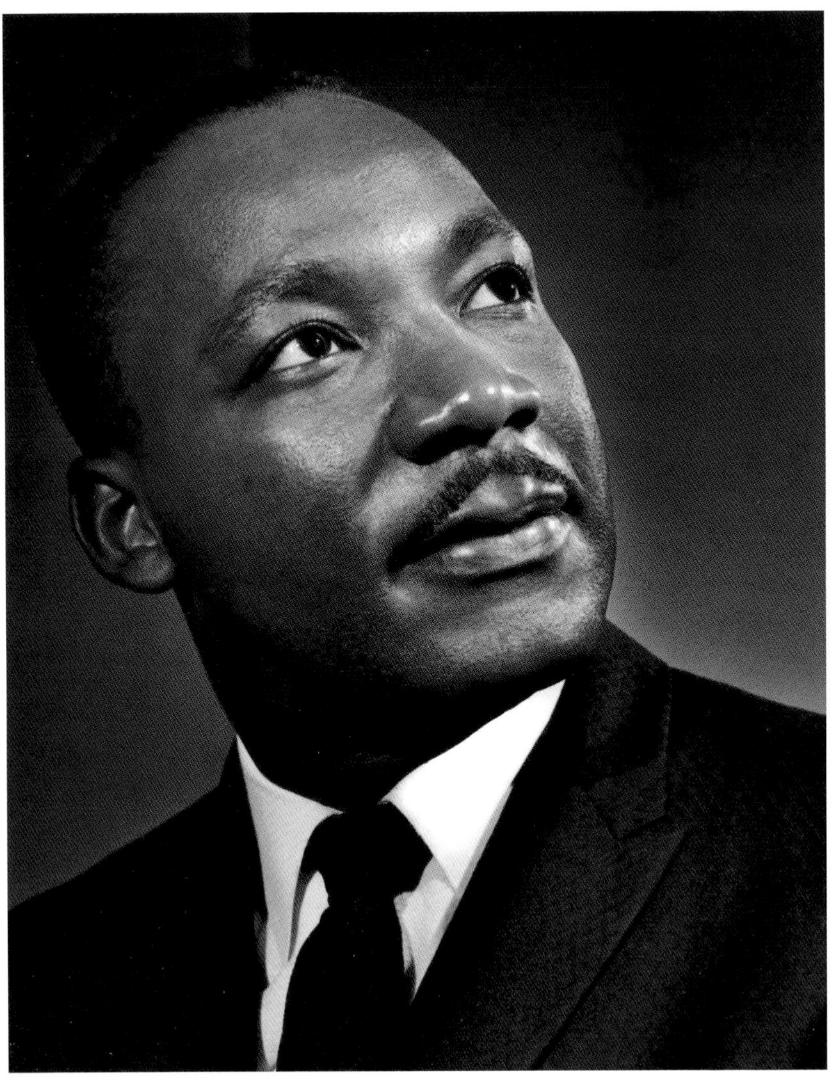

Yousuf Karsh
Martin Luther King, 1962

Reverend King is shown with his face turned towards the light that falls on him from above. This pose is fitting for a Baptist minister as, like other religious movements, this denomination places God high up in the heavens and associates faith with light.

We like to look at ourselves. The most famous paintings and photographs of all time are portraits. Popular television series and films depict human beings – or animals that talk and act like us, which amounts to the same thing. Most religions and myths are structured around divinities or supernatural creatures that have similar bodies to humans or act in a similar way. And a huge proportion of the hundreds of millions of photographs that are published every hour on social networks and websites are of human beings. Mirror, mirror, on the wall, who is the most interesting of them all?

Portraits have not always been used to bring our avatars to life on social networks and in the media. In the past, their main function was to help us remember people who were absent, whether physically far away or separated from us by time – in other words, dead. Nowadays, we expect more from portraits: we want them to go beyond appearances. But that is not an entirely new development. Marcel Proust wrote in a letter dated 1915 that a successful photograph captures 'what endures in a person'. A portrait can even spark an epiphany by revealing someone's true personality. It is somewhere between psychoanalysis and an X-ray.

STRIKING A POSE

The American photographer Elliott Erwitt (1928–2023), a member of the Magnum agency, had an ingenious trick for making his subjects appear, if not intelligent, then at least alert: 'It's almost embarrassing, but I do have one trick for taking portraits on commission. I carry one of these little bicycle horns in my pocket, and once in a while, when someone is sour-faced or stiff, I blow my horn. It sort of shatters the barriers. It's silly, but it works.' But when we are faced with a famous person, someone dignified and intimidating, it is difficult to take out a bicycle horn...

On that day in 1962 (opposite), the Armenian–Canadian photographer Yousuf Karsh (1908–2002) had only a few minutes with Martin Luther King, in a more or less quiet corner of his church, which was packed with worshippers. 'What emerged in my mind and, I trust, in the portrait, was the dedication of the man and his clear vision of ultimate victory.' The subject looks up and to the right with an unassailable faith, facing his goal, the summit of the mountain that he has set himself the task of climbing. The look of inspiration is fitting, as King would later become known across the entire world for his 'I have a dream' speech. Here he is thirty-three years old. Two years later, he would receive a Nobel Peace Prize, and in another four years he would be assassinated. This picture could have been a slightly wooden official portrait, but in that case, an assistant would have rushed in to powder King's nose. The shine on his nose draws us in, reminding us that the great man is a human being after all.

How we see, especially how we see ourselves, is part of being human. Psychologists say that our vision is at once egocentric (I see what is inside me) and allocentric (I 'see myself' wherever I am). The concept of allocentric vision may seem strange, but we are so used to it that it goes unnoticed in our everyday lives – for example, I know very well where I am when I am reading this book, what position my body is in and how I would appear to anyone who came into the room. All that remains is to reconcile ourselves to the way we look, especially in photographs. In *The Book of Disquiet*, the great Portuguese poet Fernando Pessoa (1888–1935) noted down his impressions the first time he saw an unremarkable photograph taken in the offices of the insurance company where he worked, in 1930. All of his colleagues looked more expressive than him: the boss, the deputy, even the courier! Pessoa felt that he had to accept what the camera showed him, which was that he looked like a fool, staring emptily into space.

The German-born French sociologist and photographer Gisèle Freund (1908–2000) also sought to avoid creating an impassive official portrait when she took this photograph of Frida Kahlo (opposite). In it, Kahlo poses alongside a painting of her father Guillermo, a professional photographer in Mexico in the early twentieth century. She is wearing an *enagua* (skirt) with a floral pattern and a *huipil* (traditional tunic) made of cotton embroidered with a motif typical of the Tehuantepec region. A red *rebozo* (shawl) is draped across the back of her chair. There is usually no embellishment in the middle of a *huipul*, which means that the *torzales* (necklaces) stand out. Frida Kahlo's are made of gold; one of them features a bat in the pre-Columbian style. This is what she wears on a day-to-day basis. Between her fingers is a cigarette; this object, usually banished from official portraits, marks a departure from the solemn feel of this genre. We can also make out the packet, with a box of matches on top of it, under the easel.

Gisèle Freund
Frida Kahlo in front of the portrait of her photographer father, Mexico City, 1951
35mm colour film

The Mexican painter Frida Kahlo is seated; we remain standing, a little intimidated. After their first meeting, the photographer compared her to 'an Aztec princess', with every finger 'covered in enormous rings with finely carved precious stones'.

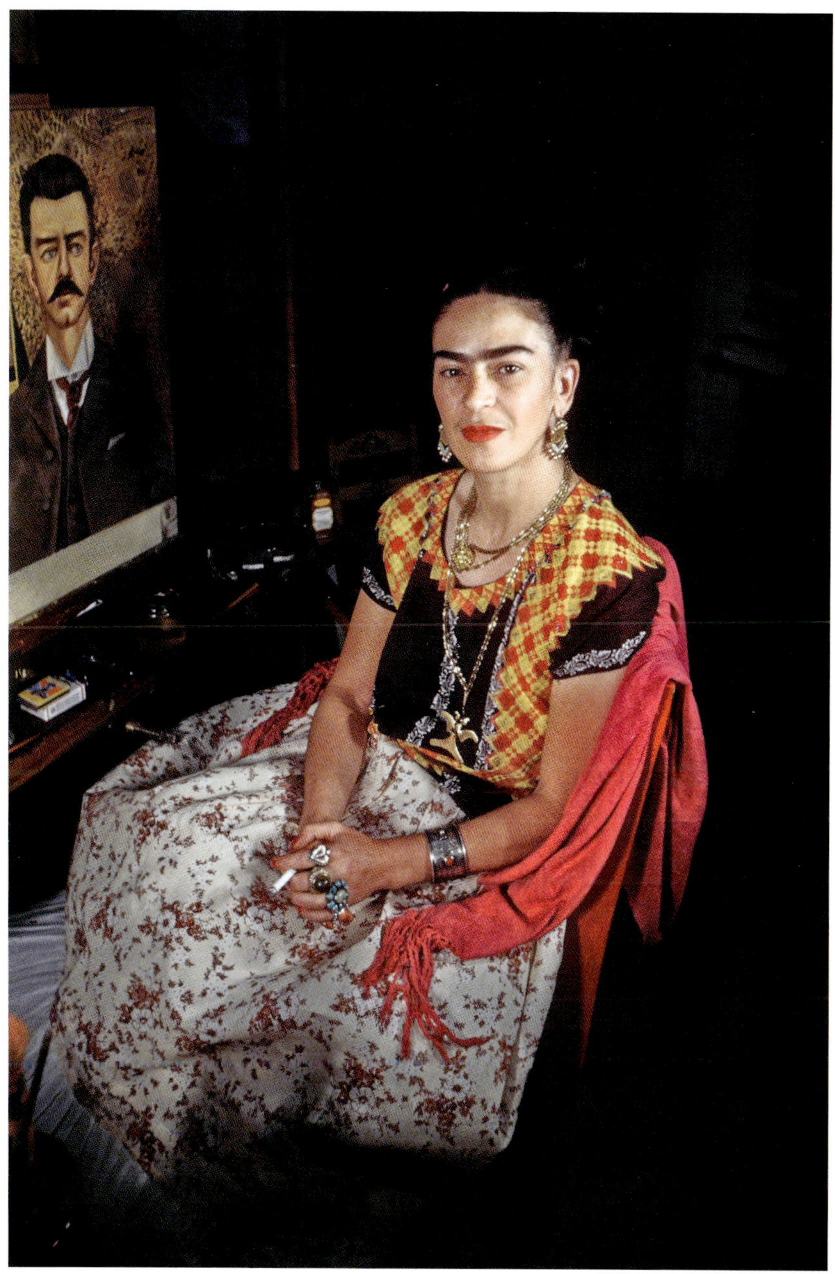

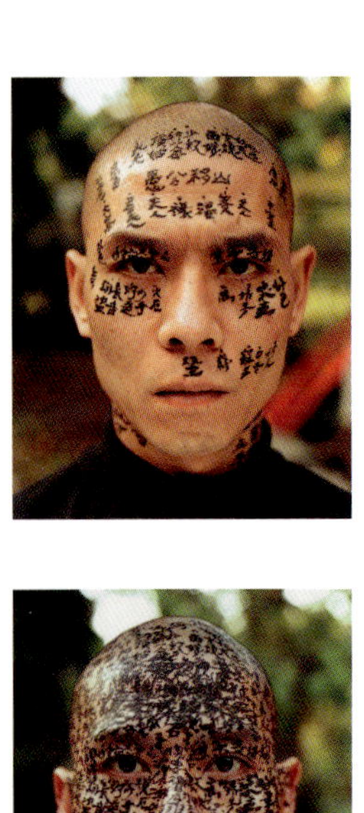
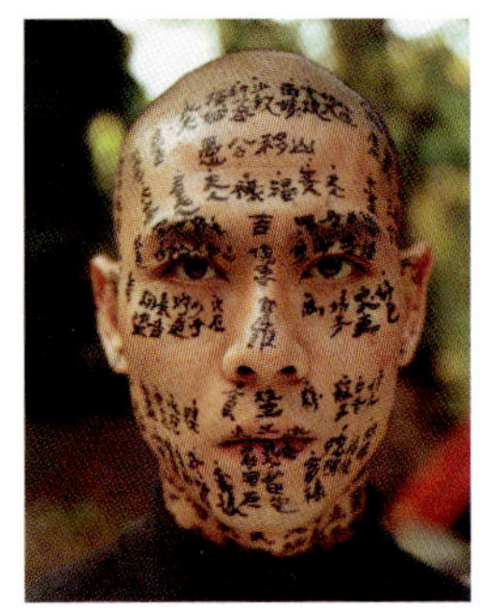
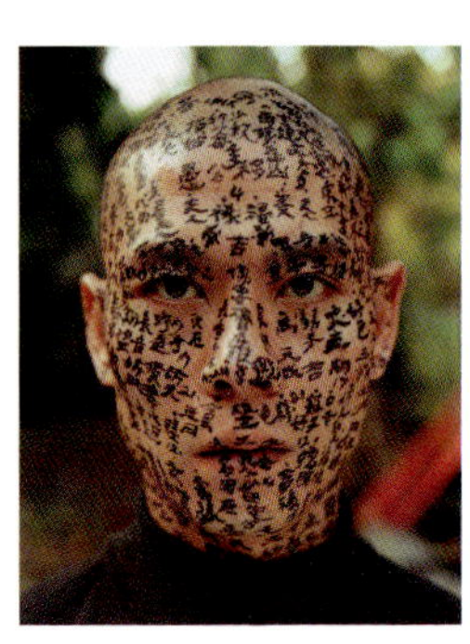
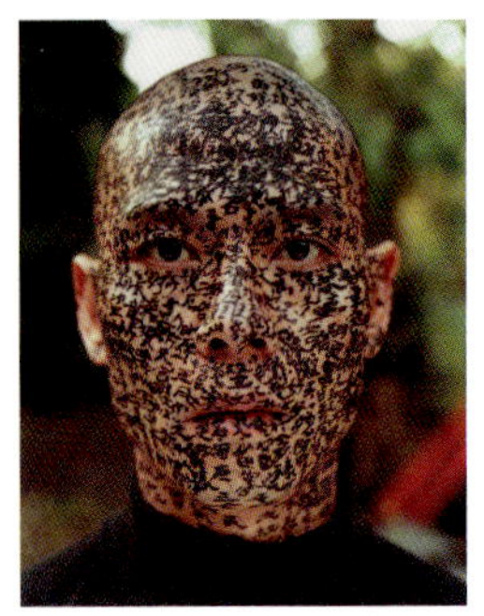
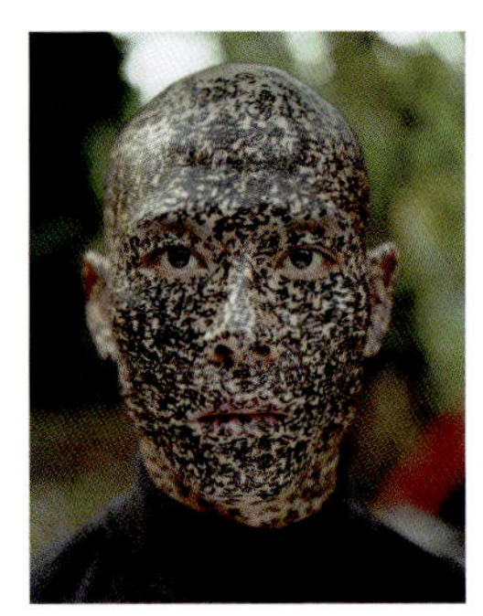
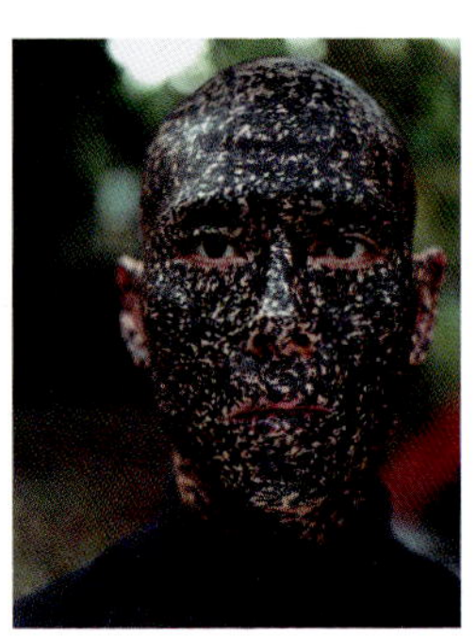
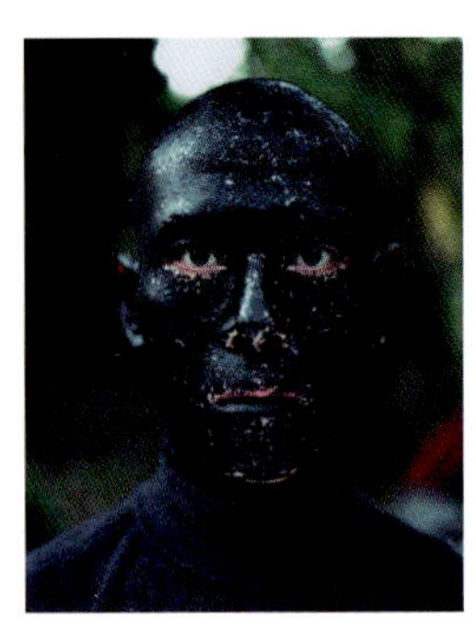
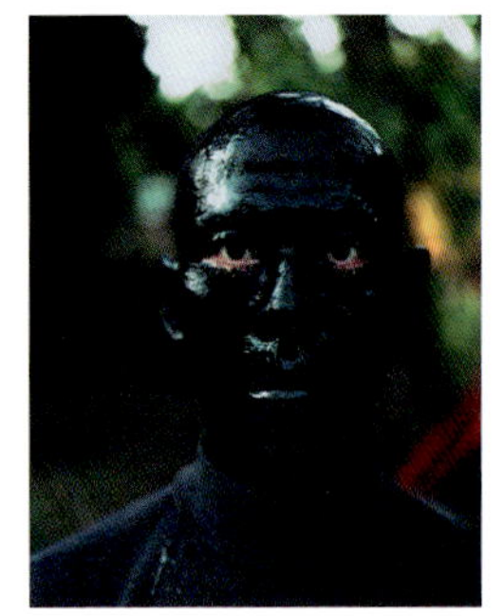
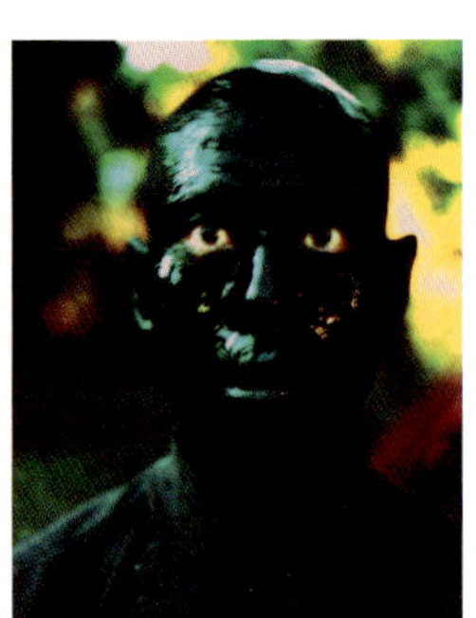

Zhang Huan
Family Tree, 2001

'More culture is slowly smothering us and turning our faces black. It is impossible to take away your inborn blood and personality,' says Zhang Huan. But there is such a thing as information overload: once we have reached saturation point, it is perhaps easier to start again from scratch.

WRITING THE SELF

As he grew older, the seventeenth-century Dutch master Rembrandt van Rijn painted a series of self-portraits that ruthlessly depicted all the traces of his physical decline, with his face growing steadily more weary and disillusioned. But not everyone turns the same pitiless gaze on themselves. Even before the First World War, portraitists made at least as many 'improvements' to their photographs as today's web users do to the flattering pictures of themselves that they post on Instagram, Flickr or other social networks. In a treatise of 1913 entitled *The Art of Retouching Photographic Negatives*, Robert Johnson wrote: 'A very skilful retoucher can make drastic changes in a face, such as closing a mouth that is opened too far so that the teeth are showing, straightening eyes that are slightly crossed or even putting into the negative eyes which may have been closed while the exposure was made.'

Today, many people living in the wealthiest countries in the world spend a lot of time and money on their own personal development, working on themselves like a muscle that can be strengthened through exercise. But not all cultures conceive of the individual in this way – Shamanic cultures, for example, or, in some ways, Buddhist philosophy, as embraced by the Chinese artist Zhang Huan (b.1965). For his performance *Family Tree* (opposite), he offered up his face to three calligraphers, who covered it with quotes taken from Huan's personal memoir and from classic Chinese literature. This work draws on the ancient art of predicting a person's future actions by analysing their facial features.

Family Tree also draws on the *non-self*, a fundamental concept in Buddhist philosophy. According to this belief, the idea that we each have an identity that is permanent and specific to us as an individual is an illusion because nothing in the universe exists independently of everything around it. A number of art critics have commented on the tragic dimension in Zhang Huan's performance – personal identity disappears, drowned in an excess of cultural symbols. But this blackened face is also a reminder that we are all identical beneath the superficial layer of culture.

Staying in the field of words, in the early 1990s the British conceptual artist Gillian Wearing (b.1963) asked hundreds of passers-by to write down on a placard what they were thinking at the moment she met them (overleaf).

It is paradoxical that a police officer, who is supposed to assist citizens, is asking for help himself. This reversal reflects the mood at this point in history, when, in certain countries and social classes,

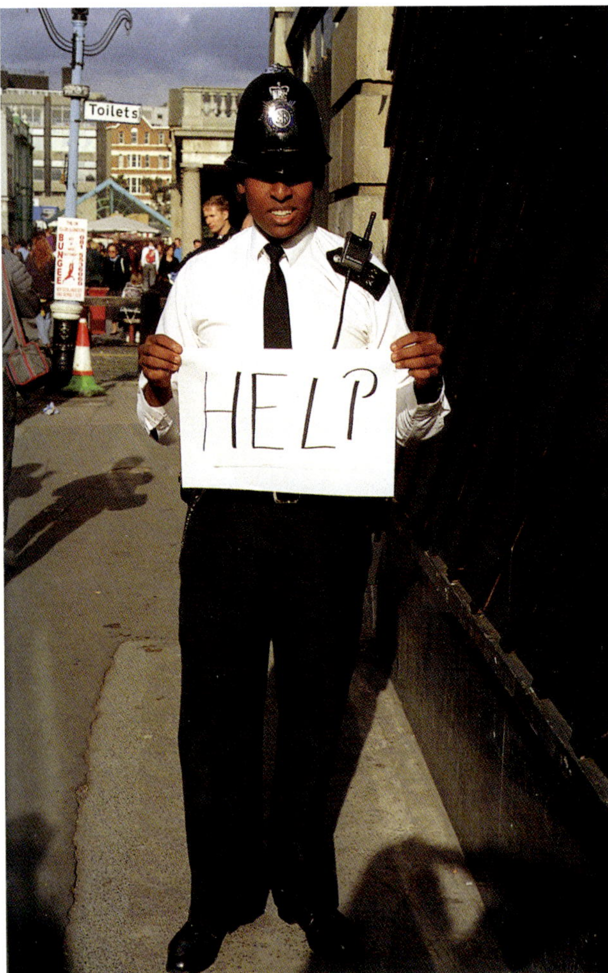

Gillian Wearing
Help, from the series 'Signs that Say What You Want Them To Say and Not Signs that Say What Someone Else Wants You To Say', 1992–93
C-type print mounted on aluminium,
44.5 x 29.7 cm
(17⅝ x 11¾ in.)

The police officer is screwing up his face, blinded by the sun, meaning that his expression seems to match the message he is holding up. The title of this series evokes a world where freedom of expression has disappeared, but it is not without its contradictions: when these portraits are exhibited on the walls of an art gallery, the messages written on the white placard may take on a meaning that was not intended by their authors.

individuals with no deeply held political or religious convictions felt lost in a world they did not understand. We can also make out an advert for bungee jumping behind the police officer, an example of an activity that offers thrills for people who are willing to risk their lives to have fun, rather than in the fight for a noble cause.

However, not everyone is equally lost, and there are those who understand the importance of fighting for recognition within societies that marginalize or oppress them.

PERFORMING GENDER

Two kiss curls on their forehead, two hearts on their cheeks, wrist supports that look like evening gloves, a leotard with nipples drawn on, between which are written the words: 'I am in training, don't kiss me': this work (below) by the French artist Claude Cahun (1894–1954) is a *performance of gender* – something that did not yet have a name in the interwar period. The large dumbbells resting on their shoulders are a prop that usually denote hypermasculinity, but the casual posture shows that they are fake, and that Cahun sees symbols of gender identity as a game: 'Masculine? Feminine? Well, that depends,' they said. 'Neutral is the only gender that always suits me.' Faced with a world that did not accept this blurring of gender markers, Cahun said: 'The happiest moments of my life? – A dream – Imagining I am different. Playing my preferred role.'

Claude Cahun
Sans titre (Autoportrait) [Untitled (Self Portrait)],
c. 1927
Gelatin silver print,
10.4 x 7.6 cm
(4⅛ x 3 in.)

With their arms forming a W shape and their feet side on, Cahun parodies the silhouettes of ancient Egyptian art. Only their face is straight on, looking at us and challenging us to react. The curtains, halfway between bedroom curtains and those seen in a cabaret show, suggest that there is not such a big difference between the stage and the city.

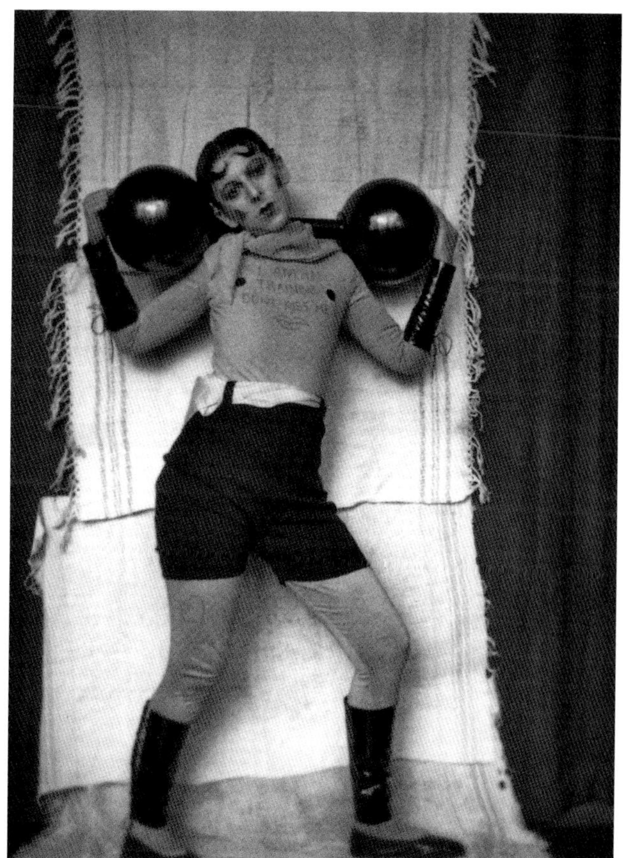

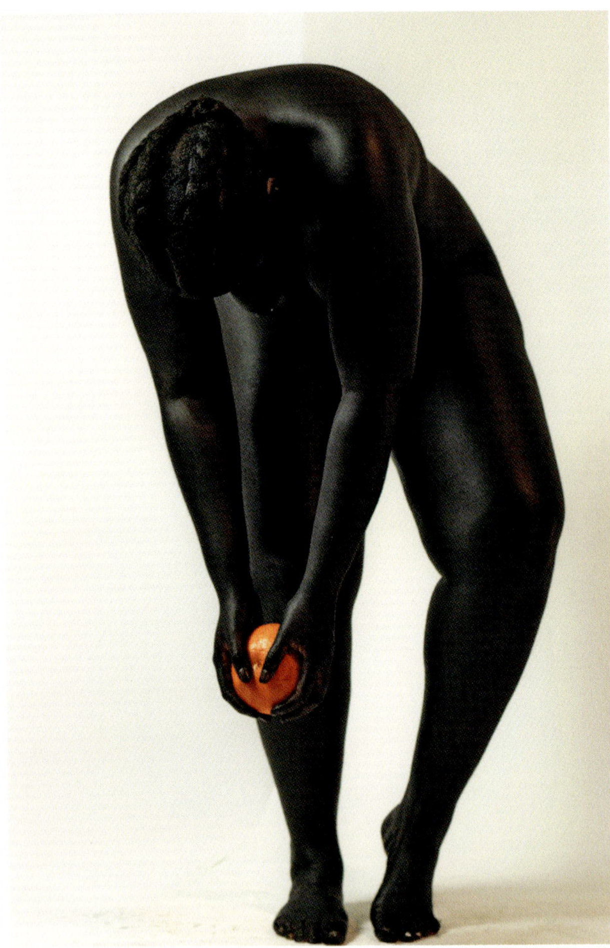

Eva Woolridge
Weight of Trauma, from the series 'Size of a Grapefruit', 2019

The photographer is holding a grapefruit as if it is very heavy – and symbolically, that is true. The colour stands out violently against her skin, emphasizing that it is a foreign object in an alien environment.

The autobiographical series to which *Weight of Trauma* (above) belongs has a more direct connection to daily life: it documents a few months in the life of the Black and Chinese-American photographer Eva Woolridge (b.1993), from the first sharp pain through her slow recovery after a major operation: the removal of an ovarian cyst 'the size of a grapefruit', which she represents here with a real grapefruit. After originally being misdiagnosed with food poisoning, she was rushed into surgery within one day of diagnosis. By displaying her personal experience in this elegant way, without trying to actively evoke pity in the viewer, she denounces the 'racial bias and micro-aggression in the medicine industry'.

Rather than starting from scratch, artists seeking to hold any given society up to the light can also make use of its iconography – such as Catholic imagery, for example. On one hand, the American artist David LaChapelle (b.1963) is faithful to the New Testament account of this scene (below): there are thirteen people around the table, Jesus Christ is easily recognizable and the work's title is in line with tradition. Even the series title echoes the depiction of Jesus in the gospels. LaChapelle says, 'if Jesus were here today, he would be hanging out with the street people and the marginalized: the poor, the homeless, prostitutes, drug dealers, gangsters, and so on.' The photographer also borrows from traditions in painting, imitating a technique used by Rembrandt in his version of *The Supper at Emmaus* in 1629: we are not sure whether the light is emanating from Jesus himself or whether it comes from a light source behind him. However, the photographer has taken certain liberties with Catholic iconography. The friends are not drinking wine, but beer and brandy, and there is a young woman bursting into the room. It is left up to us to decide whether this is Mary Magdalene, the repentant prostitute who is believed to have stayed with Jesus until his death, but who was not recorded as present at the Last Supper.

David LaChapelle
Last Supper, from the series 'Jesus is my Homeboy', New York, 2003
Chromogenic print

This photograph, in its creator's signature style, juxtaposes characters and objects that are easily recognizable. The ambiguity does not come from any photographic techniques – there are not many dark or blurry areas, for example – but from this juxtaposition itself.

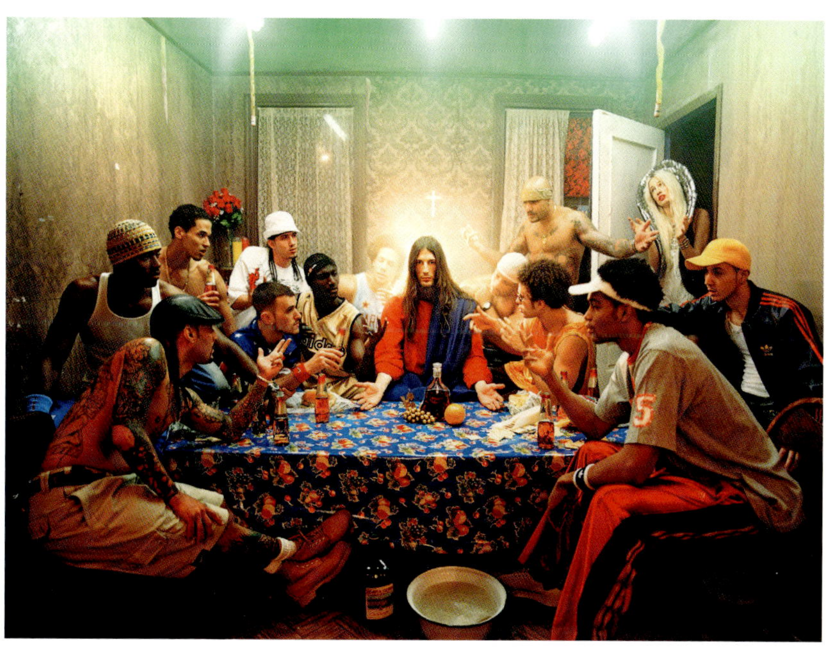

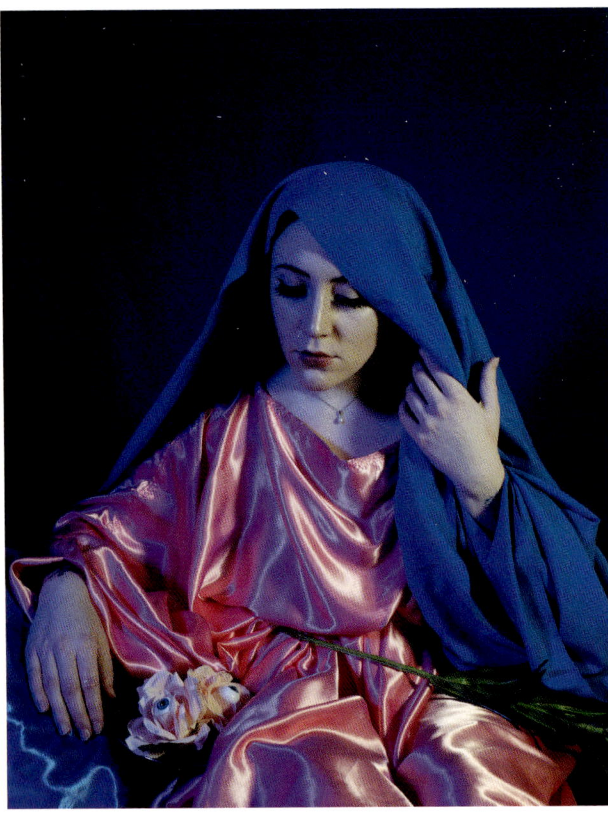

Hyacinth Schukis
Santa Lucia (After Palma and del Cossa), from the series 'Afterlives', 2020
Archival inkjet print,
61 x 76.2 cm (24 x 30 in.)

'I am white,' says Schukis in their artist's statement, 'assigned female at birth, transgender-nonbinary, raised middle-class, neurodivergent, chronically ill, and queer. All of these facets of my identity are to some degree manifest in my pictures.'

The American artist Hyacinth Schukis (b.1996) also leaves space for interpretation in their photographs. The above installation is inspired by the martyrdom of Saint Lucia in fourth-century Syracuse. The young woman refused to enter into a 'good marriage', as she wanted to take a vow of chastity and dedicate her life to helping the poor and destitute. As punishment, one of her torturers gouged out her eyes. This grisly subject inspired two painters of the Italian Renaissance: Francesco del Cossa, who depicted Lucia holding two flowers with pistils in the shape of eyes, and Palma il Giovane, who painted her carrying her eyes on a platter. Here, Schukis combines the two versions. Lucia is looking down at two eyeballs placed on rose petals, but we don't know whether they are hers, because her eyes are hidden by exaggerated false lashes. As well as evoking the martyrdom experienced by people who do not follow the path set out for them by the majority, this photograph also raises the question of how we see ourselves and others: we don't know whether the removal of Lucia's eyes was meant to stop her from seeing herself or from looking at us.

ME, ME, ME!

How should we stand in front of a camera? What should a face 'say'? The answers to these questions are always shaped by our culture. For example, family photos are associated with happiness in our collective imagination because of advertising campaigns by major companies such as Kodak. They are to blame for all those amateur photographers waiting in vain for their baby to smile, or telling people over and over again to 'say cheese', only to make them grimace harder.

The work of French artist ORLAN (b.1947) takes aim at two related targets in its quest for liberation (overleaf). The first, illustrated by this 'self-hybridation', consists of dismantling beauty

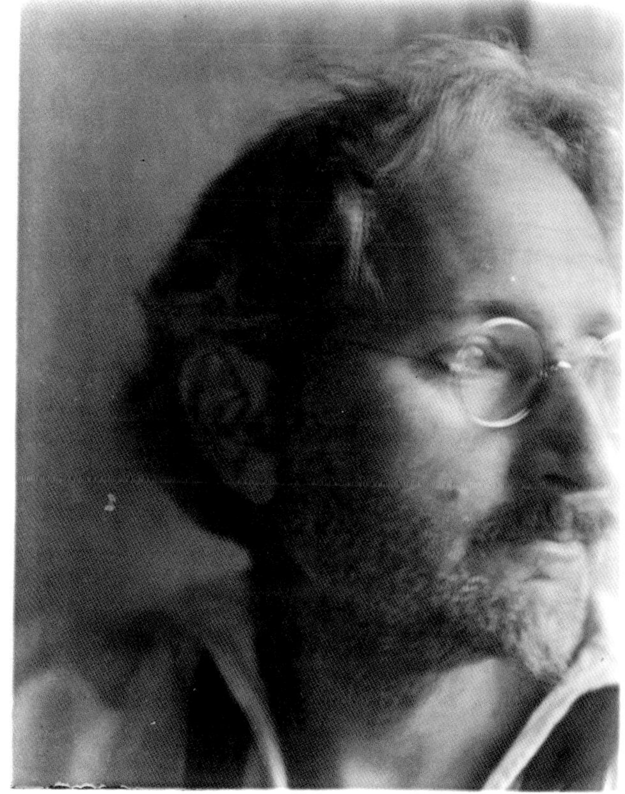

Fred Holland Day
Self-Portrait in a Sailor Suit, 1911
Cyanotype photographic print

Not only did the American photographer Fred Holland Day (1864–1933) move, which made the picture blurry, but he also turned his head too far to the side – or perhaps he did that deliberately, to remind us to be cautious. When we look at a portrait, we often think we can tell what kind of person someone is. 'This picture only shows you a part of me,' he seems to be saying in this photograph.

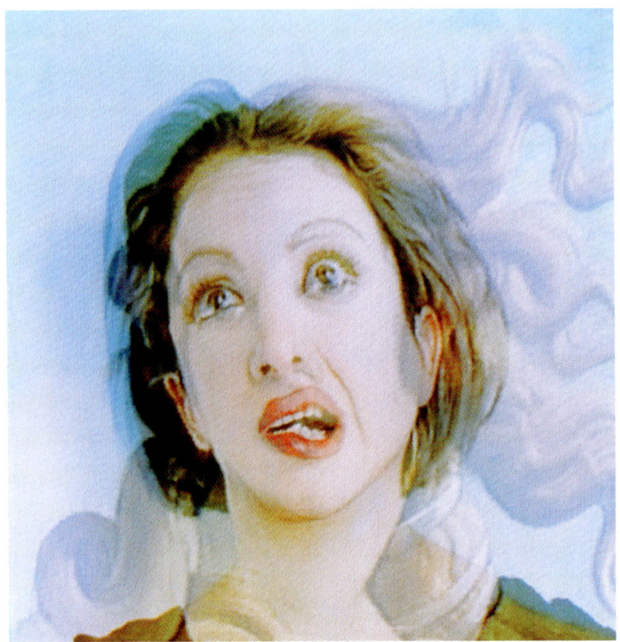

ORLAN
Self-Hybridation, In Between with ORLAN's portrait n°4, 1994
Colour photograph in lightbox, 120 x 160 cm (47¼ x 63 in.)

The artist's face is superimposed onto *The Birth of Venus* (c. 1485) by the Italian painter Sandro Botticelli. But that is not because she is trying to make herself look similar. Screwing up her mouth is a way of gently mocking the laws of feminine beauty. Cheeky kids in class photos are not the only ones who can pull faces.

standards. The second is more ambitious: it is about freeing ourselves from the genetic constraint of our natural appearance. This aim is much more complex, perhaps even impossible. To show her opposition to 'nature', ORLAN invites visitors to her website to sign a *petition against death*. Her works encourage us to look beyond appearances, as these rarely express a person's true identity. Throughout her career, this theme – the dichotomy between what a person is and what they appear to be – has dominated her work. It often focuses on her own body and identity: she is constantly transforming herself, both in her self-portraits and in her real life, even using plastic surgery in many of her performance pieces.

ORLAN is not the only female artist to interrogate the link between appearance and reality in this way. Like Barbara Kruger (see page 26), the American artist Cindy Sherman (b.1954) began her career with the Pictures Generation, an informal movement known for its critical analysis of how the media influences the way in which we construct and perceive our identity. Since then, she has taken thousands of photographs of herself, in which she never looks quite the same and yet never looks like an entirely different person. She is by turns brunette, blonde or redhead, young or old, beautiful or ugly, living or dead. But she has never sought to hide the fact that she uses makeup, prosthetics and digital technology to achieve all these transformations. Therefore these are not self-portraits but, in her own words, a way of making every day like Halloween, when we are free to dress up, to play around with people's expectations and make them question how much trust they place in appearances. Recently, Sherman published portraits on her Instagram account that had been created using artificial intelligence, through the app Lensa (below). She said that she was just playing around, that it is not art, but the idea is still the same: making us mistrust the representations we see in the media.

Everything changed after 2000, when phones that were capable of taking photographs began to be commonplace. For their users, photography became a means of communication, and even a way of creating a parallel life alongside their real one. This life is lived by an avatar that appears in videos and photographs, which has exactly the same features as the original

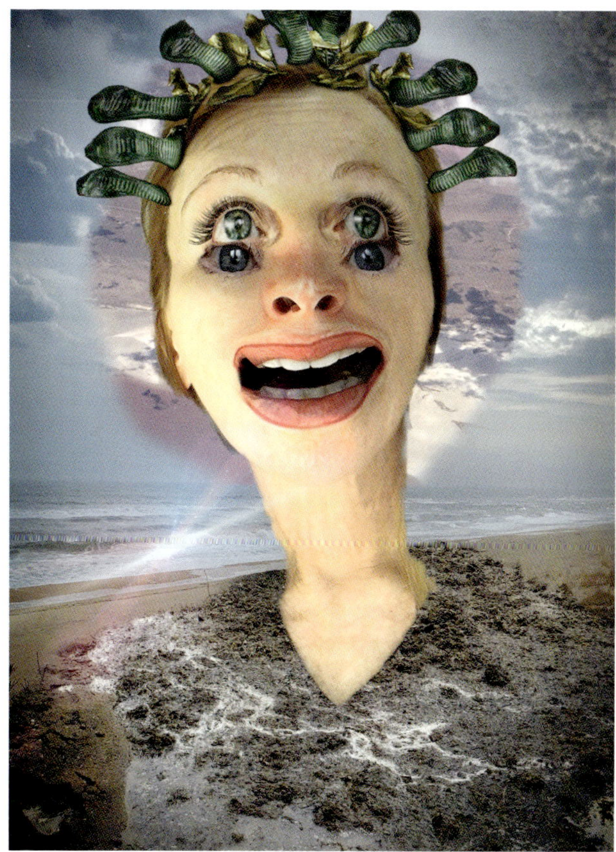

Cindy Sherman
I'm ready, March 2019
Instagram post

This photograph was created using Lensa software. 'You feed them in to this program and they make avatars out of the selfies,' Sherman explains. 'Generally, I think they are trying to make really attractive avatars of your face. But because the images that I've given them are these altered images, the results are just so much more surprising.'

person (perhaps a little retouched) and the same voice, but only exists in digital form, on social networks. One of the most common manifestations of this avatar is the selfie, a self-portrait usually taken on a smartphone. It is used for a number of purposes, some serious, some more playful. One of the simplest is to show that the photographer was in a certain place: a picture of their face in those surroundings proclaims: 'I'm here!' But because they already know where they are, the photograph only makes sense as a means of communication, sending a message to say: 'Look where I am right now!'

In general, selfies are posed. We make sure that we look a certain way, searching for the best angle, the best compromise between making our face look good and showing off our surroundings. Filters that allow us to focus on the subject minimize the risk of blending into the background. Placed side by side, selfies do not so much form a record of the lives of their creators as a kind of continuous game of hide-and-seek played by the 'true self' and the 'ideal self', all underpinned by an unquenchable desire for recognition. Every picture shouts: 'Look, it's me! I exist!'

The selfie form, which Cindy Sherman is parodying here, is the opposite of a paparazzi shot: the first expresses a desire to be seen, while the second conveys refusal, fear or displeasure at being spied on. We might think that there are not many amateurs who are tempted to play paparazzi, especially as they're not paid for it. But for some years now, people have used the tactics of professional photographers to fight back against harassment. The non-profit site righttobe.org, which encourages this practice, says it all began with a young woman in New York in 2005. 'Thao Nguyen bravely stood up to someone who harassed her. An older, upper middle class raw foods restaurant owner masturbated while sitting across from her on the New York City subway. Terrified, she took his photo with her camera and hoped to report it. When the police ignored her report, she posted the photo on Flickr.' Today, the site has picked up the baton, offering a safe space to share harassment stories.

Creating a buzz

For many years, photography has had a close relationship with advertising, and therefore with the world of fashion, which is at the crossroads between business and an individual's sense of self.

Especially when it comes to a certain type of photograph – one that has been enhanced and retouched. Advertising relies on the idea of added value: its function is to associate a product with something desirable, like beauty, happiness or luxury. The aim is to convince the customer that buying a piece of clothing or an accessory will give them access to these ideals, at least in some form. When a brand works with a major photographer (Cindy Sherman, for example, for MAC make-up products), it publicizes this collaboration, and the photographer themself becomes the added value: the brand appropriates some of their prestige for itself, business hiding for a little while behind culture.

The Italian photographer Oliviero Toscani (b.1942) understood this trade-off very well, as we can see in his collaboration with the brand Benetton, which began in 1984 (below). He saw that the added value of an advertising campaign did not have to reflect the style of the clothes being sold. That is how Benetton's relatively modest jumpers and dresses came to be associated with a whole host of provocative photos. Some of these sparked protests and even legal complaints against the brand, and most importantly – the holy grail of any advertising campaign – thousands of articles. In other words, free publicity. This strategy is even more unstoppable when it centres around a call to love one another, without making any distinctions based on skin colour, religion or sexuality – after all, we all have things in common, starting with a beating heart.

Oliviero Toscani
Hearts, advertising campaign for Benetton, Spring/Summer 1996

A few very racist people pointed out that the three hearts were not entirely identical. But did others appreciate this call for solidarity? One advantage of this kind of campaign was that it didn't rely on top models, who are supposed to make the clothes they are wearing seem desirable.

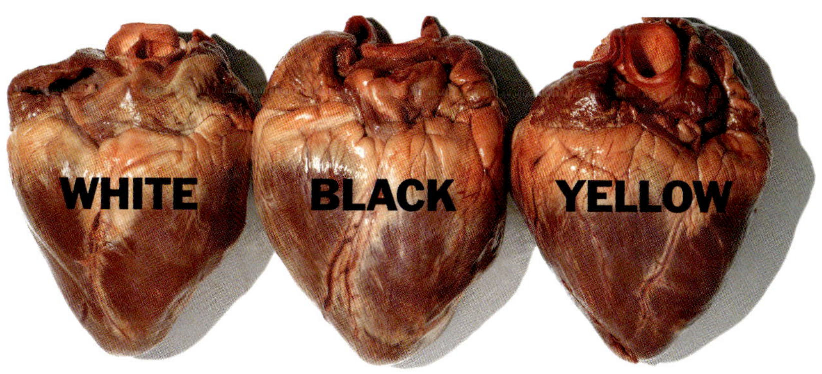

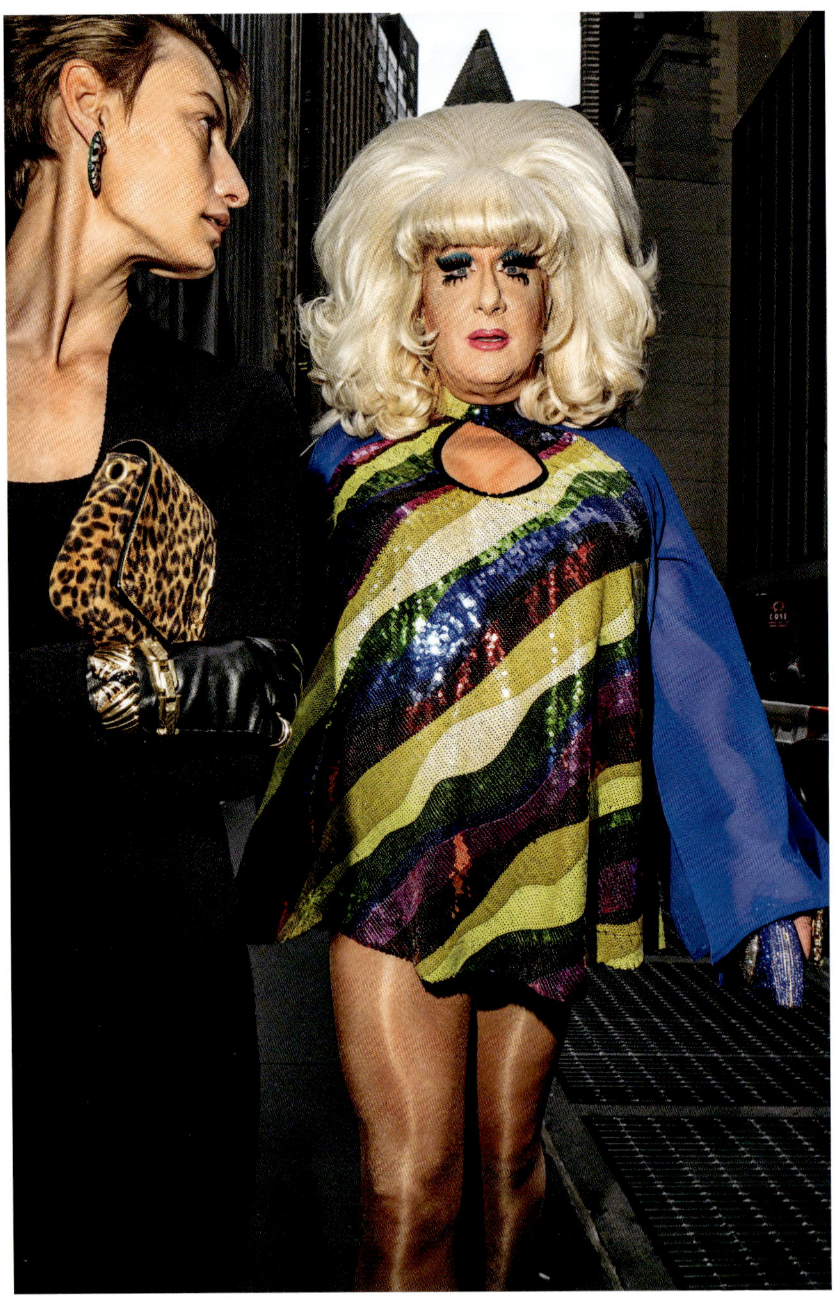

Bruce Gilden
Drag Legends Milk and Lady Bunny Show Off This Season's Most Extravagant Accessories, Fashion Shoot for *W* magazine, New York City, 2019

This photograph was taken for *W* magazine. Next to the professional model Veronika, with her luxurious accessories, the drag queen Lady Bunny is wearing her own clothes. But the photographer chose to cut off Veronika, so that half of her body is outside the frame, to concentrate on Lady Bunny, as if he recognized that the extravagance and glitter would naturally draw the eye more than the discreet chicness of a black dress, at least at first glance.

The American photographer Bruce Gilden (b.1946) is better known as a street photographer than a fashion photographer: he often works with flash to create violent, raw pictures. 'His closeups are so unforgiving and intrusive they dehumanise the subject,' said one writer in the *Guardian*. But that is not the case in this photograph (opposite). Of course, the flash and the perfect sharpness highlight the artificiality of these faces, such as the make-up and false eyelashes, and what fashion photographs usually seek to hide, the wrinkles under the chin, for example. But that is not a problem: neither of the two people in the photograph seems to be angry with the photographer for showing them as they are, and one of them is turning towards the other, as if they are having a quiet, everyday conversation as they come out of the subway in a street in Manhattan. As if they dress first for themselves, not for others.

UNINTENTIONAL STARS

It is not only fashion photographers who choose beautiful people to embody an idea or make others want to be associated with what they represent. Photojournalists are well aware that if they choose someone who possesses certain physical characteristics, at the heart of a crowd of demonstrators, for example, they will have a greater chance of getting their photograph published.

Therefore, while these two shots both capture important moments in human history and demonstrate impressive artistry, they would never have become so famous if the young women immortalized in them did not meet prevailing standards of female beauty.

Nowadays, when writing about the Spanish Civil War, the media often uses this portrait (page 143) of Marina Ginestá at the age of seventeen, taken by the German-born Mexican photographer Juan Guzmán (1911–1982). Beyond its value as a historical record, and the prestige afforded by the beauty and youth of the Republican cause, this portrait is attractive because it is posed, conforming to well-known standards – those of classic American cinema. Many years afterwards, Marina, then in her eighties, said, 'They say that in the Colón photo I have a captivating look. It's possible because we were immersed both in the mysticism of the proletarian revolution and the images of Hollywood, of Greta Garbo and Gary Cooper.'

We have the same impression of seeing familiar visual tropes in this photograph of Yuko Sugimoto, who the western media immediately dubbed 'the weeping woman of Ishinomaki' or 'the Madonna of the rubble'. Tadashi Okubo (n.d.), a Japanese photojournalist working for the major Tokyo daily *Yomiuri Shimbun*, took this picture (below right) when he was reporting on the aftermath of an earthquake in Japan in the spring of 2011. Here again, there is something more at play than mere youth and beauty: the light duvet draped hastily around the woman's shoulders is reminiscent of religious paintings of the Italian Renaissance. The contrast between this unexpected elegance and the wreckage of the disaster in the background makes this photograph very impactful. It doesn't matter that Christian iconography really has nothing to do with this catastrophe in Japan: the resemblance engages our interest.

The difference between these two young women is that one knew she was posing, while the other did not; be that as it may, their portraits have stood the test of time because they tick certain boxes in the collective imagination.

Juan Guzmán
Marina Ginestá i Coloma on the Rooftop of Hotel Colón, Plaça de Catalunya 9, Barcelona, 1936

Three elements enhance the subject's beauty: the young woman is turning her head, as if she only had a second to spare for the photographer before returning to the fighting; the wind (the winds of history, of course) is lifting her hair; finally, the barrel of the gun sits between two belltowers, implying that the fight is in some way sacred.

KEY IDEAS

We cannot tell what a subject's true personality is like from their portrait.

A portrait can become an avatar that takes on its own existence.

A portrait can even become a symbol that is no longer controlled by the photographer or the person being photographed.

KEY QUESTIONS

... to ask with a photograph in front of you:

What makes this portrait different from a simple ID photo?

Is this portrait the result of a meeting between the photographer and the subject, and was the subject aware that they were being photographed?

What are the visual elements that can help me to piece together the subject's personality?

To appreciate a portrait, do you necessarily have to understand the pictorial tradition and cultural mores that it references?

Tadashi Okubo
Ishinomaki, Miyagi Prefecture, Japan, 12 March 2011

Once again, this young woman's beauty is shown to its best advantage against a backdrop. A strange backdrop as it happens: the woman, Yuki Sugimoto, and the old container behind her are both lit by a ray of fading sunlight, and the chaos of zigzagging planks contrasts with the soft curves of the duvet that she has wrapped around her shoulders.

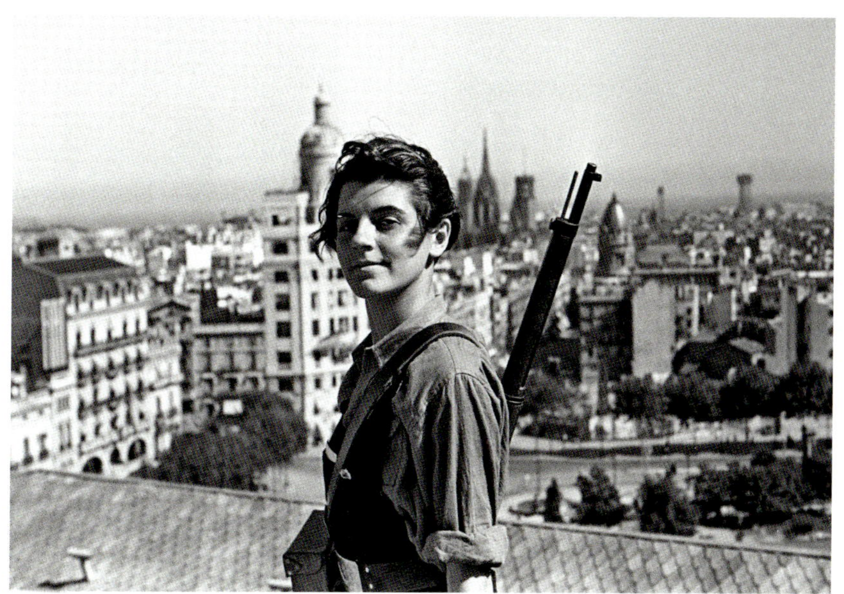

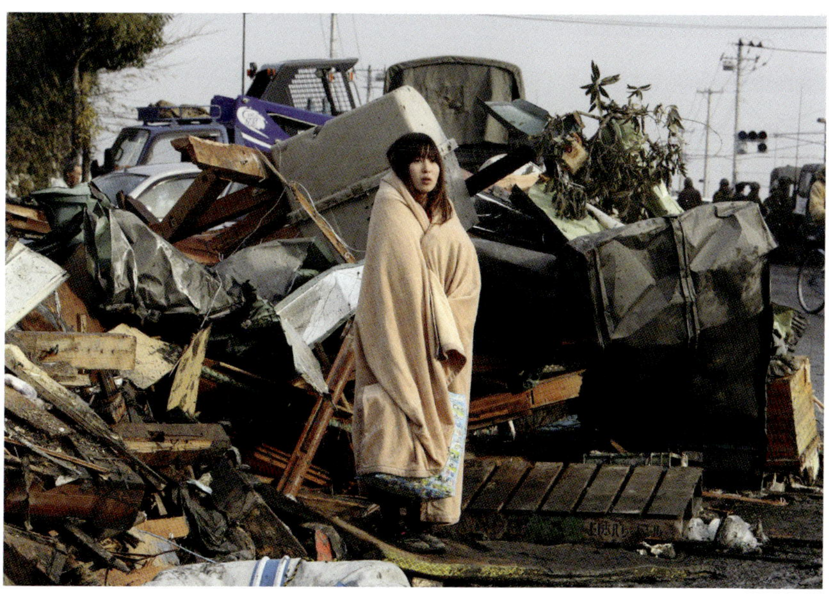

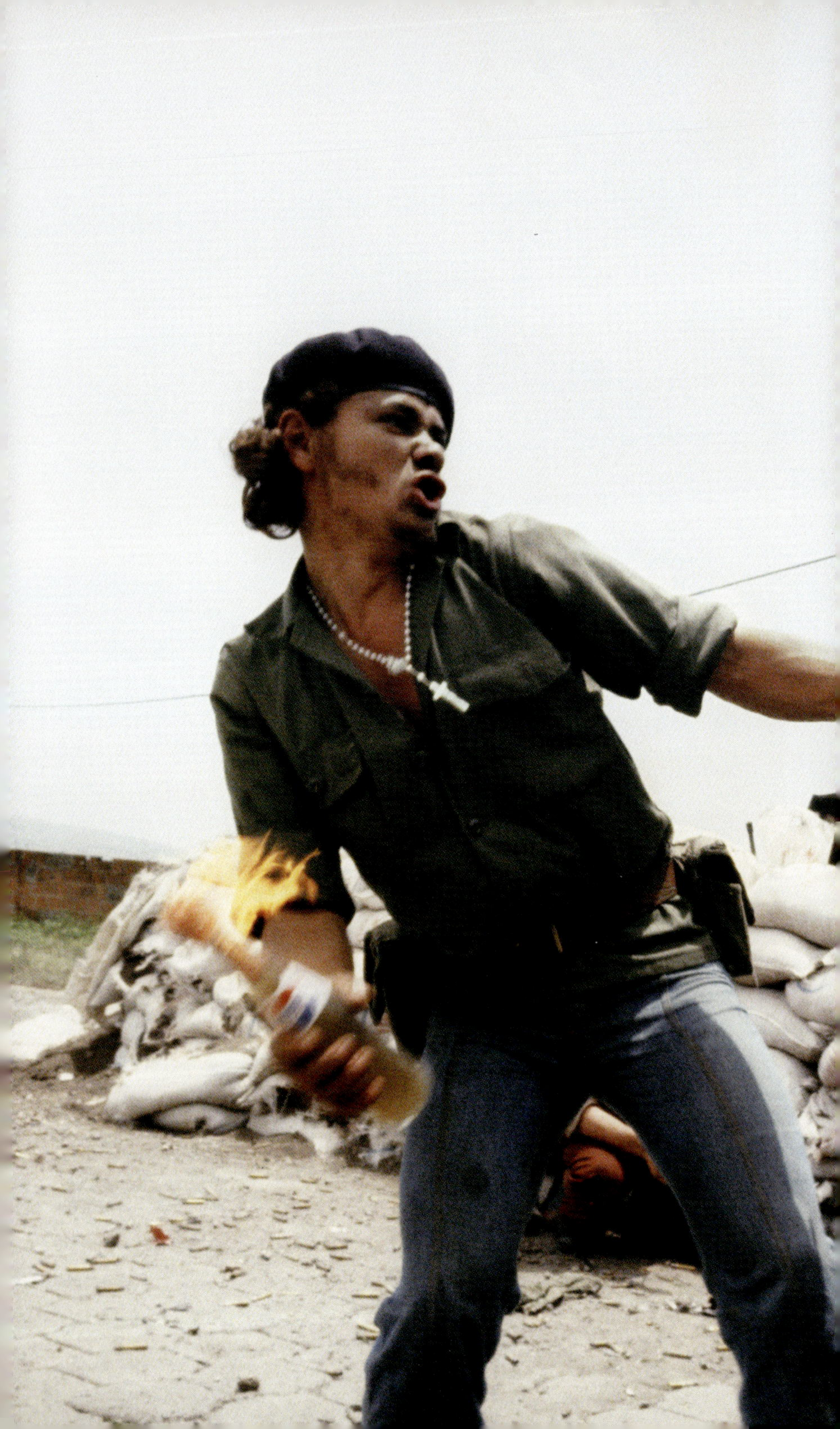

THE POWER OF IMAGES

-

Many times you don't have much control over what will happen with the image or who will consume it in the future

-

Susan Meiselas

Certain photographs make an impression on us. We can't look at them without wanting to be in the place where they were taken. Simply looking at them makes us happy. But others evoke a sense of horror, or make us feel reassured that the daily life depicted in them is not ours, and we are overcome with sadness when we think about the people who were there when they were taken. Our stomach is in knots when we look at these people, and we feel like a voyeur. There are also photographs that we cannot tear our eyes away from. Their elegance and perfection mean that they are destined to be hung in museums, alongside ancient Greek statues. Still others seem to give us access to something hidden, including other people's thoughts, and prompt us to change our minds about people or events that we thought we understood. All of these photographs belong to the family of *performative* discourses – that is how we classify symbols, words and images that have a tangible effect on the world.

Consuelo Kanaga
Eluard Luchel McDaniel, 1931
Gelatin silver print, 20 x 15.2 cm (7⅞ x 6 in.)

Born into a middle-class family in a small town in Oregon, Consuelo Kanaga was one of the first female photojournalists. She was hired by the *San Francisco Chronicle* in 1915. Over the course of her career, she met both Dorothea Lange and Tina Modotti. In this photograph, she takes her own chauffeur and handyman as her subject.

CONVEYING A MESSAGE

When we are touched by an image, we immediately start to wonder about the photographer's intention. Have we correctly understood what they wanted to convey? These doubts can be intimidating, even paralysing: instead of looking more closely at the photograph, we rush online to search for as much information as we can find about where, when and how it was taken. However, perhaps there is a better way. Not all photographers seek to communicate a specific message, and even those who do are aware that they cannot control other people's interpretations of the work. Photographs are not like road signs. The highway code assigns a specific meaning to each sign, but there is no *photography code*. Once we have more or less identified a photograph's subject, we are free to interpret it however we wish. We can't be fined for reading it wrong.

That is why, when a photographer wants to make us feel something, they don't rely on things that can only be understood by the learned few. They concentrate on what we call *universals*, traits that are present in all human beings, whatever their language, sex, age or skin colour. 'Everything has to be personal in order to be universally understood,' said the Canadian photographer Barbara Cole (b.1953). 'At least, that's when I know a photograph is doing something right.'

One of these universals is the attention we pay to other people's hands. They draw our eye, as the American photographer Consuelo Kanaga (1894–1978) was well aware (opposite). Indeed,

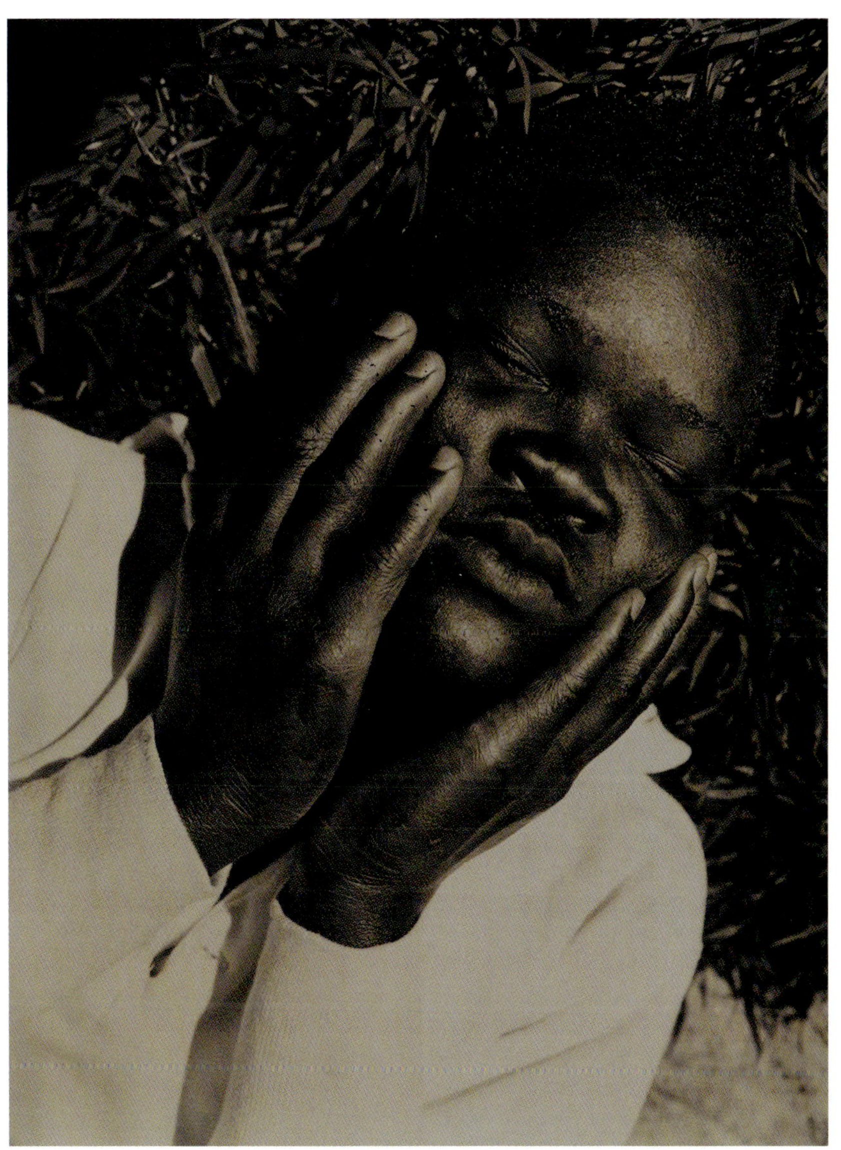

all photographers know this. Instead of perpetuating stereotypes associated with the figure of the Black domestic servant, often shown in uniform and going about their work, Kanaga simply depicts *a man*. To achieve this, rather than emphasizing his hands, she draws on three very simple elements: the pose, the framing and the background. The pose, because Mr McDaniel's pose is familiar to us. We all adopt it, but it doesn't have a specific meaning. McDaniel seems to be relaxing in the sun, forgetting all his cares, or, in contrast, resting his head on his hands to concentrate. Next, the framing on the diagonal makes the photograph feel as if it is tipping over, perhaps suggesting a desire to escape from the cares of everyday life, or even to no longer be a domestic servant. Finally, the jumble of vegetation behind McDaniel's head evokes the complex thoughts at play in this photograph.

How photographs can change the world

Many activists believe that it is important to highlight issues, to make them visible, so that people recognize the urgent need for change. The South African photographer Neil Aldridge (b.1982), for example, remains convinced that his photographs of animals at risk of extinction have contributed to slowing down this disaster: 'I guess I have been able to reach a considerable audience with the pictures I think people need to see and, in the process, hopefully creating greater empathy for a natural world under strain.' But it is not always as simple as that. To start with, we cannot be certain that this photograph (opposite) will automatically evoke a feeling of empathy. Aldridge, who used a telephoto lens, was probably many metres away from the elephant when he pressed the button. This creates a shallow depth of field, which has the effect of isolating the animal from its environment; this is both unnatural (because elephants are part of the savannah ecosystem) and paradoxical (the savannah disappears in the blurriness, but it is not at risk of extinction). What's more, no one can ever be certain that an image, even a very powerful image, will prompt people to act. There is a big difference between realizing something is not right and taking action to make it better – the situation does not change simply because we know what we need to do, but because we decide to act.

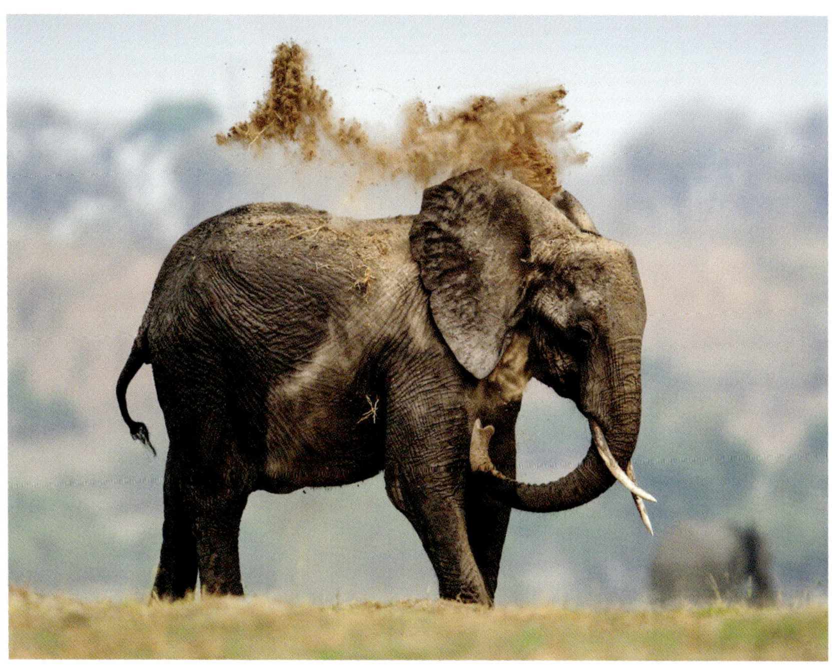

Neil Aldridge
Elephant, Chobe, Botswana, 2013

The dust that the elephant is spraying over its skin, frozen in place by the photograph, makes the animal look like it is disintegrating, disappearing in a puff of smoke. Which is true, in a figurative sense, when we consider that the species is at risk of extinction.

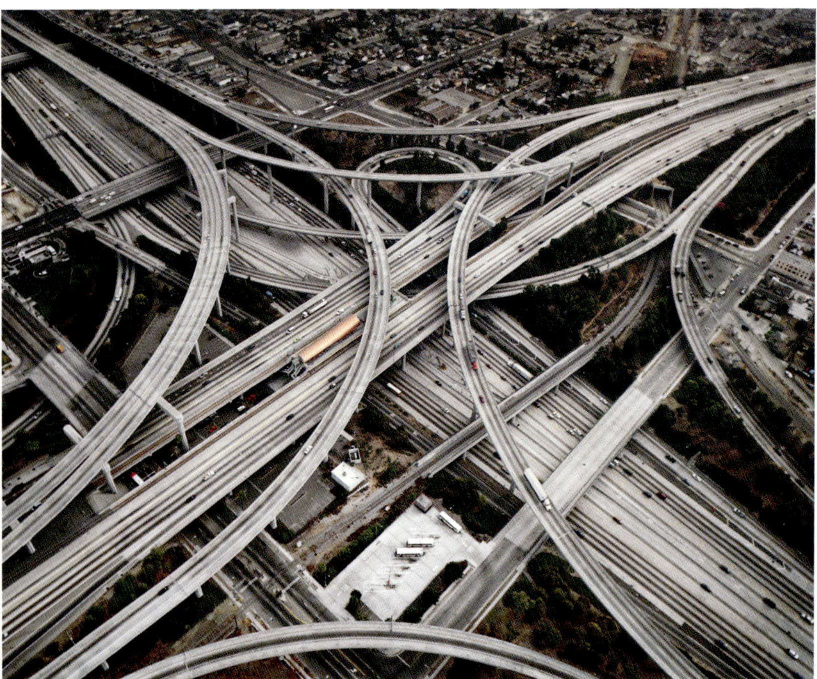

Edward Burtynsky
Highway #2, Intersection 105 & 110, Los Angeles, California, 2003
Digital chromogenic print

The highway ramps seem to be growing on top of each other, beyond all rational logic, unless the idea is to eradicate all traces of vegetation; but the drivers, glued to their steering wheels, don't notice this.

Now for a different approach. While the elephants of Botswana don't have a significant impact on what their ecosystem looks like, that is not the case for humans. Many scientists use the term Anthropocene to highlight the way in which urbanization and our unchecked exploitation of natural resources are changing the planet as a whole, to the point that we have moved it into a new geological era.

In the Anthropocene, nature and culture no longer exist in harmony with one another. Culture, or rather technology, has won. As we can see in these two photographs, it even seems to have broken free from its inventors, to no longer be under their control. In the above picture by the Canadian photographer Edward Burtynsky (b.1955), nature has been overcome by concrete. The trees at ground-level are scarcely visible: they have been sacrificed at the altar of human transportation – or rather, since the overhead view has also made humans disappear from the scene, they have been sacrificed for cars. By contrast, the Quebecois photographer Robert Polidori (b.1951) adopts a more familiar perspective (opposite): we are going into a classroom. But that is the only human element in this scene. Because we are,

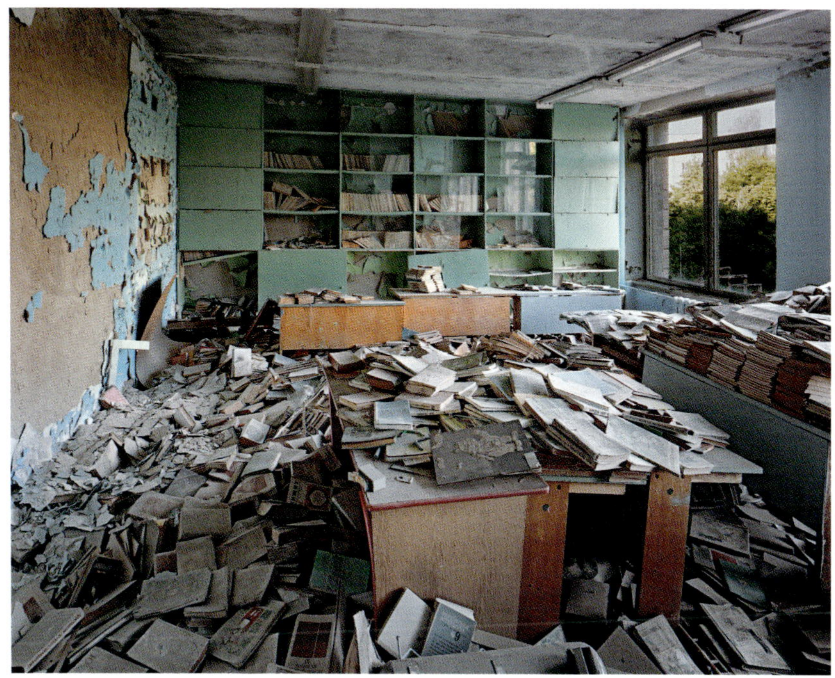

Robert Polidori
Classroom in School #5, Pripyat, from the series 'Zones of Exclusion', 2001

A photograph cannot show the radiation in the air after a nuclear disaster, but the chaos here speaks volumes about its impact. It is as if the school books, which are supposed to pass on knowledge from one generation to the next, had already been thrown away, in a refusal to embrace the unthinking drive of technological 'progress'.

by special permission, in Pripyat, Ukraine, two kilometres away from Chernobyl. The classroom, which was intended to be used by children, symbols of life, is now contaminated by invisible, deadly radiation, while, ironically, outside the window, trees are starting to grow back.

IN SEARCH OF EMPATHY

But photographers are not always trying to change the course of history: they can have far more modest aims. Sometimes a photographer is simply – although even this is very ambitious – seeking to replace the impassive gaze of the lens with an authentic human response, less perfect but more intimate. They are not trying to explain complicated things, but simply to make us *feel*. The human eye is not capable of being objective, especially when we are looking at our fellow humans.

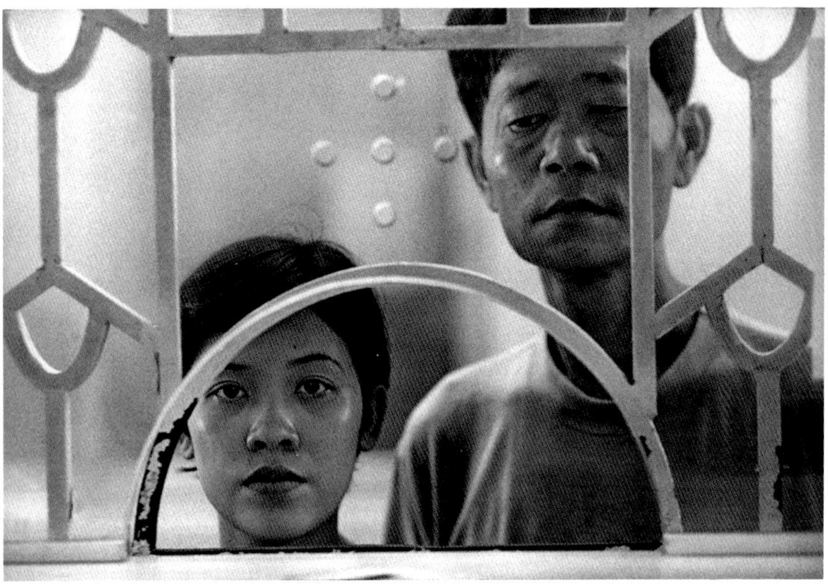

Chien-Chi Chang
Double Happiness, 2005

The small holes in the counter window are reminiscent of the bubbles used by comic strip artists to show that their characters are thinking. The flaky paint shows us that this system has been in place for a long time.

What were they thinking when the photograph was taken?

Unlike writers, photographers cannot get inside the heads of their 'characters'. But they can use their surroundings and wait for the right moment to press the button. That is what Chien-Chi Chang (b.1961), a Taiwanese photographer and member of the Magnum agency, did in this photo story (above) about 'express weddings' in Vietnam, where marriage brokers offer weddings concluded in the space of three days. That is not very long to get to know the person with whom you are going to spend the rest of your life. Chang knows that, armed only with his camera, he will not be able to show us these people's motivations. Therefore, he is content simply to appeal to our emotions by suggesting that they do not take this decision lightly.

In order to convey this, first Chang highlights the differences between the two people. The man is older and a head taller than the woman; he has not tried to make himself look good by putting on a nice shirt, and is looking down – perhaps at a piece of paper that he needs to sign. The woman has taken great care over her hairstyle and is looking straight at us, calling on us to witness what is happening, her neutral expression like those carefully adopted by people in photo booths. Next, Chang uses the surroundings to emphasize the contrast between the future spouses. The metallic uprights of the counter's window create horizontal symmetry, but not vertical. A half-circle seems to enclose the young woman's head, containing it within a small, tight space, while the man's body is also partly within this frame. He, however, is alone in his small section: she isn't tall enough to reach it.

Another asymmetrical pair appears in this work (below) by the Austrian photographer Inge Morath (1923–2002). They are the classic duo at opposite ends of the social spectrum. Mrs Nash's relaxed pose and sumptuous furs contrast with her chauffeur's stiff uniform. She seems quite at ease, whereas he is clenching his teeth, trying to maintain a neutral expression. Their eyes do not offer us any clues to help decode their feelings: hers are half hidden by a veil, his are shaded by his cap.

Behind them, the columns on the right and the trees on the left are perfectly aligned, creating a sense of order. However, the photograph is on a slight angle – you can tell simply by looking at the edge of the pavement on the left. We feel a faint sense of unease, and perhaps of violence, at the inequality between this pair: the rope handle attached to the door looks like a truncheon, and a part of the hood forms the shape of a devil's horn on top of Mrs Nash's hat. Nothing is said directly; it is a vague feeling.

Inge Morath
Mrs. Eveleigh Nash with Her Chauffeur at The Mall, London, 1953
Gelatin silver print

Two men are passing by in the background, two equals: a way of emphasizing by contrast the inequality that reigns between the couple in the foreground.

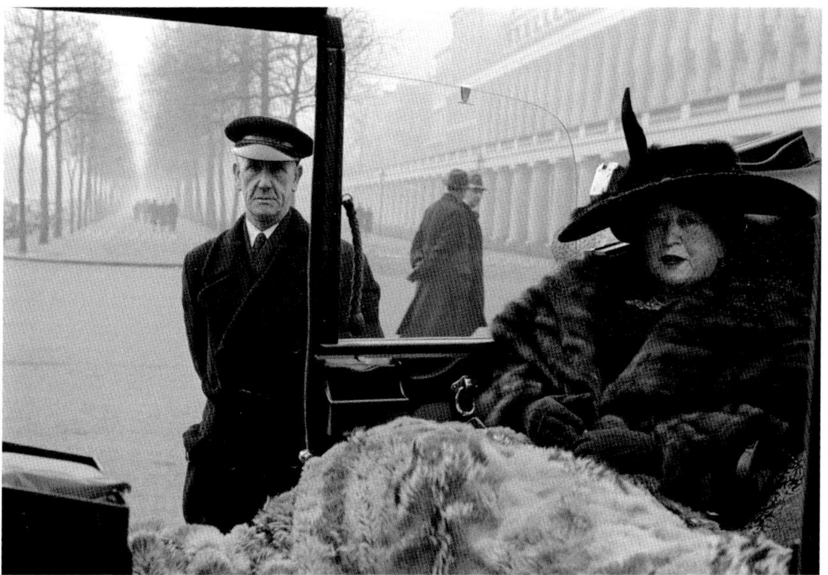

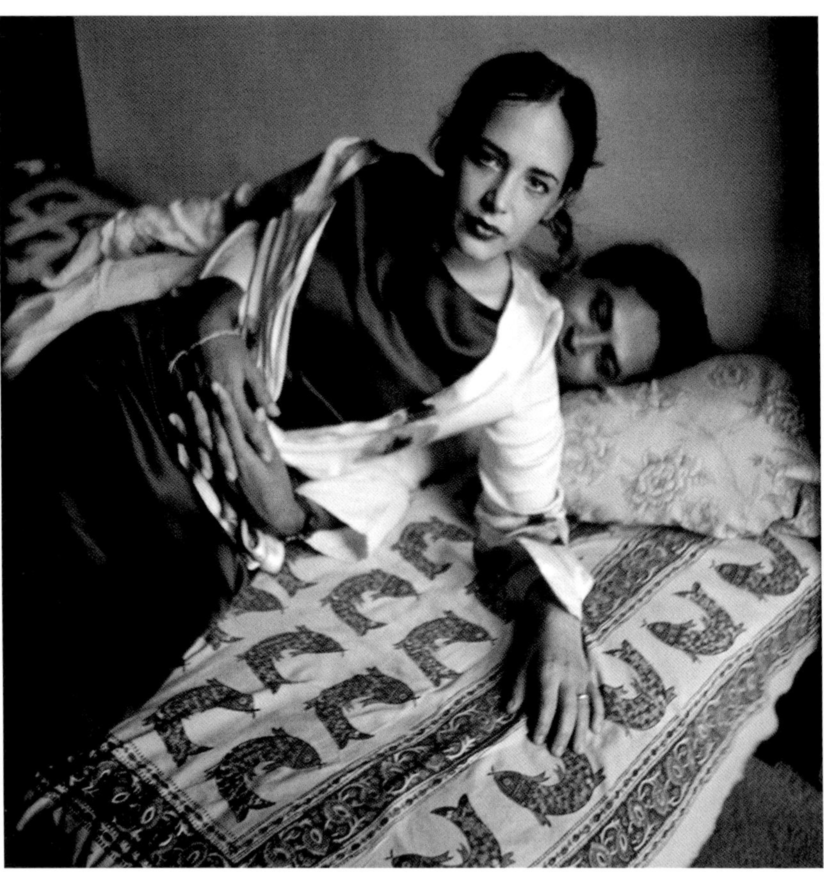

Dayanita Singh
Zeiss Ikon, 1996, from the series 'Go Away Closer', 2013

The title of this series is a paradox in itself. The photographer knows that once her work is exhibited, every person who sees it will have their own interpretation.

Empathy versus attraction

The subject of a photograph does not have to be attractive to evoke empathy in the viewer; often, in fact, the opposite is true. But artists who are aware of the ambiguous nature of beauty, such as the Indian photographer Dayanita Singh (b.1961), are able to evoke emotion in us by choosing subjects for their appearance (opposite). This young woman's face is undeniably attractive. It conforms to dominant beauty standards in many parts of the world, starting with the most universal of all, symmetry. But the photograph is a far cry from the world of fashion shots, even though the folds of the satin dress form interesting curves. Two elements that we have already seen elsewhere, diagonal lines and hands, draw the eye.

A body arranged diagonally is always in an 'impossible' position: we spend most of our time with our bodies either vertical or horizontal. We only bend over or lean down to carry out brief actions, as we risk losing our balance and falling over. Here, it takes a few seconds to understand the position of the subjects' hands. No, those interlaced fingers accentuated by the lighting do not belong to the woman, but to the man. He is holding her tightly against himself. Her hands convey a far more ambiguous message: her right hand, which fades into the blurry background, rests reassuringly on the man's body, while her left hand is supporting her weight. Is she trying to get away? We don't know if she is in the process of getting up or lying down, just as the fish on the bedspread could either be rising to the surface or descending to the depths. Therefore, is this a denunciation of male domination or a depiction of a great love story? It is left up to us to decide.

EVERYTHING LEFT UNSAID

Most of the photographs that we see, especially when we are browsing online, are texts without context. Who are these people? What are they doing? Where are they? Even the most famous photographs cannot speak for themselves. They can never convey everything on their own, and if they have an impact on us, it is partly (often especially) because we also know a whole host of facts about the events and people depicted in them.

A good photograph often goes hand in hand with a good story

The internet and printed media are overflowing with lists of 'photographs that changed history'. But did they truly change history, or did they provide our collective imagination with pictures that help us to understand what words cannot fully express? This photograph (opposite), taken by the American photojournalist Eddie Adams (1933–2004) is one of those often credited with turning the tide of public opinion in America about the Vietnam War. The man shown pulling the trigger of his revolver was supposed to be an ally of the United States. How could someone who was on the 'right side' execute a prisoner in cold blood, a man with his hands tied behind his back? In the middle of the street, what's more, and in front of the press (there was also a television camera present).

However, it is not as simple as that. General Nguyễn Ngoc Loan, the chief of police of South Vietnam, did execute this Vietcong fighter, but it was because he was overcome by a terrible rage. The prisoner had just killed one of his men, as well as the man's wife, mother and six children. But the photograph doesn't tell us that. In fact, it implies the opposite. In the act of killing, the general seems unmoved, as if it is an everyday occurrence. His left arm, which is hanging loosely at his side, implies a certain detachment. A white stain on the back of his jacket subtly suggests that, whether we want to admit it or not, this war is something dirty. There would be many struggles to come for Loan, as this sad story would follow him throughout his life. 'The general killed the Vietcong; I killed the general with my camera,' Adams would later say bitterly.

Photographs as wake-up calls

Art should not be confused with communication, and there are very few artists whose ambition is to send the clearest possible message through their work. We prefer to draw our own conclusions from what they present. However, photographs sometimes convey explicit messages. Adverts are one example, of course, but they are not the only one. Some photographers are activists, and when they press the button on their camera, they hope that the shot they

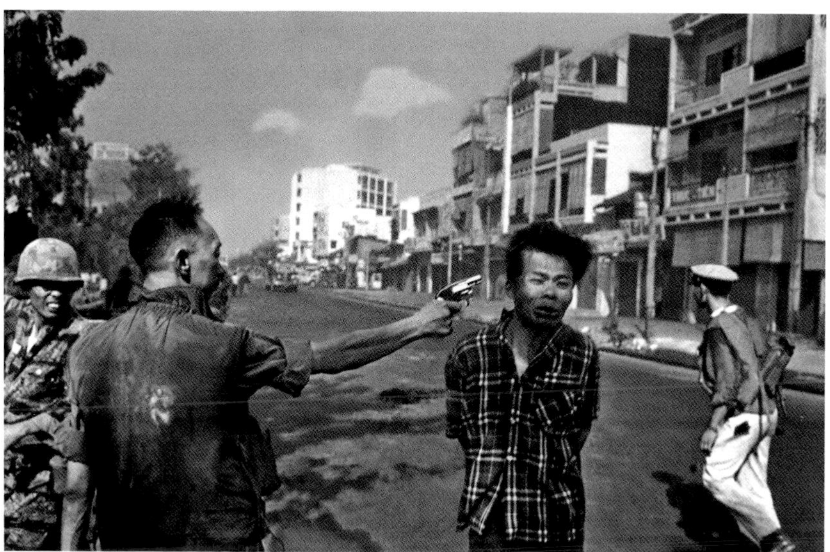

Eddie Adams
Nguyễn Ngoc Loan Executing Nguyễn Văn Lém, Saigon, February 1, 1968

This photograph is on a slight angle, which accentuates the violence of the moment, as if the wind from the bullet made the vertical lines of the street tilt to the side.

create will reduce suffering in the world. Others capture certain aspects of society at a specific point in history, whether to celebrate or criticize them. In both cases, they have something political to say.

The word 'political' here is understood in its broadest sense. It is not only about legislation being debated by representatives in parliament, but about everything to do with how we live together as a community. Some photographers prompt us to reflect on this by freezing time so we can stop and think more deeply, by putting the world on pause so we can examine how we live our lives in society. Especially when our differences seem to form unbreachable divides – although sometimes these photographs transform people into symbols when they did not necessarily want to be seen that way.

In the below image, the French–Moroccan photographer Fatima Mazmouz (b.1974) focuses on Bousbir, the brothel quarter used by the French army in colonial-era Casablanca in the interwar period, where many of the prostitutes were underage Moroccan girls. Mazmouz's pictures, which show female subjects in neutral, stereotypical poses, seem to imitate the chromolithograph prints used to convey images of Empire to serve the Western colonial imagination. In fact, they are based on contemporary postcards: Mazmouz did not ask anyone to pose for her; instead she photographed photos. At first glance, it might look like she has recreated them in small red hearts, like the ones that web users add

Fatima Mazmouz
Casablanca Mon Amour!, from the series 'Bouzbir', 2018
Photography and graphic intervention, 50 x 75 cm
(19¾ x 29⅝ in.)

A record of the past, a piece of history – as always, written by the victors – is recycled and rewritten in the light of values that differ from theirs.

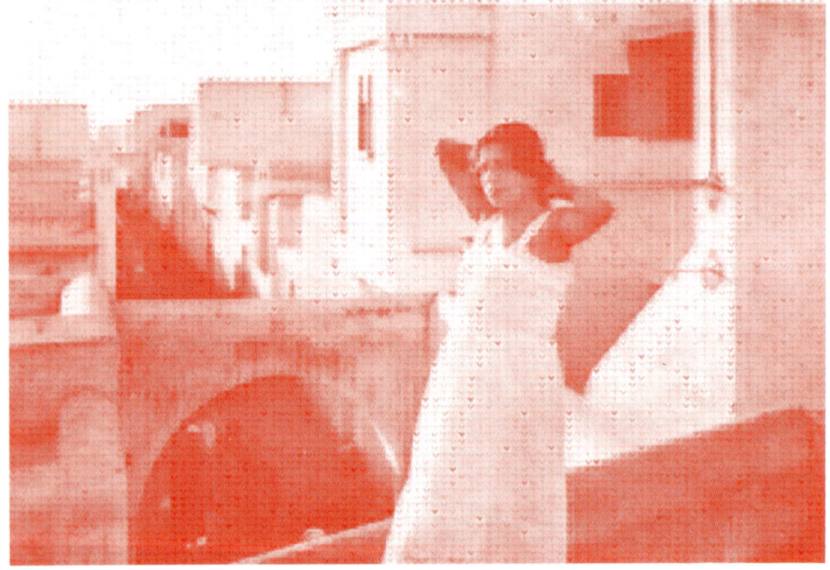

Gordon Parks
Untitled, Shady Grove, Alabama, 1956
Archival pigment print, 40.6 x 50.8 cm
(16 x 20 in.)

We can clearly see anxiety on this mother's face; she is turning around as if danger might spring up behind her. In a world where justice is rarely on your side, you quickly learn to be on your guard. But it is only a photographer.

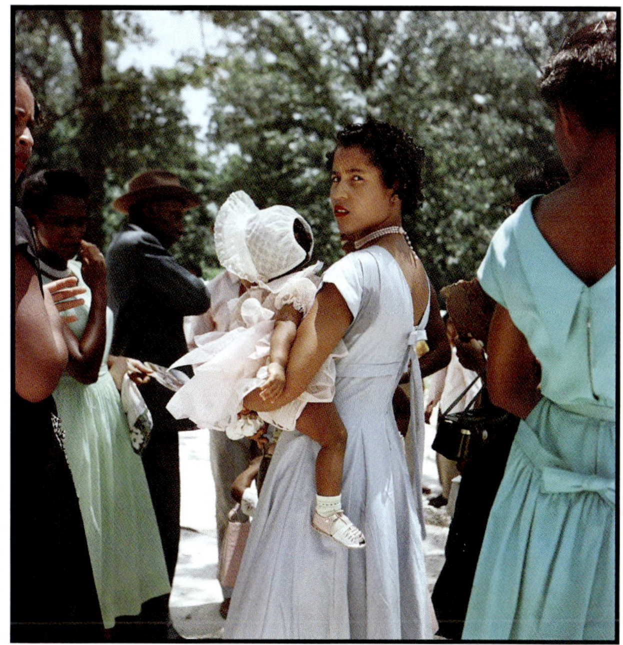

to a post to signify that they like something or someone. But that's not the case. This texture is made up of tiny images of diseased uteruses and vulvas. In this way, Mazmouz uses digital technology to convey the horror of the brothels.

Gordon Parks (1912–2006) also uses ambiguity rather than directly denouncing his subject (above) in his photographic reportage about Alabama, a state where racial segregation was still in force in the 1950s. By taking a photo that is, in essence, banal – because these figures are doing nothing extraordinary – Parks seems to be conveying to those white spectators who support segregation: 'You see, they're just like you. On Sundays they put on fashionable, well-ironed clothes, they socialize and they go out with their families. Why not live together rather than apart?'

PHOTOGRAPHS AS MYTHS

A myth is a story that is passed down by word of mouth and helps us to make sense of what is happening in the world. Thanks to the myth, we see links between things that seem unconnected, including within ourselves, and become more aware of our relationship with our own beliefs and desires. It doesn't matter whether the story is true or not, because it helps us to live our lives. Certain photographs also have this power to illuminate: they crystallize what was unclear by making us focus on what really matters, or by capturing something that we had only a vague sense of and making it concrete.

First, let's look at a photograph that became famous for all the wrong reasons, due to the court case it sparked in 1992. It seemed to show a couple being reunited, and posters of the photograph were sold in huge numbers, bringing in a lot of money. The photographer had to explain to a court that he had not in fact captured an intimate moment between two unknown people, but hired actors to pose all around Paris, not just in front of the town hall. A large swathe of the public was dismayed to learn that the photograph had been staged, instead of being a snapshot of everyday life.

Instead of disappointment, we might do better to reflect on the theme of this photograph (opposite) by Robert Doisneau (1912–1994) and how it is portrayed. His subject is the irrepressible nature of romantic love. True love means feeling an urgent desire to kiss even when it is not the time or the place. In France in the 1950s, kissing on the lips in public was frowned upon, and couples hid in doorways or cinemas. We often say that lovers are lost in their own world, and this couple has forgotten the city traffic all around them. Everyone is in a rush, except for them – the passers-by are blurry or cut off, the cars are zooming past. This contrast is accentuated by the man in the beret, on the left: he looks serious, almost sad, and is pretending not to see them. He seems to be gritting his teeth and thinking that he has never loved someone like that, seeking safety in disapproval rather than allowing himself to feel envy.

We could perhaps criticize the portrayal of gender roles in this photograph: the man's right hand, resting on his partner's shoulder, suggests a kind of possessiveness, which contrasts with the sense of reckless abandon conveyed by the woman's right hand. However, we should also note the elegance of their pose, which creates a reversed S shape between the man's hand and the woman's, following the white line of her blouse.

After love, our greatest source of myths and legends is, sadly, war. Like *Kiss by the Hôtel de Ville*, *Death of a Loyalist Soldier* (page 162) by the Hungarian-born American photographer Robert Capa (1913–1954) was the subject of an unhelpful controversy. Is this man a soldier in training, or a fighter hit by an enemy bullet in the middle of the Battle of Cerro Muriano? Countless experts –

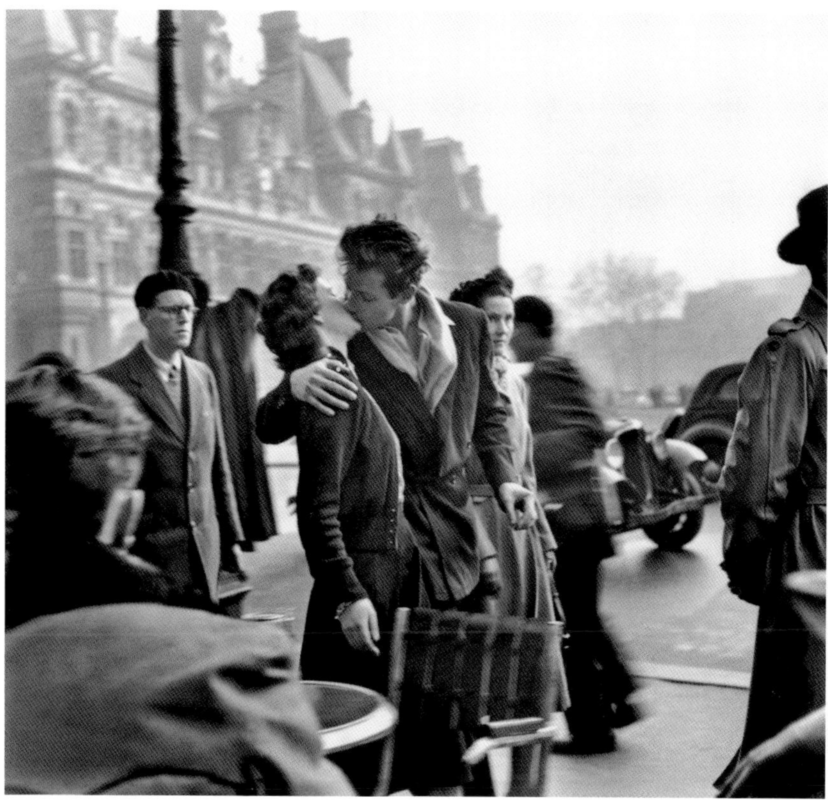

Robert Doisneau
Le Baiser de l'hôtel de ville
(Kiss by the Hôtel de Ville),
Paris, 1950
Gelatin silver print

The framing draws us in – who wouldn't want to sit idly on a Parisian terrace and watch people go by? This is an over-the-shoulder shot, to use a term borrowed from the world of cinema, as if we are sitting next to the man on the left.

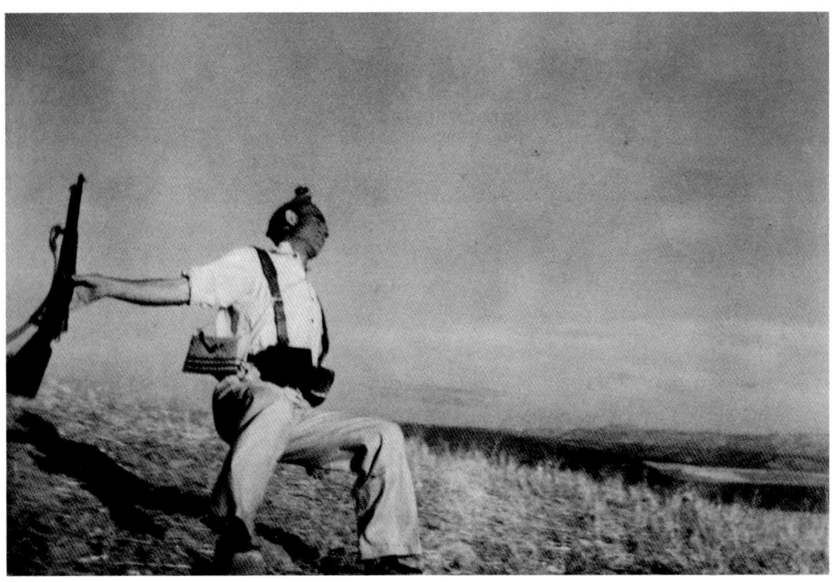

Robert Capa
Death of a Loyalist Soldier, near Espejo, Córdoba front, September 1936
Gelatin silver print, 24.3 x 40.6 cm (9⁴⁄₇ x 13³⁄₄ in.)

There is a sense of style in this image of loss. This battle scene has the feel of contemporary dance – the soldier is falling elegantly, like a dancer. His left arm disappears behind him; only his hand is visible, emerging from the top of his head and reaching towards the sky, as if to point his soul in the right direction as it leaves his body. His eyes are already closed.

from journalists and historians to forensic pathologists – have debated the plausibility of each possible answer. But again, this is a waste of time, at least when it comes to Capa. The photograph's subject is not the death of one brave man, one individual. Since the guns fell silent in Spain, this photograph has come to represent the defeat of the Republicans by the far right in the Spanish Civil War. More broadly, as the years passed, it has come to symbolize the capitulation of democracy to dictatorship, and even the defeat of the forces of good by the forces of evil. The framing, on a slight angle, reinforces this impression – the grass forms a descending line between the two sides of the shot, like the line on a graph that indicates decline, deceleration, impoverishment.

Is such an elegant death worth more than a wretched life? The fallen fighter is beautiful, like Jan Rose Kasmir, the young American woman who was captured by the French photographer Marc Riboud (1923–2016), offering a flower to the intimidating soldiers pointing their bayonetted rifles at her during a protest against the Vietnam War in Washington on 21 October 1967. In both cases, one side's defeat is more beautiful than the other side's victory – although that may be scant consolation.

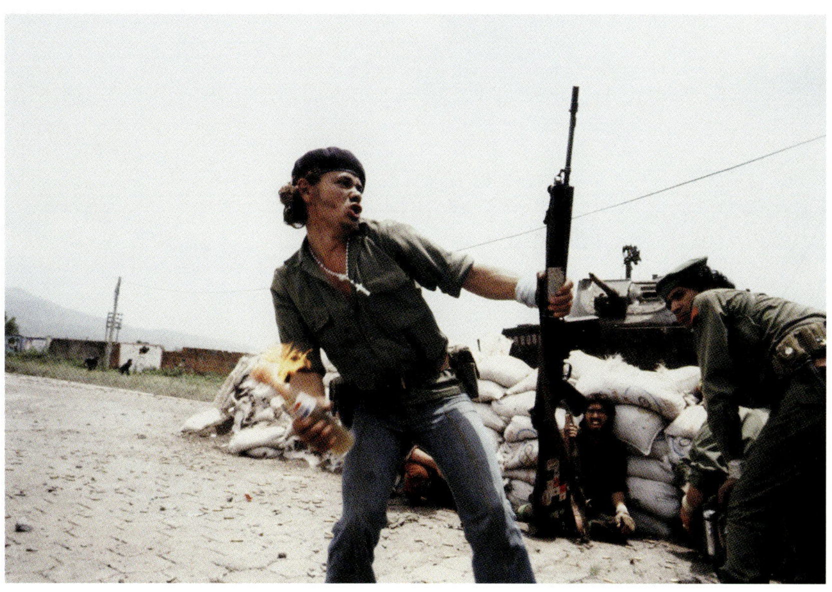

Susan Meiselas
Molotov Man, 1979

While in Capa's photograph all is lost, here everything remains possible. The determination on Aráuz's face is undeniable. He is throwing a Molotov cocktail in a Pepsi bottle – a symbolic detail, as the United States would continue to support President Somoza's regime, against which he is fighting, for a few more days.

An unstable situation

There is no time for melancholy in *Molotov Man* (above) by the American photographer Susan Meiselas (b.1948). It shows the first Sandinista revolution in Nicaragua, poised on the brink of success thanks to help from neighbouring countries (we can make out the flag of Panama on the gun). The bottle of soda, imported from the United States, is not the only paradoxical element of this picture: Pablo Aráuz is wearing a beret in the style of Che Guevara, with a Catholic rosary around his neck, and he pairs his uniform with flared jeans. His comrades are equally mismatched: one sits, grimacing as if anticipating the violence of the explosion, while the other, on the right, seems to be wondering if it's a good idea to throw this Molotov cocktail. Even more strangely, the tank's gun is pointing towards us. The composition suggests that this is an unstable situation, both literally and figuratively: the framing is angled, but the telephone line, which seems to anticipate the flight path of the Molotov cocktail – straight at the enemy – is slanted in the opposite direction. It forms an ascending line, a classic symbol of progress, growth and improvement.

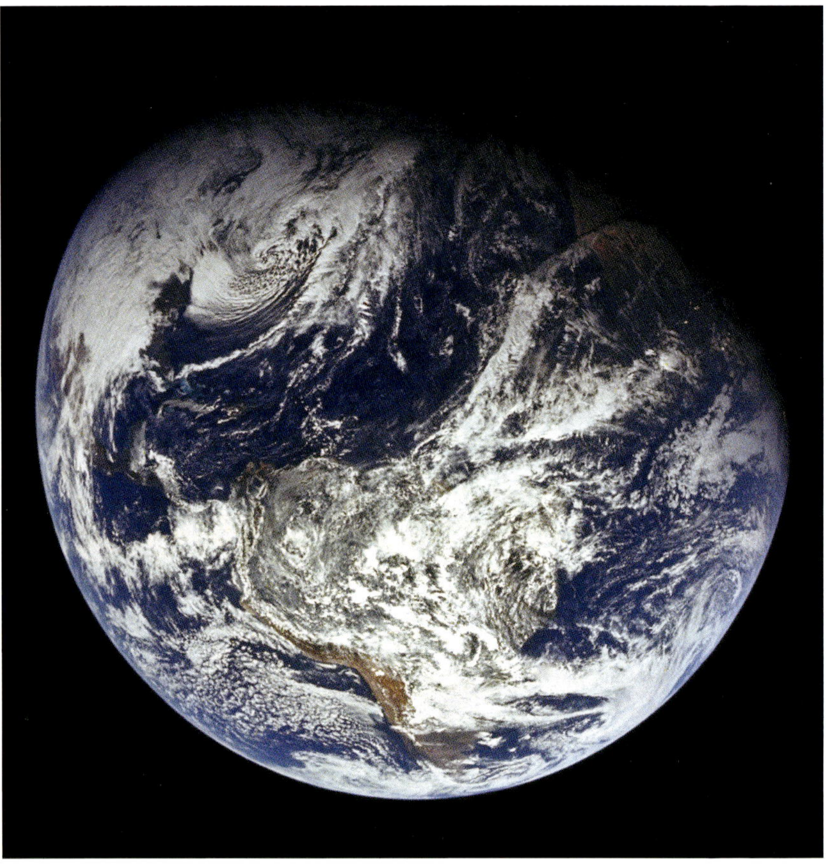

William Anders
First full-disc image of Earth from space taken by a person, 22 December 1968
Photographed with a 77mm camera

A selfie showing all of humanity. South America is visible on the lower part of the photograph, but further up, night is already falling, because the sun, the photographer and Earth are not all perfectly aligned. We would have to wait for the Apollo 17 mission to see Earth in its entirety.

Let's take another step back to the American Apollo 8 mission. On Christmas Eve 1968, the astronaut William Anders (b.1933) decided to take a photograph of us (opposite). All of us, each and every one. All together. But in context: in our natural habitat.

None of the borders between nations, those invisible lines for which millions of people have died, and for which they are still dying today, appears in this photograph. We can only make out water, land masses and clouds. Despite the myth that the Great Wall of China is visible from the moon, there is no trace of humans. All we can see is the outline: the circular line that confirms that Earth is a sphere, isolated in space. And this also shows that the ideology of infinite growth is ridiculous. Our unchecked exploitation of resources can only lead to our own destruction.

As soon as this photograph was published around the world, it should have spelled the end of all wars, all waste and pollution. But that was not the case. A photograph can do many things, but we shouldn't expect the impossible.

KEY IDEAS

Some photographers are like seismographers, recording shifts in society.

Some photographs can change our minds, even about important subjects.

The effect that a photograph has on us does not always match its creator's original intention.

KEY QUESTIONS

... to ask with a photograph in front of you:

Do I understand what is happening here, or do I need to find out more about the context in which this photograph was taken?

Do I feel empathy for the photographer or the people being photographed?

What does this photograph make me want to do?

GLOSSARY

Analogue photography: An analogue photograph is created by manually exposing film to light.

Aperture: Adjustable opening through which light focused by the lens passes into the camera.

Belinograph: A device used to send photographs over great distances, via telephone or radio, especially used by newspapers from the 1920s to the 1960s.

Binary code: A code made up of 0s and 1s, used to encode data in bits. A pixel is generally made up of 24 or 32 bits.

***Camera obscura*:** A box with a small hole in one of its sides. When light passes through the lens in this opening, the scene in front of the *camera obscura* is projected onto the opposite side.

Camera shake: Blurriness caused by the camera moving while the photo is being taken.

Chronophotography: The process of taking a number of photographs at close, regular intervals, with the aim of making the movement of an animal or object visible by breaking it down.

Compositing: A range of digital techniques used to combine elements taken from different images, to create the impression of a consistent whole that exists within a single frame.

Composition: How a photographer arranges the main lines and shapes within the frame.

Daguerreotype: Photographic process that consists of exposing silver-plated copper sheets to light, patented by Louis Daguerre in 1839.

Definition: The number of pixels in a digital photograph or on a screen. Not to be confused with sharpness: a photograph can be blurry while still being very high-definition.

Depth of field: The part of the field in line with the camera within which the image is sharp.

Developer: Chemical bath that acts on the photosensitive crystals in the film that have been exposed to light, converting them into a visible image that forms the negative.

Developing: Treating the exposed film with chemical solutions called developer and fixer, to prepare it for printing.

Digital photograph: A classic digital photograph is made up of pixels and created by exposing a sensor to light.

Digital software: Computer technology and programs used to edit or create images.

Exposure: The amount of light absorbed by the film while the shutter is open.

Exposure time: The length of time needed to take a photograph, during which light passes through the aperture.

Field: The space depicted in a photograph when we view it as a window opening onto a three-dimensional world. Traditionally this contains the foreground (the subject) and the background (the surroundings).

File: A digital photograph (or an analogue photograph that has been scanned) can take on a non-physical form as a digital file made up of binary code.

Film: A supple material that contains photosensitive crystals.

Fixer: Chemical bath that stabilizes the image by making the film no longer sensitive to light.

Focal distance: The distance between the film (or the sensor) and the optical centre of the lens. The longer the focal distance, the more it feels like you are looking at the scene through binoculars.

Focusing: Adjusting the camera to define the area within the field where the image is sharp.

Format: Ratio between the length and width of the frame. Sometimes, this is misused to mean the size of the print (e.g. 'large-format').

Frame: Everything that is included between the four sides of a photograph, when viewed as a flat rectangle. The frame is two-dimensional, unlike the field, which is three-dimensional.

Frame within a frame: An effect created when a frame, in the physical sense of the term (all or part of a window, for example), is visible within the framing of the photograph.

Glitch: A mistake in a digital file. The term 'glitch art' is used to refer to works that take advantage of the aesthetic possibilities of these kinds of mistakes.

Grain: *see* Resolution

Greyscale: All the different shades of grey, from the lightest to the darkest, that exist between white and black.

High-angle shot: A kind of framing in which we are looking down on the subject. A 90-degree angle is called a God's eye view.

Lens: The part of a camera, or a smartphone, that focuses light on the film or the sensor.

Low-angle shot: A kind of framing in which we are looking up at the subject.

Motion blur: Blurriness caused by an object in the field moving while the photo is being taken.

Negative: In traditional analogue photography, a developed film in which black and white (or colours) are reversed. This is a unique original, but it is possible to create many prints from it.

Paparazzi: Photographers who specialize in taking photos of celebrities. The word comes from the name of a character in Federico Fellini's film *La Dolce vita* (1960).

Pixel: An acronym for 'picture element'. Pixels are tiny squares that, when lined up side by side, form a digital photograph. We also use this word to mean the dots in a digital screen.

Polaroid: Instant cameras first sold in 1948, with which users can develop and print photos within a few seconds.

Post-processing: Editing a digital photograph using computer software.

Presentation: A photograph can be presented on paper, on screen, by projecting it on a slide, in an illuminated chamber, etc.

Print: In analogue photography, a print is created by projecting and fixing an original negative onto photosensitive paper. In digital photography, a print is created from a file using a printer.

Process: Different technical processes, from daguerreotypes to digital, that allow us to create photographs.

Resolution: The ratio between the definition of a digital photo (or a screen) and its size. The resolution is measured in *ppi* (pixels per inch). In printing, we refer instead to the grain, as a measure of how close together the dots of colour are.

Retouching: In analogue photography, modifying a negative (by using a paintbrush, scratching it, etc.) or changing a photograph at the printing stage. In digital photography, we tend to speak instead of 'post-processing'.

Reverse angle: A way of framing that consists of turning round to show the 'other side' of a particular scene. A 180-degree reverse angle shows the fourth wall.

Rule of Thirds: A compositional convention that consists of dividing the frame into nine equal parts, using two horizontal and two vertical lines. According to artistic tradition, the horizon should be placed along one of the horizontal lines and the main subject along one of the vertical lines.

Sensor: In a digital camera, this is a photosensitive cell that captures light and converts it to binary code.

Shutter: The part of a camera that opens to allow light to pass through the aperture and land on the lens or sensor.

Telephoto lens: A lens with a long focal distance, popular with paparazzi.

Timer: A mechanism that allows us to extend the time between when the photographer presses the button and when the photograph is taken.

Viewfinder: The part of a camera that the photographer holds close to their eye so that they can accurately determine the framing before pressing the button. It is not present in certain cameras, such as smartphones, where the framing is done using a screen.

Wide-angle lens: A lens with a short focal distance.

FURTHER READING

Barthes, Roland, *Camera Lucida: Reflections on Photography* [1980], trans. Richard Howard, London, Vintage Classics, 1993

Bate, David, *Photography: The Key Concepts* [2009], New York, Bloomsbury, 2016

Benjamin, Walter, *On Photography* [1931], trans. Esther Leslie, London, Reaktion Books, 2015

Berger, John, *Understanding a Photograph*, London, Penguin Classics, 2013

Bright, Susan, *Art Photography Now*, London, Aperture, 2005

Campany, David, *On Photographs*, London, Thames & Hudson, 2020

Chéroux, Clément, *The Perfect Medium: Photography and the Occult*, New Haven, Yale University Press, 2005

Ford, Colin (ed.), *The Kodak Museum: The Story of Popular Photography*, London, Century Hutchinson / Bradford, National Museum of Photography, Film and Television, 1989

Freund, Gisèle, *Photography and Society* [1974], London, Gordon Fraser, 1980

Hacking, Juliet and Campany, David, *Photography: The Whole Story* [2012], London, Thames & Hudson, London, 2021

Ignatieff, Michael, *Magnum °* [exh. cat.], London, Phaidon, 2000

Jeffrey, Ian, *Photography: A Concise History*, London, Thames & Hudson, 1981

Lardinois, Brigitte (ed.) *Magnum Magnum*, London, Thames & Hudson, 2009

Noble, Andrea, *Tina Modotti: Image, Texture, Photography*, Albuquerque, University of New Mexico Press, 2000

Séclier, Philippe, *Magnum Photos 75 Years*, Paris, Atelier EXB, 2022

Sontag, Susan, *On Photography*, London, Penguin, 1979

Thompson, Jerry L., *Truth and Photography: Notes on Looking and Photographing*, Chicago, Ivan R. Dee, 2003

Whelan, Richard, *Robert Capa at Work: This is War!* [exh. cat.], Göttingen, Steidl / New York, International Center of Photography, 2009

Whiston Spirn, Anne, *Daring to Look: Dorothea Lange's "Photographs and Reports from the Field"*, Chicago, University of Chicago Press, 2008

INDEX

Main entries are in **bold**.
Illustrations are in *italic*.

PICTURE ACKNOWLEDGEMENTS

2, 93 Ernst Haas/Getty Images **4, 90** Commissioned by Wateraid and supported by H&M Foundation. © Aïda Muluneh **8, 16** © Harry Gruyaert/Magnum Photos **10** J. Paul Getty Museum, Los Angeles. Acc. No: 86. XM.722.3 **13** Spencer Collection, The New York Public Library. Acc. No: 1850-12 **14** © Robert Mapplethorpe Foundation. Used by permission **18** Musée de l'Élysée, Lausanne **19** Société française de photographie, Paris **20–21** © Andreas Gursky/Courtesy Sprüth Magers Berlin London/DACS 2024 **24, 25** Library of Congress Prints and Photographs Division, Washington DC, Acc. No: 2017762891 **26** Courtesy the artist, The Broad Art Foundation and Sprüth Magers **27** © Lee Jeffries **29** © Cristina de Middel/Magnum Photos **30–31** © Stuart Franklin/Magnum Photos **32 above** © Adrian Sonderegger & Jojakim Cortis **32 below** Courtesy Pavel Maria Smejkal **34, 47** Courtesy of the artist and Jack Shainman Gallery, New York. © Richard Mosse **37** The Royal Photographic Society, Bath **38** J. Paul Getty Museum, Los Angeles. Acc. No: 84.XP.218.71 **40** © National Science & Media Museum, Bradford/ Science & Society Picture Library. All rights reserved **42** Barbara and Willard Morgan photographs and papers, Library Special Collections, Charles E. Young Research Library, UCLA **43** © Ministère de la Culture – Médiathèque du patrimoine et de la photographie, Dist. RMN-Grand Palais/André Kertész **45** Nick Knight/Trunk Archive **48** Courtesy of Kasmin, New York. © Daniel Gordon **49** Philadelphia Museum of Art. Purchased with funds contributed by the American Museum of Photography, 1971. Acc. No: 1971-117-32(400) **51** Courtesy the artist and Sprüth Magers/Matthew Marks Gallery/Esther Schipper, Berlin/Taka Ishii Gallery. © Thomas Demand, VG Bild-Kunst, Bonn **52** Jacques Henri Lartigue © Ministère de la Culture (France), MPP-AAJHL **54** © Center for Creative Photography, The University of Arizona Foundation/DACS 2024 **57** © Juno Calypso **58, 77** © Susana Moyaho **60** Société française de photographie, Paris **63** Courtesy Gallery KUZO. © Byung-Hun Min **64–65** Courtesy Matthew Marks Gallery. © Heirs of Luigi Ghirri **67** © ARS, NY and DACS, London 2024 **68** © Mohau Modisakeng **69** National Gallery of Art, Washington DC, Patrons' Permanent Fund. Acc. No: 1995.36.67 **71** © Roger Mayne Archive/Mary Evans Picture Library **72** Published by Crown Point Press. © ADAGP, Paris and DACS, London 2024 **74–75** © Alison Jackson **78, 95** © Martin Parr/Magnum Photos **80** Berenice Abbot/Getty Images **83** © A. Abbas/ Magnum Photos **84** Musée Carnavalet, Paris. Acc. No: PH5471 **86–87** © Luca Campigotto **89** Courtesy the Estate of Vidyavrata **91** Courtesy of Nailya Alexander Gallery, New York. © Arkady Shaikhet Estate **92** The Metropolitan Museum of Art, New York. Ford Motor Company Collection, Gift of Ford Motor Company and John C. Waddell, 1987. Acc. No: 1987.1100.499 **97** National Gallery of Art, Washington DC, Corcoran Collection (Gift of Harry H. Lunn, Jr., through Graphics International Ltd.). Acc. No: 2015.19.4167 **98** © 2024 Woodman Family Foundation/ Artists Rights Society (ARS), New York **100** © Saul Leiter Foundation **101** Courtesy the Estate of Fred Herzog and Equinox Gallery, Vancouver. © The Estate of Fred Herzog, 2024 **102, 109** © Corinne Vionnet **105** Courtesy Robert Klein Gallery. © Paulette Tavormina 2010 **106** Courtesy Gagosian. © Sally Mann **108** Courtesy Hamiltons Gallery London. © Erwin Olaf **110** Courtesy Doug Rickard Estate **111** © Fondation Henri Cartier-Bresson/Magnum Photos **112** © Raymond Depardon/Magnum Photos **113** © Anup Shah **114–115** © Xavi Bou **117** Library of Congress Prints and Photographs Division Washington DC, Acc. No: 2006684217 **118** The Royal Photographic Society Collection at the V&A, acquired with the generous assistance of the National Lottery Heritage Fund and Art Fund. Acc. No: RPS.611-2020. © Mervyn O'Gorman **119** Bayerisches Nationalmuseum, Munich **121** Courtesy of the artist and Marian Goodman Gallery. © Hiroshi Sugimoto **122, 136** © ORLAN **124** Yousuf Karsh, Camera Press London **127** © IMEC, Fonds MCC, Dist. RMN-Grand Palais/Gisèle Freund. © Banco de México Diego Rivera Frida Kahlo Museums Trust, Mexico, D.F./DACS 2024 **128** © Zhang Huan Studio **130** © Gillian Wearing, courtesy Maureen Paley, London, Tanya Bonakdar Gallery, New York and Regen Projects, Los Angeles **131** © Claude Cahun **132** © Eva Woolridge **133** © David LaChapelle **134** © Hyacinth Schukis **135** The Louise Imogen Guiney Collection, Library of Congress Prints and Photographs Division, Washington DC, Acc. No: 00651847 **137** Courtesy the artist and Hauser & Wirth. © Cindy Sherman **139** © Oliviero Toscani **140** © Bruce Gilden/Magnum Photos **143 above** Juan Guzmán/Agencia EFE/Shutterstock **143 below** AP Photo/The Yomiuri Shimbun, Tadashi Okubo/Alamy **144, 163** © Susan Meiselas/ Magnum Photos **147** Brooklyn Museum. Gift of Wallace B. Putnam from the Estate of Consuelo Kanaga. Acc. No: 82.65.389 **149** © Neil Aldridge **150** Courtesy Flowers Gallery, London. © Edward Burtynsky **151** Courtesy Kasmin Gallery, New York. © Robert Polidori **152** © Chien-Chi Chang/Magnum Photos **153** © Inge Morath/Magnum Photos **154** © Dayanita Singh **157** AP Photo/Eddie Adams/Alamy **158** Archive Carte Postale DR © ADAGP, Paris and DACS, London 2024 **159** Courtesy of and copyright the Gordon Parks Foundation **161** Robert Doisneau/Gamma-Rapho/Getty Images **162** © Robert Capa/International Center of Photography/Magnum Photos **164** NASA

SOURCES OF QUOTATIONS

page 12 Karl Marx, 'Introduction', *Critique of Hegel's Philosophy of Right*, Cambridge, Cambridge University Press, 2009; **page 15** Robert Mapplethorpe quoted in Franca Falletti and Jonathan Nelson (ed.), *Mapplethorpe: Perfection in Form* [exh. cat], Kempen (Germany), teNeues, 2009, p. 20; **page 16** Harry Gruyaert, 'Le Maroc en Kodachrome par Harry Gruyaert', interview by David Ukaleq for the online magazine *Yonder*, 30 October 2017 (www.yonder.fr/en-images/photographes/interview-harry-gruyaert-maroc); **page 16** Harry Gruyaert quoted in Laura Havlin, 'East / West', Magnum website, 19 October 2017 (www.magnumphotos.com/arts-culture/travel/harry-gruyaert-east-west-magnum-photos); **page 17** William Henry Fox Talbot, 'Introductory Remarks', in *The Pencil of Nature, London*, Longman, Brown, Green & Longmans, 1844; **page 18** Susan Sontag, *On Photography*, London, Penguin, 1979, p. 5; **page 27** Barbara Kruger, interview by Jori Finkel, *The Art Newspaper*, 16 August 2021; **page 29** Cristina de Middel, extract from the caption accompanying the work on the artist's website, 2009 (www.lademiddel.com/poly-spam.html); **page 36** Extract from the rules of the World Press Photo competition, 2023 (www.worldpressphoto.org/contest/2023/verification-process/why-manipulation-matters); **page 36** Thomas Hoepker quoted in Clément Chéroux and Clara Bouveresse (ed.), *Magnum manifeste*, Arles, Actes Sud, 2017, p. 382; **page 46** Richard Mosse quoted in Tom Seymour, 'Richard Mosse – Incoming' *British Journal of Photography*, 15 February 2017; **page 49** Daniel Gordon quoted in Claire Barliant, 'Photography and the Objet Manqué', *Art in America*, 23 February 2012; **page 53** Viktor Shklovsky, Theory of Prose [1925], Elmwood Park (United States), Dalkey Archive Press, 1990; **page 56** Juno Calypso, 'Juno Calypso checks in solo at a surreal honeymoon hotel', interview by Sam Warner, *Huck Magazine*, 1 October 2015; **page 60** Elizabeth Eastlake, 'Photography', *The London Quarterly Review*, vol. 10, 1857, p. 442, 460–461; **page 62** Sally Mann quoted by Danna Singer in 'How Danna Singer shot one of *The New Yorker*'s best photos of the year', interview by David Walker, *Photo District News*, 27 November 2019; **page 66** Ming Smith quoted in 'Ming Smith receives lifetime achievement award by International Center of Photography', *Contemporary And*, 11 January 2023 (contemporaryand.com/magazines/ming-smith-receives-lifetime-achievement-award-by-icp); **page 66** Mohau Modisakeng quoted by Keisha Jacobs, 'Mohau Modisakeng: The Materiality of Dreams, Violence and Black African Kinship', *ArtsHelp*, June 2022 (www.artshelp.com/mohau-modisakeng); **page 69** Clément Chéroux, *Si la vue vaut d'être vécue : miscellanées photographiques*, Paris, Textuel, 2019, p. 148; **page 73** Alison Jackson, description of the 'Disaster' series on the artist's website, 2010 (www.alisonjackson.com/disaster-series); **pages 73, 76** Susana Moyaho quoted in Kellye Eisworth, 'Digital Mediations: Susana Moyaho: Misremember Me Correctly', *Lenscratch*, 29 September 2021 (lenscratch.com/2021/09/digital-mediations-susana-moyaho-misremember-me-correctly); **page 82** Susan Sontag, *On Photography*, p. 81; **page 89** Aïda Muluneh, extracts from the description of the 'Water Life' series on the artist's website (www.aidamuluneh.com/water-life); **page 90** 'L'œil-caméra va où l'œil humain ne va pas' : Dziga Vertov, manifesto 'Kinoks-Révolution' ('Kinoki. Perevorot'), *LEF* (journal of the Left Front of the Arts, founded and edited by Vladimir Mayakovsky), no. 3, June 1923; **page 93** László Moholy-Nagy, *Painting Photography Film* [1925], London, Lund Humphries, 1969, p. 28; **pages 94, 96** Martin Parr, *Parr by Parr: Quentin Bajac meets Martin Parr: Discussions with a promiscuous photographer*, Amsterdam, Schilt Publishing, 2010, p. 61 and 70; **page 104** Susan Sontag, *On Photography*, p. 15; **page 108** Erwin Olaf quoted in 'Jonathan Turner on "Grief"', 2007 (www.erwinolaf.com/art/Grief_2007/artist_statement); **page 108** Henri Cartier-Bresson quoted in Clément Chéroux and Clara Bouveresse (ed.), *Magnum manifeste*, Arles, Actes Sud, 2017, p. 363; **page 109** 'La Terre a rapetissé', *Le Journal*, 28 September 1935, p. 1; **page 110** Doug Rickard, 'Screen Captures: Americans on Google Street', interview by Spring Warren, *Boom*, vol. 2, no. 4, Winter 2012, pp. 18–26; **page 117** Gertrude Käsebier quoted in 'The camera has opened a new profession for women – some of those who have made good', *The New York Times*, 20 April 1913; **page 125** Elliott Erwitt quoted in John O'Mahony, 'Best in Show', *The Guardian*, 27 December 2003; **page 125** Yousuf Karsh, artist's website (karsh.org/photographs/martin-luther-king); **page 126** Fernando Pessoa, *The Book of Disquiet*, trans. Margaret Jull Costa, London, Serpent's Tail, 2018, p. 8; **page 126** Gisèle Freund quoted in Claire Wilcox and Circe Henestrosa (ed.), *Frida Kahlo au-delà des apparences* [exh. cat.], Paris, Palais Galliera / Paris Musées, 2022, p. 95; **page 128** Zhang Huan, extract from the description of the work on the artist's website (www.zhanghuan.com); **page 129** Robert Johnson, *The Art of Retouching Photographic Negatives* [1913], revised edition by T. S. Bruce and A. Braithwaite (ed.), Boston, American Photographic Publishing Co., 1936, p. 5; **page 131** Claude Cahun quoted in *Claude Cahun* [exh. cat.], Paris, Jeu de Paume / Hazan, 2011, p. 55 and 65; **page 132** Eva Woolridge quoted in Zarita Zevallos, 'Photographers on Photographers: Zarita Zevallos in Conversation with Eva Woolridge', *Lenscratch*, 13 August 2020 (lenscratch.com/2020/08/photographers-on-photographers-zarita-zevallos-in-conversation-with-eva-woolridge); **page 133** David LaChapelle, interview for *The Art Newspaper*, 2008 (www.youtube.com/watch?v=E8QFJgxMJuM); **page 134** Hyacinth Schukis, *AFTERLIVES. (Gender)queer Photographic Self-Representation and Reenactment*, thesis, Bachelor of Fine Arts, Robert D. Clark Honors College, June 2020; **page 137** Cindy Sherman, 'Cindy Sherman on AI experiments, lockdown pottery and being a woman in today's art market', interview by Anny Shaw, *The Art Newspaper*, 13 June 2023; **page 141** Sean O'Hagan, 'A latter-day freak show? Bruce Gilden's extreme portraits are relentlessly cruel', *The Guardian*, 19 August 2015; **page 141** Marina Ginestà quoted in 'Marina Ginestà, la memoria viva de una imagen simbólica', *Público*, 10 May 2008; **page 146** Barbara Cole, 'Exclusive Interview with Barbara Cole', interview by Sandrine Hermand-Grisel, *All About Photo*, 10 August 2021 (www.all-about-photo.com/photo-articles/photo-article/1043/exclusive-interview-with-barbara-cole); **page 148** Neil Aldridge, 'Shooting for Survival by Neil Aldridge', *Sevenseas Media*, no. 66, November 2020; **page 156** Eddie Adams, 'Eulogy: General Nguyen Ngoc Loan', *Time Magazine*, 27 September 1998

First published in the United Kingdom in 2024 by Thames & Hudson Ltd, 181A High Holborn, London WC1V 7QX

First published in the United States of America in 2024 by Thames & Hudson Inc., 500 Fifth Avenue, New York, New York 10110

Translated by Bethany Wright
Design by April

British Library Cataloguing-in-Publication Data
A catalogue record for this book is available from the British Library.

Library of Congress Control Number 2024934204

ISBN 978-0-500-29750-6

Printed and bound in Bosnia and Herzegovina by GPS Group

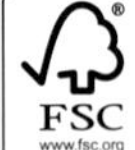

Front cover: Robert Doisneau, *Le Baiser de l'hôtel de ville (Kiss by the Hôtel de Ville)*, Paris, 1950 (detail from page 161). Gelatin silver print. Robert Doisneau/Gamma-Rapho/Getty Images

Title page: Ernst Haas, *Park Avenue Taxis*, New York, 1958 (detail from page 93). Ernst Haas/Getty Images

Contents page: Aïda Muluneh, *The Shackles of Limitations*, from the series 'Water Life', 2018 (detail from page 90). Inkjet print on paper, 80 × 80 cm (31½ x 31½ in.) © Aïda Muluneh

Chapter openers: page 8 Harry Gruyaert, *Los Angeles*, 1982 (detail from page 16); **page 34** Richard Mosse, *She Brings the Rain*, 2011 (detail from page 47); **page 58** Susana Moyaho, *Debris 20*, 2020 (detail from page 77); **page 78** Martin Parr, *Food*, 2012 (detail from page 95); **page 102** Corinne Vionnet, *Beijing*, 2007 (detail from page 109); **page 122** ORLAN, *Self-Hybridation, In Between with ORLAN's portrait n°4*, 1994 (detail from page 136); **page 144** Susan Meiselas, *Molotov Man*, 1979 (detail from page 163)

Chapter opener quotations: page 9 Harry Gruyaert quoted in Brennavan Sritharan, 'Harry Gruyaert: "There is no story. It's just a question of shapes and light"', *British Journal of Photography*, 27 July 2015; **page 35** Richard Mosse quoted in Tom Seymour, 'Richard Mosse – Incoming', *British Journal of Photography*, 15 February 2017; **page 59** Susana Moyaho quoted in Kellye Eisworth, 'Digital Mediations: Susana Moyaho: Misremember Me Correctly', *Lenscratch*, 29 September 2021 (lenscratch.com/2021/09/digital-mediations-susana-moyaho-misremember-me-correctly); **page 79** Martin Parr, 'Je suis bien plus doué pour faire des photographies que pour en parler', interview by Pauline Ngo-Ngok, *S-quive Magazine*, 13 April 2023; **page 103** Corinne Vionnet, by email; **page 123** ORLAN, 'De la self-hybridation aux cellules souches', *Les Actes de colloques du musée du quai Branly Jacques Chirac*, no. 2, 2009; **page 145** Susan Meiselas, 'Style Can't Sustain You: Notes from the Field', interview by Coralie Kraft, *Lens Culture* (www.lensculture.com/articles/susan-meiselas-style-can-t-sustain-you-notes-from-the-field)